Barbara Băcăuanu

Transgenerational Astrology

Astrology of Family Patterns and the Path to Personal Healing

Publisher Beta Aqarii
2023

TRANSGENERATIONAL ASTROLOGY
Astrology of Family Patterns and the Path to Personal Healing

Barbara Băcăuanu

@ 2023 - Publisher Beta Aqarii

ISBN 978-606-93442-7-9

web: www.reveland.net
e-mail: contact@reveland.net

social media:
FB: @thelandofrevelations
IG: /landofrevelations
YT: /thelandofrevelations

To my family

Content

Astrology and Psychogenealogy

The moment you are born your mind is already created, but it is not the mind you know as a human being, the conscious mind, it is the mind of your soul, the subconscious mind, which you create your whole life upon.
Carl Gustav Jung

Constellations

Though apparently our relationships - with the living and people we actually interact with - only take place in the physical world, the connections with our ancestors do not cease to exist. We are all connected, from our roots to our last born, and this relationship pervades the laws of the dimension we live in, and transcends time, life, and death since it happens in an elusive realm.

The roles, dynamics within the family tree, relationships between its members, and changes between generations can be unmistakably witnessed by those who are alive and experience them. On the one hand, they are faced with the parents' generation they belong to, on another plane with the times they represent, and, on the other hand, with the new generation of their children, representatives of evolution and the passage of time.

Exchanges are permanent and generations are bound together, endlessly, building up on each other, in a spiral, from the roots to the present.

The way we humans see, think and imagine the world is a continuum and, at the same time, it overlaps the way we were taught to see it by all previous generations, from the first man all the way to our parents, who have explored it, lived it, and classified it into a number of templates, beliefs, imagery, and characters, into guidelines and rules about how we should or shouldn't live our life.

When a man is born in this great archetype, the world, being connected to it and driven by instinct, his life unfolds exactly according to one of its plays and scenarios, with not a trace of freedom, attracted and led by invisible strings of unconscious rules, which he follows without drifting from the pattern. Because he is not aware of and does not know anything outside it, his individual goal is to adjust himself to a collective model, to be part of it, and to identify himself with one of the roles available in the system and generation he is part of.

His boundaries are well defined by whatever exists and everyone else knows, by casts already made, by patterns perpetuated from time immemorial.

This universal image of the world, with all its experiences and adventures, exists in a dimension of the human psyche, in the collective unconscious, as a concurrent and parallel world, as vivid as the conscious one, but with the ability to guide us unseeingly. It is the voice of the pattern, of the inexorable fate, a track on which man walks out of inertia, asleep in unconsciousness, the trans-generational line that follows up the path of his ancestors. He carries forward a dowry chest that contains the set of experiences, beliefs, customs, traditions, connections, and emotions that define his family's identity and behaviour.

Family consciousness can be seen as a form of collective consciousness, an invisible but powerful structure that shapes the behaviour and relationships within the family, including its communication patterns, power hierarchy, rituals, and laws.

It contains joy, love, understanding, compassion, and high ideals, as well as suffering, grief, secrets, and bitter experiences.

By unveiling patterns and issues that repeat themselves across generations and becoming aware of the family unconscious, one can begin to better understand one's own history and identity, break free from the pattern, and become one's authentic self, healing oneself. When it occurs, this healing not only changes one's personal life and pathway but also the family's pathway, balancing an entire branch of the system.

The healing not only occurs in the physical world but also in the subtle world, being a therapy for the entire family tree.

Family tree therapy

The unconscious content of the family tree can be accessed directly, by learning the life stories of the ancestors and correlating them, but also by decoding the subtle systems, which are laid out in the form of constellations.

Constellations are in the sky in the form of celestial bodies, just as constellations are inside us as pathways between parts of the psyche and reactions, emotions, feelings, and actions in the conscious plane. When confronted, the two types of constellations, the astral ones in the sky at the time of birth and the inner ones, are not only identical but also work in perfect synchronicity.

The moment of birth of each member is not random, but occurs according to unconscious laws within the system, creating a sequence that goes in line with the family saga. A natal chart is a single snapshot of a whole series of birth charts that make up the astral saga of a family, and although static, it is in constant motion and evolves along with the life of each individual.

Look in the family album of the astral charts and you will notice that they are dynamic, in motion, and complete one another or repeat themselves, like a film played on slides or like the pages of a diary. The interpretation of the archetypes that make up a birth chart opens a gateway to an ocean of meanings about the personal and generational biography that takes place in the unconscious.

Family tree chart

Although it is a very old science, which over time has branched out, developed, and sought to show its usefulness and truthfulness in several forms, astrology is still in continuous evolution, and its understanding is available to humans according to their knowledge.

The astral chart, with each of its symbols, embodies both the present universe of the native and those that preceded him or her, showing a configuration that can be interpreted multi-dimensionally. With each perspective approached - natal, karmic, predictive, relational, medical, mundane, and so on - it shows itself differently, on a different frequency.

When all these dimensions align in a larger pattern, one can see that they are not actually separate, but together make up a longer story that did not begin now, but long before birth.

It began with our parents, with their parents' parents, and their parents' parents, in a chain of lives that were created one from another.

To solve the mysteries of a man's behaviour, experiences, and facts of life, his life story must be read from the first page, which begins not with him, but with that of his ancestors. Much like the genosociogram[1] drawing, the astral chart - by the outline formed by the interaction between the personal and the transpersonal, generational planets - provides the blueprint of the way the set of experiences have flown between generations, where both the

---

1   Genosociogram, the main tool for genealogical diagnosis, in which the design of the genealogical tree is enriched with the dates, facts, and significant events of the ancestors

beneficial and harmonious patterns, as well as the dissonances, took form! The theme that appears repeatedly throughout the life stories of the predecessors creates a red thread that runs through the existence of each branch that originates from the same system.

By recognizing and addressing the red thread of the family saga, its members can understand how to improve their relationships and find solutions to overcome the unconscious problems that affect them.

Transgenerational Astrology

The idea of writing this book grew in me during the 15 years of astrology practice in the consulting office. Over the last two years, its vision has been supplemented with studies on genograms and ongoing participation in family constellation sessions, where I understood that the interpretation provided by the birth chart, superimposed on the life story of its holders and their family history is amazingly similar!

We cannot choose to detach ourselves and decide we do not come from a certain system, because that would mean disconnecting ourselves from the source, life, and roots. The past continues to exist in the present, from the present the future is born, and this trans-generational passing of information forms a long line of patterns that make up evolution and life.

For those who study astrology, these pages can bring new insight into how the universe works and provide a foundation in a field now forming - transgenerational astrology. At the same time, they can be a useful guide for psychotherapists, as they help decode and understand the scripts, patterns, and traumas in people's lives (as described in Parts III and IV).

Relating to both astrology and psycho-genealogy, the book describes throughout its contents the universe of the family with all its members, the dynamics inside the system, the way the family develops its beliefs, structure, and patterns, and how all these are transmitted trans-generationally.

The system formed by the five personal planets - Sun, Moon, Mars, Venus, and Mercury (Part I) symbolizes - at the archetypal level - the members of the present family, as well as the members of the larger family, of the ancestors. They make up the primary individual personality, that is, a reflection of what has been extracted from the quintessence of the entire family tree.

The transpersonal planets, Jupiter, Saturn, Uranus, Neptune, and Pluto (Part II), stand for the broad concepts of life, the information that transcends time and is transmitted through the members of a family across the generations.

The unintegrated traumas of one generation are unconsciously transmitted to future generations, who, not knowing why, face certain fears, behaviours, and actions that are inexplicable for the events they experience. They have to overcome an inner conflict between their own desires, needs, thoughts, emotions and those of their predecessors.

The pathway to the ancestors

Although the history of the genealogical tree flows from the ancestors' times to the present day, the study of the evolutionary path of man should first consider the reverse path, from him to the ancestors.

It is the only way that he can truly understand his roots, who he is now, and who he wants to become, and the only way that he can get a full perspective of the history that created his dowry chest.

The process of individuation[2] is a quest for the authentic

____

2   Concept developed by the doctor, psychologist, and psychiatrist Carl Gustav Jung, individuation involves the process of differentiation, making up, and particularization of one's own essence

self and development of human potential, which takes place throughout life and involves the integration and balancing of all aspects of the human personality, including the conscious and unconscious, masculine and feminine, and the intrapsychic oppositions between them.

Part I - The Family

Mercury

The matrix of psychic structures is the set of mental activities, conscious and unconscious, said and unsaid, the words, but also the phantasms, which made possible the encounter of the two cells and the formation of an embryo.
J'ai mal à mes ancêtres - Patrice van Eersel, Catherine Maillard

Family scenario

The motivation of two people deciding to become parents creates an energetic imprint on the child since its birth: a child who is desired, expected, and loved by both partners has a different astral signature than a child brought into the world as a bargaining chip, for fear of losing the other, or in order to obtain social or financial advantages, or as a result of manipulation on the part of the larger family, of an accident, incest or rape. At the same time, the role assigned to the child who is about to be born in a family is established even before conception in the imagination of its parents, in their idea of children, in the way they portray in their mind their features, abilities, personality, even in the way they imagine they will outline their destiny.

Therefore, on the one hand, there is an imaginary child, created from the desires, ideals, and frustrations of all family members, on the other hand, a real one, with its own thoughts, feelings, and emotions. If the real child does not resemble its image, a great distortion is created - between the parents' projection, the motivation of the child's conception, and his true personality - which can have long-term repercussions, over several generations.

As the child grows up, if the parents stick to their fantasy, the child has to comply more and more with their expectations, learn the roles assigned to it, and play after a script written beforehand, the family script. He is a prisoner of the pattern assigned to it, and if it does not fit, if it is reproached to, forced, blamed, or removed from the system for what it is or is not, it ends up feeling guilty, unloved, and not belonging anywhere.

On an unconscious level, willing to be accepted and to remain loyal to the family, the child will align itself to their wishes, and in adulthood, he or she will not understand why (s)he is not happy, what is that (s)he misses and what is (s)he actually looking for, that is, him(her)self!

The ghost

The transmission of life consists of a cycle of three generations: grandparents, parents, and children, who change their roles permanently as time goes by.

The things that were named, said or unsaid, the thoughts and projections, and the words and statements that flowed between them, compose the psyche of the genealogical tree and the structure according to which the entire family novel is written. In this chain of life progress and transmission of information, a child does not learn to speak and think, but takes over the language and thinking of the parents, which it unconsciously integrates and later passes on to his/her children.

In the bosom of a family and in the interaction between its members there are always rules about what you must say or what you must never talk about, the facts that deserve to be praised and remembered over time, and facts that must be swept under the carpet and concealed by all means. The labels, the appellatives, the diminutives, the cuddling, the naming, come from the family unconscious, from the parents' desire to create new versions of themselves. Therefore, what is communicated may or may not be true, and how things are said helps shape a family story and program its descendants.

The lies, the secrecy, reluctance to bring up what caused pain, forgetting, as well as repressing some thoughts or hiding some stories, distort reality over time. The unvoiced or unthought is like a ghost that haunts over several generations and produces the destabilization of the entire family system. Usually, this ghost hides the silence over some unintegrated events - abortions, lovers, divorces, crimes, dispossession of money, etc., and its presence stores unknowns, missing links, and information, pages torn from the story, unfinished chapters in the lives of parents and their ancestors.

These gaps and everything that was not expressed in words create psychic discomfort and tend to be expressed later in the life of the offspring, through gestures, somatizations, or events of an inexplicable nature. Everything that has been blocked in terms of the flow of transmission of truth can be felt in mental health, in blockages at the level of verbal expression or cognition, and in the intelligence, cleverness, and learning patterns of children and their descendants.

The archetype of the planet Mercury symbolizes the respiratory system of the family tree, the inhalation and exhalation, its lungs, and the whispers that its members transmit to themselves, beyond space and time.

Brotherhood

As far as the family structure is concerned, Mercury represents the siblings, the extensions of the parental couple, the branches of the family tree. The more children are in a family, the more it branches out and, therefore, the more kinship ties and hierarchies are created between its members: cousins, brothers-in-law, uncles, aunts, nephews, and godfathers.

Feelings of love, competition or rivalry, attitudes and behaviours between siblings, intensified by those of parents, such as comparison, favouritism, or imposing expectations, create a complex in each of the children.

Brotherhood is an important relationship within the family and is a key element of the family tree, because the way each was received into the system, the chronological order of births that differentiates between older and younger siblings, and the relationship between them, configures the way the family tree is arranged, and the laws governing it.

In order to sustain itself, sustain life, and to be able to evolve, the family tree system always tends to remain in balance. Like a real tree, it needs strong roots, symmetrical growth, and preservation of proportions between the trunk, branches, leaves, and flowers.

Single-parent step-siblings or those who believe they have the same parents but don't, adopted siblings, hidden and unknown siblings, bastards or siblings excluded from the system give rise to unknown paths in the family tree, tangled or broken branches, unsuspected entanglements with other families and unnaturally evolving genealogical lines.

Hate, jealousy, anger, envy, unexpressed emotions, but also excessive love, the feeling of complicity, unhealthy attachment, and incestuous relationships can be consequences of how every sibling received love and attention from the family, but also of some unconscious patterns, inherited from generation to generation.

To keep symmetry, a mistake can be perpetuated for a

long time by an unconscious algorithm and balanced only many hundreds of years after it occurred, by subsequent generations, who are faced with similar situations without knowing why!

The law of order, belonging, and balance

The law of birth order reflects the fact that depending on the position at birth in relation to brothers and sisters, each person has a distinct role within the family system, and, along with the place they occupy, they also receive from their parents the related responsibilities.

The first child is the firstborn and will always have a special place in the family because it is the first child of the parents and may be considered the natural leader of the younger brothers and sisters. The second child may be considered the "middle one", and the last child may be seen as the "baby" of the family. The eldest sibling may be considered responsible for protecting younger siblings, and the youngest child may be considered more vulnerable and treated with more care or pampered. A child may be the grandparents' favourite grandchild or be the firstborn in a family with a long history of first-born women or men, which gives them a privileged role.

These distinct positions can have an impact on how each child relates to other family members and what role they play within the family system. Since all members of a family are linked together through a system of membership, the family being an interdependent unit, the actions and behaviours of one member affect and influence the entire family, both positively and negatively.

When the individual needs of a family member become too great or too important compared to those of others, this can lead to an imbalance in family relationships and affect the well-being of the entire family. For instance, if a family member suffers from a chronic disease, this can affect the emotional state of the whole family, causing a change in roles and responsibilities within it - the mother takes over the father's role or, on the contrary, the father takes the mother's duties, the children take care of their parents, they grow up too fast and miss their childhood. Or, if one of the parents decides to move to another city for a job opportunity, this choice can have an impact both on the children, who would have to adapt to a new school and a different social environment, and on the spouse, who in the new location may no longer feel fulfilled or able to find his or her place.

Each member of the family has unique needs and desires, so there must be a balance between these and the needs or desires of the family as a whole.

In a healthy family system, there is a balance between give and take, between self-support and membership, and between stability and change, as needed to enable the family to adapt and grow over time. When a single member feels left out, unimportant, unseen, misunderstood, or unloved, the whole family suffers, if not visibly and consciously, more than likely on a much deeper level over time.

Pattern inheritance according to the order of emergence in the system

It is important to note that in a family consisting of the parental couple and several children, the patterns shown by every single brother/sister are different, and this is explained by the tendency of the family tree to maintain balance and to replicate the same characteristics or personalities on the vacant places in the system.

For instance, the first-born of a family can conform to the pattern of the first-born from the parents', grandparents', or great-grandparents' family, the second-born aligns with the second-born from the lower steps, and so on, respecting the algorithmic law of the order and hierarchy.

Things get more complicated when the patterns are repeated, but not in people of the same gender (for example, the first-born is a boy but takes over from a branch where the first-born before him was a girl), where between living siblings there are also miscarriages, abortions, stillbirths, single-surviving twin births (as these all add to the order of siblings in the system and identifications or projections), or when there are also children outside the couple, from previous or later marriages, abandonments, and adoptions.

Each birth takes a distinct role in the family system and is bound by a unique red thread, which it receives and follows, so that what may be called fate, as well as the personalities and unconscious modes of manifestation differ in the members of the family, even if they are siblings and are born, raised and developed in the same environment.

Therefore, if we want to understand the roles that each member of a family receives, we need to study the number of brothers and sisters in the predecessors' systems, as well as the circumstances, context, and manner in which they experienced life.

In the chapter on planetary aspects and unconsciously inherited life patterns - even if siblings of the same family have similar astral configurations - it will be considered that the interpretations may vary depending on the order and the way they belong to the system.

Hermes

Mercury, or Hermes, is the only god who can move quickly and freely between all dimensions, universes, and worlds (levels of the psyche) to convey messages and information. In transgenerational astrology, his archetype represents extended family ties, siblings, ramifications created by them, cousins, the way they communicated, the social relationships they developed, and the binder and script by which life experiences and family history unfold.

It is by him that the teachings of each generation were passed on, and the conscious memory of the entire genealogical tree was formed. He contains truths and untruths, communicated, hyperbolized or distorted facts, and also hides secrets, unsaid things, kept or unkept promises.

Mercury is the keeper of love letters or declarations of war, it is the sum of thoughts and words, spoken or written testimonies, diary pages, and photographs in the generational album.

He symbolizes what has been preserved on the mental level, the Psyche of the family tree.

What are the questions answered by the study of planet Mercury?

◊ How was the information passed along the system?
◊ What is the structure of the genealogical Psyche?
◊ How did family members express themselves?
◊ How did they communicate with each other?
◊ How were people encouraged to think, to express themselves?
◊ What is the relationship between brothers, sisters, and extensions of a system?
◊ What is the natives' psychic and rational structure?
◊ How did they listen, look at, and respond to the world?
◊ What filter did they use to see and judge?
◊ What is their conscious reality?
◊ What is hidden in their mind and what direction are they focused on?
◊ What are their abilities to pass knowledge and information onward, to the system and to the world?

The Sun and the Moon

*The world will ask you who you are, and if you don't know, the
world will tell you.*
Carl Gustav Jung

The parental couple

A child's life is largely programmed during childhood when it becomes the mirror of those who raised it, that is, an extension of the parental consciousness.

To really know him/herself as an adult, he/she needs to understand, accept, and cure the relationship with the parents, who represent the relationship with life itself, with the source, and with the creators.

Conscious - Unconscious

In the early part of our life, we build alter-egos for ourselves. It is a period of life that takes place mainly externally when we seek to satisfy our needs, desires, and goals related to integration and success in society. By the end of this stage, we build strong personalities and think we know who we are, defining ourselves by our status, achievements, wealth, degrees, or titles. But what we think we are is an identity that shows only one side of the coin, the outer one, an illusion, Maya. Because we are half awake, we are not aware of the tension between the inner side and the outer one, the conflict between what is hidden in our soul and what we see in reality, a tension that can make us unhappy or that, more often than not, leads to somatization and major existential crises - unhappy relationships, jobs or professions unsuited to the soul, frustration with decisions made, or anguish projected onto life situations and people around.

The second part of life can represent for many the desire for inner discovery, to access the soul, and this first step triggers the process of individuation, that is, to know and complete the two parts of oneself, to access the shadow. The process of individuation, as the psychologist Carl Gustav Jung called it, involves the way, simple or complex, by which every person becomes what they were destined to become from the beginning of life, by which they become complete!

Failing to unleash your inner side means repressing and killing a part of yourself! Failing to unleash our inner side makes us only half alive, and whatever lies in the unconscious will demand its rights. When we fail to make peace with what is within, all the illusions and fantasies of the Ego are projected outward!

The Outer and Inner side

In astrology, the Sun archetype symbolizes the outer and masculine side of the astral chart, representing the father, his personality, the concept of paternity, and the content inherited from him along his systemic line.

At the opposite pole, the Moon archetype is the bridge to the inner and feminine side, representing the mother and her personality, motherhood, how she positioned herself and was received in the system, and the information transmitted along her genealogical tree.

The Sun and the Moon are a quintessence of all the experiences and life situations that the fathers and mothers of an entire family system have experienced. Their archetypes carry within themselves, at a subconscious level, the informational imprint of how they have over time exercised their paternal and maternal functions and the way they have passed on these values.

The way parents behave with children is a copy of the way their parents were, who in turn are a copy of their parents, who tend to copy their parents, and so on in a long chain of information, which goes through the entire family tree, from the most distant roots to the last bud.

Father-Sun

Family-wise, what is seen on the outside and the primal mask we try to copy is that of the father hero, the masculine energy, and the authoritative father figure.

The Sun is the archetype of the father and his systemic line, as well as his connection with the child, from which the inner child is born, but also the future adult. The Sun shows the link between the fatherly figures in the bloodline and their relationship with the children.

The way the child was encouraged to express itself, the freedom it was given in play and in finding its own identity, the ability to create and recreate, all can be seen in the way the personal Sun shines and in what was passed down from the father! The ability to move in the external environment is given by his influence. The Sun is the heart of the astral chart, the nucleus which all the other planets revolve around, representing the self, the external identity of the individual, but also all his egoic masks. It is the way it shines in the world, the way it explores and faces the world.

The Sun is the hero, the embodied self, who sets out on the

journey called life and goes through all its stages, from childhood to adulthood, seeking to become, to be, to live, to experience, to answer the questions: who am I and who I want to become?

He is the eternal inner child who wants to play and integrate himself into the countless roles he can play on the stage of life. It is the desire to be genuine, beyond the inherited patterns, to find oneself, the true self, beyond what he was taught or what was passed on him to be.

Through the Sun flows vitality, vital energy, self-confidence, courage, and the desire for autonomy, individualization, and freedom. He represents the ability to be his own master, the king of his own kingdom, and the central figure in the story, the father.

Psychologically, the Sun represents the trilogy between the parts of the self: the id (the instinctual part, what we feel inside), the superego (the moral, controlling part, what we display externally), and the ego, the part that tries to find a balance between the first two.

The ego is responsible for the perception of the self as a separate entity and the need to protect and maintain our identity in the world around us. When it fails and feels unable to cope with the world, it may create an alter ego, that is, a character who expresses himself in a different way than he normally would, who has no fears, traumas, or blockages, and who is characterized by traits and abilities by which it can cut trough. An alter ego is a second personality or alternative identity, developed later and perceived as reality.

The need to be seen

In order to grow harmoniously and develop, children need to be seen, enlightened, and valorised. A child who receives light from a strong, bright Sun, which emanates plenty of energy and heat, gains self-confidence, while the one who does not receive the light of valorisation and has a weak, slowly flickering Sun by its side, is devitalized. In this latter case, throughout its life - since it does not have enough strength to develop - the adult child either gives up its goals and hides in the shadows, or tries to compensate for the shortcomings it has by own resources and to draw attention to itself, placing itself in the spotlight!

The need to be seen means to be considered, to be received, to be correctly positioned in the family, to be accepted, to be welcomed and loved, to feel joy from others when they learn the news that you are, to be guided, listened to, and understood.

Systemically, the children unseen by their parents, abandoned, unaccepted, or left alone hang heavy in the family tree as their Sun tends to fade while they want to survive.

At the same time, the aborted children, those who died at birth, during pregnancy, or, much more dramatically, those who were killed by their parents because they were not wanted, have their place in the system as entities that should have existed, as offspring whose existence lasted very little. At an informational level they existed and were supposed to be born, but, for various reasons, this right of them was denied. Like children who live, they need to be known, remembered, loved, and seen by their parents, siblings, family, and descendants. They exist as dead members of the family tree, they are present in it and waiting to be recognized as members.

In their turn, the pain, guilt, and resentment of mothers who gave up their children or who lost them, are passed on at an unconscious level, creating a trauma across future generations, that face infertility, difficulty in sustaining more pregnancies, the impossibility of creating a family or sadness, depression, and anxiety when faced with the idea of becoming a parent.

The Sun, the self, and the ego

Any child, in order to detach beautifully, to be released, and to become an autonomous self - in the material or subtle space - needs the blessing of its parent.

The position of the Sun in the natal chart, depending on the sign, house, and aspects, provides information about the patterns and transgenerational complexes that were inherited from the male lineage, of the father, and which are highlighted in the current personality of the native through self-esteem and respect, the feeling of self-worth, confidence in one's own strength, the postures of the self and the ego.

What are the questions answered by the study of the Sun?

◊　How is the father figure seen throughout an entire system and what is its legacy?

◊　What is hidden in the father's family tree and how does it leave its mark on future generations?

◊　Were there hidden, infamous, outcast parents?

◊　How were the children seen, how were they welcomed into the family, and how much encouragement or guidance did they receive to cope in the outside world?

◊　How well prepared were they for life or how was their existence blocked?

◊　What is the native's relationship with his/her father?

◊　What is the manner in which the native's ego is expressed?

◊　How does their inner child manifest?

◊　What are their joys, passions, and loves?

◊　How does it play on the stage of life?

◊　How can the native express his/her success and what is his/her visibility in the world?

Mother - Moon

The mother sustains life within her and nourishes the child for it to survive. The connection between her and the child is intimate, close, embrace, and depth, a connection by means of which the child receives the grounding and rooting it needs to begin to grow. The mother contributes to the growth of the roots, ensuring nourishment in the earth, and the father ensures the extension in height, above the earth, towards the light and the sun.

Through the roots we take in a certain family, the feeling of belonging to the entire genealogical tree is born, through which we connect physically, and emotionally, but also unconsciously to all its parts.

In the past, before the development of the big cities, life was lived in small settlements, in villages. People knew each other, children grew up together, families saw each other every Sunday at church, respected traditions, celebrated unions, welcomed newly arrived children with joy, and buried their dead together. The community is a cell, with its own rules of operation, its own conduct and interdependence between elements, delimited borders, and safe bases. The community is a family, to which you feel you belong, in which you feel contained, protected, and safe, just like in a womb.

On the lands of the birthplace are our ancestors and roots, there is our origin and mother. Many times, we feel its call home as an inner echo of longing, which embraces us due to the strong emotional ties that keep us attached to the memory of that place.

From a systemic point of view, every child needs to know that it belongs to a certain family, that it has an identity, a nationality, it has roots, and that can return home at any time. Only this way is it connected to the source of life, is emotionally nourished, and has the inner stability to set off confidently towards the Sun!

Belonging

In antithesis to the Sun, which is related to the obvious, visible genetic inheritance, the Moon refers to the long history of the family, to its roots, and all that has been stored in the unconscious of the family tree.

The Moon is a symbol of the mother's warm womb, the inner, intimate, and emotional environment within a family, for the invisible and subtle bond that unites all generations.

The Moon is the gateway to understanding the family picture, the mother's dowry chest, and the maternal line. Archetypal traits flow through it such as compassion, care, empathy, fertility, the ability to provide care and support on an emotional level, being an indicator of the basic needs and how we attach ourselves, build our nest, and open our soul to others.

The moon stands for the space of childhood and the connection with the parents, with the ancestors, with the places of birth, with the kin, and with the entire family tree. It is the sense of belonging to the family and to the sacred space that builds up along with it, to the community, country, or humanity.

It is on the Moon where all the emotions, pains, and sufferings endured by both the family and the mothers are encoded. It is by it that we can comprehend the accumulation of feelings gathered at an unconscious level and the inner, hidden motivations of the present!

Psychologically, the Moon is the unconscious, a part of the human psyche that is inaccessible to consciousness and that contains hidden information, thoughts, feelings, and desires that impact our emotions, relationships with others, and behaviours.

Circumstances such as children who were estranged at birth, bastards, children raised by a grandmother, sister, or aunt as if they were their own, cases where paternity/maternity is hidden as a result of infidelity, rape, or incest, children kidnapped, killed or sold, create deep holes in the family system, which will tend to bring the traumas to the surface in order to heal them!

The Moon, unconscious family patterns

The mother-child bond transcends time and is passed on in the form of patterns that influence the manner, time, and attitude of the offspring in procreating and raising their own children. The way in which we choose to make a family, the fears in the face of the idea of being a parent, the fertility of a woman, as well as the house we have are a continuity of the past, still present in the inner unconscious memory.

What are the questions answered by the study of the Moon?

◊ How did the mothers of this system dedicate themselves to the growth and evolution of the family tree?
◊ What is the reason they became mothers for?
◊ Did they assume the role of mother?
◊ Did they give love?
◊ Were they or did they know how to be mothers?
◊ In what context did they do it?
◊ How is the inner life of the native organized?
◊ How do they express their emotions and what is their attitude towards the family?
◊ What is the native's relationship with his/her mother?
◊ What is the native's degree of fruitfulness, of fertility?
◊ How does their inner universe transform into the ability to care for others?
◊ What are their subconscious desires, emotions, motivations, and reactions?

Parental complexes

The child's relationship with its parents, with the family environment and the feelings it develops in childhood shape its personality and have an impact on its entire existence as an adult. The relationship between the two genealogical trees represented by the parental couple, i.e., the two families to which the child relates, the father's and the mother's, the emotional connection between the parents and their level of interaction, can be analysed in the aspects between the Sun and the Moon, as well as in the aspects between them and the other planetary archetypes.

The aspects show how the information is transmitted along the family tree and how the situations or relationships between its members were integrated, the dynamics within the family.

The harmonious aspects show a harmonious transmission, while the hard ones show an information transmitted distorted, a mental or emotional load that must be integrated and released.

When a planet is involved in several aspects, its archetype and symbolism are essential in the family system, because they reveal a nodal point, a family member or situation on which all others depend, a constellation of complexes.

Psychologically, the astrological aspects translate into parental or ancestral complexes, i.e., the sum of unconscious thoughts, feelings, and behaviours, positive or negative, resulting from interaction with parents or other parental figures of childhood (grandparents, uncles, aunts, cousins, brothers).

A negative parental complex can arise as a result of the feeling of inferiority, abandonment, guilt, authority or dominance, etc., and in adulthood, it somatises physically in diseases, depression, anxiety or personality disorders, and difficulties in relationships with the people around.

Once identified with one of the maternal or paternal complexes, detailed in parts III and IV of the book, the individual can develop an emotional dependence on it, helplessness and inadequacy, as well as poor development of their own identity.

In order to function individually and evolve into its own version, the Ego complex needs to detach itself in due time (around the age of 14) from the maternal and paternal complex, otherwise it will be subjugated to them, it will tend to repeat the same transgenerational patterns and be a copy of one of the parents.

Any complex that is not recognized and worked upon is projected externally, creating a strong imprint in personal reality.

Mars and Venus

To a man, the Anima is the mother of God who gives birth to the Divine Child. To a woman, the Animus is the Holy Spirit, the procreator. He is at once the light and the dark God.
Carl Gustav Jung

Men and Women

While the Sun and Moon represent the parental couple, the archetypes of the planets Mars and Venus are an extension of them, symbolizing men and women throughout the system, the concepts of masculinity and femininity down the ages, and how they found and exercised their function in the family.

Mars and Venus are equally the husbands, brothers, uncles, brothers-in-law, and sons, as well as all the wives, sisters, aunts, sisters-in-law, and daughters that make up the family tree.

How are men or women remembered in the system? What kind of relationship did they have with each other and how were the unions formed? Were there marriages of convenience, arranged, were they happy, did they love each other, what was the context they lived in, and what were their experiences?

Venus stands for the attitude towards women and the way they were valued, the value attributed to love, and the way the feeling of love was perpetuated. She symbolizes all the poses of the woman - child, virgin, partner, wife, or lover and it is in her where love, desire, beauty, femininity, and harmony, but also the suffering, disappointment, and frustration of unfulfilled relationships are coded.

Mars symbolizes the attitude towards men, the value attributed to bravery, masculinity, heroic deeds, virility, and the strength to be a fighter, defender, leader, partner, husband, or lover. It is also pervaded by its hard side, the shadow, aggression, anger, war, struggle, trauma, or destruction.

For a woman, Venus symbolizes her femininity and what she has inherited on the female line, and Mars portrays the man she unconsciously seeks, the pattern she needs in order to continue, understand, and heal her story.

For a man, Mars is his phallus, his masculinity, his male heritage, and Venus is the woman he seeks to complete himself.

Mars is the Animus and Venus is the Anima of the entire family tree.

Masculine - Feminine

In the process of individuation, everyone has to become acquainted with the two energies within oneself, because if one is lost, the other is in distress.

The integration of the feminine and the masculine in one's own person means balance, a fulfilled relationship with the Self, and therefore also love! When the two are brought together, the soul is complete, a complete human being.

This alignment produces the first step toward self-accomplishment, healing, liberation, and spiritual evolution.

The gifts

The woman has the ability to beautify the place where she is, to give colour to the home, to spread scents, and to attract with her charm. She is the one who inspires and creates, muse and fairy, gentleness and mystery. She is the one who seduces and the man is the one who conquers.

On the feminine side, Venus is the wealth of the family system, the treasure that engulfs all the talents, skills, and crafts the ancestors have developed and which they passed on to the descendants to use as inner resources.

On the masculine side, Mars symbolizes the ability to use our inheritance, enrich it, and exercise our power in life. He means determination, strength, ambition, courage, honour, and the way each individual acts. The Martian energy can be constructive, bringing courage and discipline, or destructive, cruel, brutal, and aggressive, depending on how it has been and is mastered.

Venus symbolizes the bounty of the family system, balance, and peace, while Mars governs passion, desire, and sexuality, but also weapons, accidents, and operations, being like a volcano full of vitality that lies within us waiting to be released and directed.

Love

The relationships we have with other people are projections of our relationship with ourselves, in fact, a relationship that continues to exist from another time in ourselves. The attitude toward love, the ability to maintain relationships, to understand the other, and love that appears for certain people fit the pattern that we feel unconsciously.

Venus symbolizes the love between our parents, the love they received and the way they passed it on to their children and future generations, the way we love and know how to maintain relationships.

Following this lead, we will find that we tend to repeat the theme of past love until the tree is freed from it, that is, until the moment when the alliance between two partners does not mean trying to replace their mother or father, and they cease to project the parental figure on them.

The "destructive" relational patterns, if any, will repeat themselves cyclically until the aspect is understood, realized, resolved, and integrated until the chain is broken and its ghost released.

Most of the time, it is necessary to learn self-love, personal empowerment, freedom in relationships, and love.

Venus is the feminine energy in each person, built on the basis of the relationship with the feminine side of the family, especially with the mother, grandmother, sister, and close female relatives. At the opposite pole, Mars is the male energy and it materializes especially on the basis of the relationship with the male side of the system, with the father, grandfather, brother, and close male relatives.

What are the questions answered by the study of the planet Venus?

◊   How was femininity manifested in the family system?
◊   How were women viewed throughout time and what role did they play in the family?
◊   How was love transmitted and what is the inherited relational pattern?
◊   How was the relationship between the native's parents?
◊   What are the relational patterns that they saw in their family?
◊   What are the inherited personal talents and resources?
◊   How love and self-worth are expressed?

◊   What about artistic and aesthetic sense?
◊   What is their capacity to give and receive love?
◊   By which criteria do the natives fall in love?
◊   For a woman, what is her type of femininity?
◊   For a man, what is the type of woman he is looking for on an unconscious level?

What are the questions answered by the study of the planet Mars?

◊   How was masculinity manifested in this system?
◊   How were men viewed across the family system and what role did they play in the family?
◊   How is personal freedom expressed and what motivates the person unconsciously?
◊   How is the energy released, how does the native act and react to internal and external stimuli?
◊   What is the native fighting for?
◊   Practicality and endurance
◊   For a man, what is his type of masculinity and virility?
◊   For a woman, what is the type of man she is looking for on an unconscious level?

*

The answers to these questions show what are the subtle mechanisms by which we fall in love and form relationships, what is our behaviour when we are in love and why, what makes us attract a certain type of person and what is love at first sight, i.e. that magical impulse that makes us see a man as the most wonderful on earth.

Part II - Family's dowry chest

Saturn

*Until you make the unconscious conscious, it will direct your life
and you will call it fate.*
Carl Gustav Jung

The decisions

We all have to make decisions in life: we choose one path over another, one person and not another, a certain school, a job, a lifestyle, how to live, and so on, and this has an impact not only on our own destiny but also of those who are involved in our lives, in the destiny of the family.

How do we know we've made the right decision, especially when we're faced with hard, life-and-death choices? But what if we have no choice and life forces us? Or, if we violate our conscience and know that we are doing something against our nature or desire, what are the consequences?

In the past, many decisions were made as a result of needs, conditions, or conditioning: for example, wounded abandoned on the battlefield to save their own lives, arranged marriages to restore honour or improve the financial status of the family, children given up for adoption by mothers far too young to support them, educational support for a single child in a home with several siblings, killing someone in defence of one's own life or that of loved ones, dispossession of property as a result of arguments, or other intense situations and experiences. All of these decisions carried an emotional or mental burden that was hard to endure by those who had to make them, causing a lot of pain, suffering, loss, guilt, humiliation, sorrow, frustration, or feelings of helplessness.

Unfortunately, there is no such thing as an unblemished history, and they can all be part of a "once upon a time" in any family tree. They are objective reality, hard facts that happened, and real history, recorded over time. Unintegrated, they remain embedded in the structure of the family tree until they are realized, healed, and released.

The pattern

If we look at nature, we can see that every species of tree has a geometry of its own, according to which it forms its structure, grows, and branches. The way the branches, twigs, leaves, and buds are arranged is not haphazard and random but follows an algorithmic pattern, which keeps everything in a perfect symmetrical balance. Likewise, from a genealogical perspective, like a mathematical system that works according to a certain logarithm, any family system has its own structure according to which it reproduces, its rules and laws of operation, existence, and evolution, which have been perpetuated throughout time and built the skeleton, shape, and dynamics of the entire family tree.

Everything evolves according to a pattern, which tends to reproduce the same shapes endlessly, in fractals. When a gap, error, or blockage occurs in the system, the system tends to fill it up, to correct, or heal it. If this is not possible, the wound is further transmitted to the new, replicated forms, where a new attempt at healing occurs. If even at this younger stage it fails, what remains is passed on in an endless string of patterns.

Anniversary syndrome[3], repetitive dates or ages, synchronicities[4] - everything aligns to respect the structure. When nothing can be done and the whole system gets infected, the chance for life, evolution, and growth decreases, until it fades away!

From a transgenerational perspective, the geometry of the family tree follows the rules formulated by the ancestors at its base, by the authoritative family members, by the elderly, the experienced and wise, by those who have preserved the spirit of the time in traditions, known or forgotten, conscious or unconscious.

There is, beyond time and space, an invisible duty, a family loyalty, and if a positive or negative pattern repeats itself over generations, it happens because law and order must be complied with!

Structure, organization, and rules

A right frame of reference, where the child feels safe, well-guided, and where conduct is followed, creates a solid basis to grow and develop on, whereas an authoritarian, absolutist, restrictive frame of reference, with strict, but also absurd rules, with limits that if crossed there are also consequences, limits the child's growth and leaves it with deep frustrations.

Even though rules like - the young must take care of the old, the first-born male is the head of the family and takes over the household, girls are not allowed to meet boys until they are

---

3   The anniversary syndrome is a repetition of some past events, which happened on certain significant dates for the genealogical tree and which require to be brought back to life whenever necessary for them to be integrated
4   Synchronicity, a concept elaborated by Carl Gustav Jung, refers to the significant coincidence in time of two or more causally unrelated events

18, the younger girl must marry only after the older one, the boy must follow his father's career or the girl her mother's - are no longer spoken, they are still transmitted unconsciously. The consequences can span generations and those who reach the right age get sick, and the burden falls on the younger members of the family, a younger brother cannot afford to grow financially, certain girls are inhibited, a younger sister conditions her life after the older one, boys and girls unconsciously choose a certain path that is not their own (see the section with the analysed examples).

Unfinished business, unbuilt relationships, injustice towards someone who is no longer living, and unpaid physical, emotional, and financial debts, all are passed on to be recalibrated. What has to be recovered, repaired, or replaced demands its rights, and debts are paid according to the law of compensation and balance.

The obligation to the family

Many times, in exchange for the right to life offered to him by his parents, the child has certain obligations towards the family, which obediently it must accept as laws, and take them for granted.

Phrases of reproach such as:

I sacrificed myself to give birth to you.
I've done so much for you.
I gave up a certain status for you to be.
I didn't remarry to raise you.
I got sick working so you could eat.
I grew old providing for your tuition, and so on,

condition one's life, creating the feeling of guilt and, with it, the obligation to return something in exchange, to make an equally great sacrifice, to compensate for all the accusations which they feel guilty of.

Trapped in this conditioning, forced to assume responsibilities and pay for what it thinks it has received, the child misses its own purpose, deviates from what it has to do, no longer has personal freedom and joy, and the dissatisfaction, the discontent leaves a big void, in which depression settles down!

The escape from obligations and rigid family structures, already transformed into patterns, can only be done by rebellion and getaway, by a desire for independence and individualization.

Cycles of Saturn

Psychic contents can be transmitted between the members of a family in two ways: intergenerationally, i.e., between generations that know each other and consciously transmit information, or transgenerationally, i.e., the exchange is made between distant generations, where unconscious content and those kept secret, hidden, unknown, unstated and even unthought of are transmitted.

Like a wave that travels through time, the patterns are inherited from one generation to another, growing layers in the structure of the family tree: children take from their parents and pass on to their children, over a long string of years.

This transgenerational exchange can be traced in astrology through the cycles of the transpersonal planets, especially the cycles of Saturn.

A full cycle of Saturn around the Sun takes about 28 years, so during one's lifetime the beginnings of at most four cycles can be marked:

- the first cycle: 0-28 years of age - generation 1
- the second cycle: 28-56 years of age - generation 2
- the third cycle: 56-84 years of age - generation 3
- the fourth cycle: 84-112 years of age - generation 4

Biologically, while children grow and develop through the first cycle, their parents go through the second Saturnian cycle and their grandparents through the third. If there are great-grandparents alive, they are already in the fourth cycle.

As time passes, the children become adults and enter the second cycle, while those in the second cycle advance to the third, and those in the fourth become ancestors. The first cycle is occupied by the new children of the tree and, this way, every seven years, the tree grows both a layer of branches and a layer of roots.

Intergenerationally, the generation in the first cycle picks up information and patterns from the generations in the higher cycles, and when they advance into the second cycle they are ready to pass it on. Unsolved matters on the upper floors are left to those to come.

1st Cycle: 0 - 28 years of age

During this 28-year period, four cycles of seven years each, the child who is about to become an adult assimilates patterns and knowledge from the higher generations, who are in the second and third, maybe even the fourth cycle.

It is a cycle of waiting, growing, and taking over and many things still depend on the activity and dynamics of previous generations. The child's parents and grandparents are still alive, active, and interacting with each other. What (s)he sees and receives now is deeply imprinted on his mind.

During these years, the ages of 7, 14, and 21 are very important because in these moments their patterns are restructured, depending on what happens in the upper floors and their attitude towards paternal figures.

The child, in turn, can also bring reconfigurations to the upper generations.

Until the age of seven, the child is totally dependent on those who take care of it, since it cannot satisfy its personal, physical, emotional, and social needs by itself. In the first years of life, it is driven by instincts, such as hunger, thirst, rest, play, and love, but at the same time, it is a being with huge potential, waiting to be discovered, shaped, and refined.

The feelings experienced in childhood, the love or hatred between parents, kind or naughty words, certain behaviours and events in the family environment, will be felt in future cycles, as frustrations or personal traumas, as well as virtues or principles of life.

A parent's views will be adopted by the child if it hears them for a long time, views that it will take for granted and integrate, without investigating or questioning them until later, when it is compelled to.

The square of the age of seven corresponds to the first separation from the mother and the family, the age when the first self-accomplishment begins to appear, and the child begins to show its newly discovered personality. One of the first signs of transition from one stage to another is the loss of baby teeth and the growth of adult teeth.

The period of up to 14 years continues the growth, conceptions, and associations of ideas and feelings which begin in the first cycle, 0 - 7 years. The habits the child has acquired in the first cycle of life become an integral part of their behaviour.

The age of 14 marks another transition, the one towards puberty and a time when the desire to break the dependence on parents appears much more acutely. It is the age when a lot of questions, curiosities, interests, and desires appear in the child, while also forming their own opinions. From a physical point of view, the period begins for the majority of girls with the onset of menstruation, and for boys with the awareness of their sexuality, the appearance of hair, sweating, or other hormonal changes that take place to prepare for procreation.

During the next seven years (14-21), those who have not been able to socialize and fully integrate into society may isolate themselves, feel misunderstood, or adopt extreme forms of protest (in the way they dress, the music they listen to, the sexuality expressed in an obvious way, etc.). For others, these are the most beautiful years, the years when they still experiment with teenage innocence, build the longest-lasting friendships, live the most beautiful love stories, and interact with others on a higher level.

If in this first cycle, there are unclear or painful situations, traumas, and separations, that remain unprocessed, and if the parent-child relationship is defective or non-existent, or if the child has not separated properly from the parents, they can develop complexes, such as the Oedipus complex[5], anguish, frustrations, wounds (e.g., abandonment, attachment, dissociation or fragmentation wound).

2nd Cycle: 28 - 56 years of age

Once the first cycle is completed, the child has assimilated what it had to assimilate from the higher floors and is ready to pass it on to its children. During this period, grandparents are usually lost, and the parents step forward in their place.

Although the patterns they took up until the age of 28 are grounded, they still are in a relationship with both their children and their parents, and the dynamics of the relationship between them are evolving and are in motion.

In this cycle, they struggle on the one hand between the patterns and debts received and, on the other hand, between the expectations, dreams, and desires they have. Depending on how they succeed in life, they project their accomplishments or failures onto their children, and also, are grateful to or resent their parents.

Until the age of 56, when a new Saturnian cycle closes, things go both ways - from them to their children and vice versa, as well as between them and their parents.

5   The Oedipus complex is a central theoretical concept in psychoanalysis. Sigmund Freud described the concept referring to the Theban hero Oedipus of Greek legend, who unknowingly slew his father, Laios, and married his mother, Jocasta. In psychoanalysis, the Oedipus complex symbolizes the unconscious erotic bond with the parent of the opposite sex and rivalry with the parent of the same sex, which develops from childhood and causes opposite feelings

The ages of 35 and 42 mark important moments because in these transitions all their patterns are restructured. Besides the Saturnian aspects, around the age of 42, Uranus opposes its own natal position and squares Neptune, which is a moment similar to that of the full Moon (halfway through the cycle between the Sun and the Moon).

Uranus brings the challenge of breaking free from patterns and old beliefs, and Neptune breaks the filters created. It can be a liberating and positive time in every way, when wings are taken, or there can be a reluctance to change and a deeper dive into patterns, frustrations, and fears.

In the case of liberation, what has not been experienced needs to be recovered, and the individual feels a desire for play, brilliance, independence, and focus on one's own person. Some of his relationships break at this point and others are built, on a much sounder structure.

By the end of this cycle, at age 56, the consequences of past actions and decisions are very important. If there is no more purpose and motivation, the person begins to age, and from then on, has to adjust to other demands, and cope with decline and loss of vitality.

3rd Cycle: 56 - 84 years of age

What do people pass on and what is the legacy they leave behind? It's a question that everyone should ask themselves in this last life cycle, where they come face to face with all the choices they made so far.

Depending on how they lived the first two cycles, in this period people can be fulfilled and satisfied with their lives, have a good relationship with their children and themselves, or can be burdened with many regrets, tired, angry, and sick, in competition or at war with the newer generations.

Being in this cycle they can still share directly their life experience, and those in cycles one and two still receive from them.

It is a time when they can still pay off their debts, releasing their children and grandchildren from them.

If they fail to do it and leave with regrets, frustrations, unfulfillments, and secrets, the next generations will feel indebted to pay them in their memory and will tend to follow their steps unconsciously.

Saturn in Transgenerational Astrology

◊ Indicator of structure, rules, and laws within the family
◊ Conformity
◊ The mathematical logarithm by which the tree was formed
◊ Limitations, conditionings, inabilities, boundaries, duties, responsibilities, family blockages
◊ The patterns and traditions that define the family
◊ Invisible fidelity
◊ Maturation, determination, the spirit of endurance, patience
◊ The passage of time
◊ The authoritarian figures, the elders of the system
◊ Negative emotional or mental load

Jupiter

*Often the hands will solve a mystery that the intellect has struggled
with in vain.*
Carl Gustav Jung

The questions

In order to please our parents or to show our anger against them, maybe we once put on a mask, the face of perfect children, or rebels in search of justice.

In order to be accepted among friends, maybe we once put on the mask that the entourage required of us.

In order to be respected at work, we may once have put on the mask of the perfect employee, the man who knows how, who is good at everything, or who must be respected.

Due to the requirements and standards we are required to comply with, or we think are appropriate - to be seen, validated, loved, wanted - we may put on, day in, day out, mask after mask.

But there comes a time when all the masks start to hang too heavy and burn. We are suffocated by this weight, by what others want, by their words and judgment, by what they want, not us, not you.

What mean to be yourself?

Who are you really and who do others think you are?

How can you be genuine when every day you add another veil to the masks and costumes you've learned how to wear?

Who are you if almost everything you know has been taught by others, and how can you be yourself if so many people are inside you?

To be well, you need to be yourself, you need joy, truth, and genuineness, to get rid of masks and show your face.

The journey to the self is, in fact, an adventure where you strip yourself of others so that you can see yourself.

But even so, when do you know you've got to yourself and how will you know to recognize yourself?

Freedom, adventure, exploration, new horizons

How far does a man's horizon extend and where are its boundaries?

How far can be its reach if his view of the world is narrow?

What is the truth, in essence?

What does it mean for everybody?

How many really go in the pursuit of it?

We are born into a truth of others that becomes a certain reality. What we are told by society, teachers, parents, and people who train us and guide our first steps becomes law and is rarely challenged.

What you believe about yourself, the world, and life sets up the profile of the actors you will play with, the script and the stage you will play on. The greater the ability to step out of the play already written, to explore and have the freedom to push the boundaries further, the more the world will be a place of infinite possibilities and multiple truths, constantly changing depending on time, people and place.

Education

Access to and emphasis on education differs for each individual according to the era, place, family, and opportunities of the times when they were born.

For a simple family in the countryside, who raise their children in the spirit of their own needs, in order to carry on the traditions of the home, work of the fields and the family wealth, education may not matter at all, while for a family where the parents, grandparents or others members are literate, erudite, intellectual, education can be more than important, indeed a prerequisite or a true blazonry.

There have been periods in human history, and in many parts of the globe there still are today, when only the privileged, wealthy or of a certain social class had access to education, study or travel, where they came into contact with other cultures, broadened their horizons and evolved.

Polar opposite, those from the disadvantaged class were illiterate or had only access to primary knowledge, received in the family, or acquired through their own experience.

In the case of the privileged or noble, the education received may be an asset, a chance, may be beneficially integrated or, on the contrary, may be felt as a pressure to do something or to become someone, to follow the father's, mother's or grandparents' career, as well as an obligation to family identity and the social class to which one belongs. The one who fails to live up to expectations may be disregarded, ridiculed or labelled as an unworthy descendent, therefore excluded, which can generate one's guilt, shame, fear of not knowing, and the feeling of being unimportant, worthless and unloved.

On the other hand, as far as the underprivileged are concerned, a descendant's dream to study and evolve may be treated with hostility and hindered by the parents, instilling a sense of alienation and a desire to go their own way.

In both situations, the repressed ideals, the frustrations and the wounds inflicted, travel through time and influence many of the following generations.

Social Class

Education separates people into different social classes: people with education, high moral values, principles, and ethical conduct, and people who are uneducated, illiterate, of easy virtue, common, uncultivated, in conflict with the law, of low caste, etc.

Each social class operates as a system, with its own rules and values, and the interconnection between them has long been forbidden, blamed or considered bad. For instance, depending on social identity, it was not accepted for someone of noble descent, literate and educated, of a certain religion or wealth to marry a servant, someone uneducated, from an ordinary family, a poor one, or who was born with other beliefs. This, despite love, has destroyed relationships, created frustration, resentment, guilt, and blame, and led to suicides, bastards, family breakdowns, disinheritance, and even murder.

Keeping up with their rank and social class has created order or disorder in many families, and also created many beliefs that have turned into boundaries, separating and blocking entire generations.

In the bosom of each family, community or nation a personal motto and declaration is created that binds all its members. Beliefs such as rich people are bad, miserly, cold; he who learns the most earns the most; you must become somebody; it is not the coat that makes the man; you have to marry someone of your status, like your father, mother or grandfather; we must not make a laughing stock of the family; it is a sin or not good; having children this way is not a thing to do; the man must only know you from the neck down; and so on, lingers in the collective unconscious of the genealogical tree and resonates in the minds of those connected by it, who tend to follow them and, meaningless as they are nowadays, carry them on.

Religion, dogma and the Church

The first of the most important beliefs which a newborn in the family is greeted with is the religion to which it belongs, and depending on it, the traditions, customs, and philosophy of life that are passed on to it are different.

Those who come from Orthodox families are raised, educated and taught in one way, and those from Catholic, Islamic, Jewish or, for example, atheistic traditions in a completely different way. Depending on the dogma followed, each family has its own rules and laws, which feed fear, guilt, sin, judgment, prejudice and imprisonment into a perpetuated personal truth.

The fear projected on God is actually the fear a child feels in the family, and it is entirely related to the idea of being accepted or rejected by them because simply belonging to a system excuse it of all the actions it does in their name. This is how the hatred between the races was born, which over time has created many wars, murders, pain, broken families, unfulfilled loves and deep frustrations.

Conversely, the marriage with a partner of a different culture or nationality, motivated by the awareness of exclusion from the system, may show the need to get out of the origins of one's own habitat and to approach a completely new and unknown way of adjusting to another social and cultural environment.

The beliefs branded in the unconscious of the family (such as it is a sin to break up; for better or for worse; the woman must obey the man; dogmas; superstitions, etc.) ingenerate strange, compulsive behaviours in the following generations, which obey them to the letter, without having logic explanations for them.

To break free, one needs to challenge such beliefs, ask

questions, judge them by one's own research or experience, and find a truth that is personal.

Jupiter in Transgenerational Astrology

◊ Indicator of beliefs and moral and social laws that have been passed down from generation to generation
◊ The values, the motto and the blazonry that define a family
◊ Proverbs and sayings transmitted within the family, stories about the past and ancestors (related to emotional, financial, social and family life), which end up being idealized, hyperbolized, taken as reference and transformed into beliefs
◊ Family beliefs related to religion, politics, life, dos and don'ts
◊ Encouraging education or limiting it
◊ Chance in life
◊ The ideals, the culture, the capacity for evolution, the intellect broadening
◊ Spreading across the globe, travel and values borrowed from other nationalities and peoples
◊ The ability to find one's own truth

Uranus

Life not lived is a disease from which you can die.
Carl Gustav Jung

The unpredictable

Regardless of the plans, expectations and comfort we create for ourselves, there are always unpredictable things in life. Some developments do not end as we imagined, the plans we made with someone fall apart, events occur that we did not take into account, life turns upside down or, conversely, when we expect less and everything seems lost, a chance, a miracle, a possibility that we didn't expect may emerge, that changes everything in the twinkling of an eye.

Insecurity can create strong attachments or, conversely, a total lack of commitment.

Actually, in order to evolve, things need to escape linearity, routine and comfort zone, to install chaos in the created order, to find new solutions to move forward, to try other options, to let go of the old to embrace the new.

So is life.

Old structures, when they rust and are superfluous to the system, are replaced by new, young ones, atypical from the previous ones. Lingering in the past ultimately causes death, and breaking away from the past brings a new path.

The Atypical

We call something or someone atypical when it deviates from the classical patterns we are used to when it does not obey the traditional, when it does not belong to our limited sphere of perception and does not fit the frame or reference we are normally used to.

Genealogically speaking, the atypical is present in a man or a woman who strikes a wrong note in his/her family, who breaks the rule of the system and stands out with something. (S)he is simply different or, outside his/her family (s)he wants to be different, to be free, unique and genuine.

The atypical persons startle with their unusual presence, their progressive ideas, shocking attitude and their personality, which is labelled as crazy, strange, abnormal or random, and directionless.

If the family supports them and allows them freedom, they are able to breathe new life into the whole family tree, break patterns, change laws and issue evolutionary and progressive rules that would help them, both in their individuation process and in the pattern healing process.

Otherwise, if they are not understood or, worse, not accepted or forced to be compliant, the atypical people have only two options for survival: escape from the absolutist and authoritarian system, take it on their own and free themselves, or revolt against it, becoming rebels, anarchists or the black sheep of the family, who shake the family's foundation, hit hard, tear down walls and structures, taking upon themselves the struggle and the fact that they can be repudiated at any time.

Breaking free

In happy circumstances, when you break away from something that holds you back, there are no more emotional attachments, regrets or guilt, only freedom, achievement and independence. The taste of freedom gives you a new spur, a vital force and a desire to be on your own account, to do something new, in a different way.

In other cases, the escape from one's own system may come as a struggle to change and overthrow it, or it may come suddenly, as a relinquishment, as a flight, or as an expulsion. The excluded cannot find their roots, or their place in life, are wanderers with no clue where to settle, have a choleric, angry temperament and easily revolt against any external limitation. The past - about which they are not resentful - no longer matters, only the future matters. They do not belong to anybody but themselves. They do not know where they are going, they no longer have a frame of reference. All is new and they can innovate. In case of conflict, hell breaks loose inside the family – fights between generations, rebellion against the rules enforced by parents, acts of protest, the desire for dominance and control versus the desire to accept the new personality, which tends to move away from their tree. The war can last a lifetime, in which case the feeling of non-acceptance, exclusion, and non-belonging is strong.

Revolution and revolt

When something is taken from you, when you lose everything and have to start over, when you have no control and your life is moving fast, when you suffer and are not seen, you tend to revolt, to take revenge, to strike furiously left and right.

The rebel's pattern can be transmitted across generations

and can strike out with anger at others as well as at oneself because due to their loyalty, the natives will self-sabotage.

Novelty

Novelty means a step forward from the old way, structure and pattern, broader horizons and advance. The old order always tends to oppose, hedge and hold in place, while the new order has the function of breaking down and going beyond what is visible, palpable and known.

Everything that opposes evolution is revolutionized.

Uranus in Transgenerational Astrology

◊ Indicator of sudden losses/breakups and destabilizing, unpredictable situations
◊ Getting out of the comfort zone
◊ Breaking free or escaping from the mathematical logarithm of the family system
◊ Changing and broadening the former perspective
◊ Rebellions or revolutions within the family
◊ Overthrowing the authority
◊ The breaking down of the Old and the advent of the New
◊ Nonconformism, separation, schism
◊ Breaking attachments, relinquishing the ego
◊ Depersonalization, face forsaking, world's child
◊ New perspectives of evolution
◊ The future and modernization of the family
◊ Emancipation and plans for the future

Neptune

Who looks outside, dreams; who looks inside, awakes.
Carl Gustav Jung

The subtle link, the unconscious

Though apparently our relationships - with the living and people we actually interact with - only take place in the physical world, the connections in the unconscious world continue to exist with those who have passed away, and even with those ancestors of the family tree that we have never known, who lived long before.

We are all connected, from our roots to our last-born, and this relationship pervades the laws of the dimension we live in, and transcends time, life and death since it happens in an elusive realm.

After their passing away, the information contained by people at the level of consciousness merges with that of the entire family system, becoming a unique memory, shared by all. This unconscious space can be accessed using specific techniques, rituals and meditations, by elucidating dreams and the symbolism that is somatised on the body, by decoding the subtle messages that are transmitted between dimensions, because although unseen, intangible and lacking consistency, it exists simultaneously, here and now, permanently.

It bears witness to all that has been, the achievements, successes and gifts, but also the shadows, weaknesses, fears and anxieties, which give birth to great visions, inspirations, and creations, but also nebulae, chimaeras or distorted realities.

Dream and illusion

Every man has an ideal, a dream, a story that he creates, believes in and follows throughout his life. Sometimes this dream comes true, making life a story to tell, other times it flies to the winds and turns into disappointment, into vain hope. In turn, disappointment can produce pain, hopelessness, a sense of loss or failure, and wounds that need time to heal in order for one to be able to move on and build another ideal.

When the fear of pain makes him not give up the dream, when the man refuses to see the failure and identifies with the desire, the ideal ends up haunting him like an illusion, like the shadow of an unfinished story or like a dense fog that covers his reality.

The desire to be in the beautiful story and to stick to the created image, makes them hallucinate and project their own reality onto those around them. Thus, they no longer see them clearly and unconsciously attribute to them imaginary qualities, traits and characteristics, which they need for their characters.

Escaping reality and suffering creates the need to break into an imaginary world, which is envisaged to be redeeming.

The lies, the secrets, the distortion of reality

Secrets are like locked rooms or drawers, where the most intimate or the most vulnerable and priceless treasures are hidden. Whatever happens at the level of a generation between family members, between parents and children, or amongst children and is not said or revealed, remains as a void or as a fog, covering a long series of events experienced by the descendants.

Sexual secrets, those concerning origins, secrets of filiation or paternity, of death, suicide or illness, secrets that cover the shame, double lives, rapes, incest, prostitution, bisexuality, homosexuality, all leave gaps and pages torn from family history, causing further trouble.

A well-kept secret or a lie creates guilt, and duplicitous, inauthentic and dissimulated behaviour in the one who contains them. Secrets leave traces of interpretations, distort reality, and make us think or act in ignorance. Their track is lost in time, those who hid them are gone, and things seem to be buried along with the dead. But this is not true, as the unspoken things are perpetuated across generations and recoil on members who live shrouded in a thick fog that hides their true identity.

It feels like something is missing and the hidden thing continues to show itself under different visions, life situations or dreams. Its presence persists as an unseen ghost and continues to haunt the descendants until they straighten things out, uncover the truth and restore the natural order of the system.

Everything that has not been clarified and left to chance, trailing, abandoned, deserted, dissipated needs to resume its course, materialize and manifest.

Imagination

When something is hidden, when you don't know the truth, when you don't want to know it, or when you know it but can't accept it, the mind can make anything up, may imagine multiple realities, may lie to make you feel good, safe and protected.

Imagination can be the tool that helps you create a better world, in which you give yourself reassuring explanations, have faith that things are going in a favourable direction, or it can be an inner world full of monsters, conspiracies and cognitive distortions, false opinions and paranoid images about people, situations, or things.

Imagination can be the gateway to a fabulous world, which you draw inspiration from, play with and create spectacular things in the physical plane, or it can be the portal to total aberration and madness.

As a result of a lack of identity and inaccurate role-playing, of man's desire to be what he is not, to protect loved ones from the suffering of a painful truth or to defend someone in the eyes of posterity, a whole array of situations can arise - false opinions, accusations and feelings and distortion of reality - untruths, lies and secrets.

On a transgenerational line, they are transmitted as nebulae, as a lack of consistency, a break from reality, and mental and psychosomatic illnesses.

Truth intertwines with the lie, phantasm with illusion, reality with the dream, and smoke with earth until everything becomes so puzzling that it causes madness.

Fantasy

The fantasy is halfway between reality and the unconscious, being the bubble created inside the conscious dimension by the one who wants to escape to another world, where they feel more fulfilled, better, and happier. What they experience in this space cannot be taken away from them, and cannot be condemned or blamed, because it does not shine outward, it is not visible and remains only theirs.

Even if they are married, have a family, a career or an entourage, in their fantasy, they can have anything they want - position, relationship, children - they can love anyone; they can be proud of themselves and can remove mountains. In this image created by them, they can give the best replies, they can emerge victorious from everything they set their minds to, and they can test and experience everything they cannot afford in physical reality.

To those outside they show one face, but in their fantasy, they play a completely different role - they can be both good and evil, angel and demon, they can be a boss, a lover, a heart breaker, they can have everything that they failed to achieve in the real world. A man's inner universe is infinite, and in its overwhelming immensity, everything is possible. In this universe, the human transforms into the meta-human, for whom the limitations of the self are meaningless. The outer universe remains frozen and moves out of inertia, muted, while the inner one has life, passion, feeling and intensity.

Duality, parallel lives

There are cases where those who are not satisfied with their own life, but out of cowardness or being caught in its chains cannot leave the role they are playing, find escape in another story, which duplicates the first in a perfectly parallel track.

Thus, apart from what they have, they create another life situation, another relationship, another family, another job or hobby, playing a duplicitous role and totally different characters. They extract from each world the resources they need, and in each role they play, they feature distinct traits that can only be expressed in the specific scenario they play. In one world they may wear the mask of gentleness, compassion, morality, and exemplary people in terms of principles, and in the other world they may unleash or exhibit their shadows, the repressed side, totally opposite to the first. Maybe much more sexual, more libertine or even obscene, immoral, gloomy and very loose. The two dimensions don't mix with each other, and they can double, transpose, and change whenever they cross the threshold into one another. They are shape-shifting, and the lie, dissimulation, falsehood and duality, but also the devotion, faith and honesty which they play each character with are part of them, feed them, fascinate them and elevate them to the rank of god.

They can instil in the ones next to them the illusion they are somehow, they can weave around them a curtain of details and a beautiful story, meant to entice them, which germinates and makes them believe in a beautiful dream.

Appearances and illusions wrap around, and the ones who are deceived live in their turn a reality that exists only in part.

The spells

What is a spell and how can it be cast?

In life you can be bewitched in many ways, as being bewitched means not being able to take your eyes off something, doing things against your very will or having deviated from your path through subtle ways.

You can be enchanted by the look of someone you fall in love with instantly, you can be enchanted by a song, a landscape, an overwhelming emotion that guides you in a certain direction, you can be enchanted by a passion or a strong ideal.

Nothing exists outside the spell anymore, everything revolves around it, maybe even death and life, which you can sacrifice at any time for its sake.

Traditionally, spells, charms, rituals, and curses are evils that consciously intervene in the subtle world to darken the mind, to influence the feelings, thoughts and will and to deviate someone from the natural course of their life, but at the same time the lies, the deliberate distortion of reality, the hiding, disguising or duality are all spells!

Faith and spirituality

Since we lack a sense of belonging, we don't know where we come from, what our real origin is, and what our purpose in life is, we humans need to create a father, a mother, and a primordial family, a source of our family tree.

We have created ideas about good, loving, compassionate and generous Gods, who watch over us permanently, who are our Sun and Father! We have created motherly figures, deities, saints, angels, protectors, and guides, onto whom we have projected our need to be contained, watched over and protected.

To escape fear, futility, anguish and searches, we needed to simply believe, surrender and offer ourselves completely to our parents, on the one hand, kind and indulgent people, on the other hand harsh, rigid and just rulers.

Faith offers the prospect of an ideal, of a spell that we send into nothingness, of ascension to a sublime space and of resurrection after death. It brings confidence and often translates into miracles that change the course of our lives. But, at the same time, an unseen and absent God induces the idea of separation, of loneliness on Earth.

The absence of real knowledge regarding his origin, creates in man the wound of primordial abandonment, the wound of lack of identity, the guilt of having sinned and the fear of punishment, of the Last Judgment.

The wound of being expelled from Heaven forever changed the relationship of man with God, of children with their father, who feel viscerally that they have been abandoned in a world of suffering and struggle for living.

Since then, they have been constantly seeking to return home, to the source, to be received, seen and accepted, trying not to fail. To this end, they must obey and do the Father's will.

Creation

God created the world with everything that is in it and then offered it as a gift to man, who was also created in His image and likeness, with creative capacities in physical space, allowing him to create things, in his turn, after his own likeness.

What is inside is also outside, what is in the imagination and in the unconscious, can be transposed into matter and into the conscious.

But if the act of creation means that one's own unconscious materializes, creation cannot be something new or unique because it involves the birth of a pre-existing system, a system of patterns.

Therefore, in order to create a completely new reality, the self needs first to be aware of itself, to look in the mirror, and then to destructure itself, to annihilate itself. It is only by this death that it can be born again, only by relinquishing the old self and the patterns that compose it, can it be recomposed.

Life and death are composition and decomposition, spirit and matter, evolution and putrefaction, to create new and new patterns of life.

What is seen - the Son - the Creator and the subtle substance of creation, the Holy Spirit, permanently coexist in an interconnection of dimensions and actions.

Neptune in Transgenerational Astrology

◊ Indicator of hidden, clouded situations
◊ The ideals and dreams of the family
◊ Disappointments and illusions
◊ The ability to sublimate negative experiences
◊ The link between conscious and unconscious, between reality and unreality, between this world and the other world

◊   The secrets, the forgotten, repressed things
◊   Infidelities, betrayals, duality
◊   Spells, brain fog and curses
◊   Family's and native's faith and spirituality
◊   Lies, theft, hiding, bastard children, incest, betrayal
◊   The distortion of reality, the unknown, the void, the fog, the delusion
◊   The imagination, the creation, the muse, the divine help
◊   The ability to communicate with the subtle world
◊   The ability to operate with the unconscious

Pluto

Even a happy life cannot be without a measure of darkness, and the word happy would lose its meaning if it were not balanced by sadness.
Carl Gustav Jung

Destruction trauma

There are moments when life derails from the normal course and in seconds everything is thrown into a storm of illogical, dramatic events that frighten, shake profoundly and change people in a radical way.

In dealing with traumas caused by natural calamities, or by war, rape, murder, illness or the death of a loved one, people are confronted with forces and energies they cannot control, and any effort to take action or resist is impossible or useless. Shattered by pain, guilt or panic, they feel they are struggling in an ocean of emotions, thoughts and feelings, which can overwhelm or devastate them.

After a great drama and pain, the soul needs healing and all that has been destroyed, torn down, killed or desecrated needs to be mourned, balanced and integrated. Unless this alchemy takes place, it remains haunted by regrets and frustration, facing its own demons, shadows, open wounds and fears.

Life inspires pain, torment, suffering, a place haunted by monsters with human faces, who attack, abuse, kill or manipulate.

In order to survive in such a world, you have to guard yourself, to hide, and if you want to fight against them you need to enter their minds and think like them.

Personal transformation

When faced with a tragedy or a personal drama, it seems to us that everything is lost, that nothing will ever be the same, that the world ended at that moment and we will never recover.

As terrified and startled as we may be, the potential of purgatory is huge, because at the end of the process of death and rebirth, we are perfectly liberated, purified or changed, with a much deeper vision of love, forgiveness, regeneration and healing.

Descending into the lowest frequency states, becoming aware of and facing our greatest fears and dreads, breaking from the dark side and returning from the underworld forces us to fight for survival and achieve the true, deep and completely transformative experience.

Dependency and attachment

When we do not indulge ourselves in pain, our soul is tormented by destructive feelings. Loss and separation are felt very intensely, like the dramatic death of a part of one's own person, and the fear of losing something or someone creates dependence and a strong attachment to them. The people who abandon themselves to these feelings want to possess, accumulate, chain and hold. They lack the ability to perceive what is beyond fear, are reluctant to advancement, and become prey to ignorance, habit, outdated conceptions, addiction, and pain. Fear is the refusal to break free and the stalling in a toxic zone, which erodes from the inside and leads to self-destruction.

Having to choose between being the victim or the abuser in control, they choose to position themselves as the ones who never lose.

Abuse and possession

Possession can take different forms, such as physical, mental or emotional abuse, sophisticated games, sexual manifestations, jealousy, desire for control and aggression. Abuse is used to subjugate the partner, leaving them no escape and wanting them to stay possessed, and the behaviour that comes with it can include attacks, coercion into silence, threats, but also subtle tactics such as intimidation, shaming, humiliation, degradation and manipulation. The abused, often without they being aware, feel the wounds much deeper, because these wounds settle deep in their soul or thought.

You're good for nothing, you're horrible, you're a nobody, you'd die without me, nobody loves you, you're incapable, incompetent, ugly, you're penniless - are the whispers that tear apart the self and self-esteem, meant to entrust victim's life to the abuser.

For their abusers - having little price of human beings and taking pleasure in causing them suffering - the victims are nothing more than substitutes for their own insecurity and injuries, and the abusers, in turn, victimize themselves for that matter. The wound inflicted is so bitter, yet subtle, that the destabilized people end up not knowing their identity any longer, and eventually considering guilty themselves.

The relationship between the two can go on indefinitely, and if unchanged, it becomes taboo and repeats cyclically in future generations, its most serious forms even leading to suicide.

The fear

Being afraid is human, mostly because fear is a good guard against real dangers. Sometimes it is real and supported by life situations and experiences, other times it is imperceptible, irrational, and without any foundation because it is transmitted in a subtle way.

Regardless of its nature, conscious or not, fear not only paralyzes human beings, but also closes the door of life in their face, denying them any experience that would remove them from the comfort zone created by them and would help them to progress or, simply, to live!

Fear of failure and even success, fear of embarrassment, rejection and abandonment, fear of gossip and people's judgment, fear of calamities, illness and death, fear of the abuser, and even fear of God, are those emotions that make them imagine nightmare scenarios, which they will never like to experience!

Unfortunately, if not theirs, these are the unprocessed pains of their ancestors. Unhealed, they will keep them stuck in a black zone, a permanent purgatory of the dark mind.

Passing away

The system formed by the three houses of water - the 4th (Cancer - Moon) - 8th (Scorpio - Pluto) - and 12th (Pisces - Neptune) - represents the connection of the human embodied in the material dimension with the plane of the subtle world, with the unconscious dimension of his spiritual memory, with that of their ancestors, i.e. with the departed souls.

The 8th house, ruled by Hades, Pluto and the archetype of Scorpio, is the portal passed by the spirit when it separates from the body, at the final moment of its life on Earth, to enter the realm of death. In this transit, it gives up everything it has gathered, the physical, emotional, and psychic layers, stripping layer by layer of what it was as a human being.

It leaves here all the earthly wealth - houses, money, objects, its own belongings - everything it valued and loved, but also the energetic information about all the experiences it lived in its carnal existence - love, joy, acceptance, health, kindness, pain, suffering, hatred, frustration or anguish.

This realm is the dimension of death, where the spirit faces its own existence. According to its load, it sees, lives, and feels everything it has experienced. If this content is warm, beautiful and soothing, it will be able to rise smoothly, in light and harmony, in the peace and tranquillity of its soul. Conversely, if everything hangs heavy with pain, if it is impossible to understand, accept and digest if the spirit has passed beyond burdened with guilt and sin, it is heavy, and the low frequency in which it bathes, drags it down, to another dimension, that of shadows, darkness and purgatory, the place needed for the spirit to transform and alchemize its energy.

In this dimension of passing into non-being, before advancing to the next process - ascension/descent and resurrection, where they leave with the essence, the spirits discard all the baggage accumulated in life, which they leave as a legacy to their descendants, to the living world, to those who remained embodied.

In this dimension lies the dowry chest of the family system, available to the surviving descendants, but also to their descendants, to those who are not yet alive, but will be born in the system, in a future 4th house.

*

When a man is born, he enters the physical world through his mother's body, through the dimension of the 4th house, of the Moon and Cancer.

His body is formed in her womb, and his energy structures

75

are drawn from the family who received him and raised him, shaping him according to their structure.

The 4th House is the realm where he is born, the gateway from the subtle plane of spirits to the embodiment in matter, the place of his family on Earth, of the people he lives and experiences with, from whom he receives teaching and to whom he gives further from his experience.

He is born from the womb, but behind him stands a long line of souls, who were once alive, but became ancestors and returned to their roots. This dimension forms him and presupposes the start with which he sets out into the world, the gate through which time is released, that is, the time of his life on Earth, the time to be and become. With his birth, the thread of time unfolds until death, so that he too, in turn, then becomes part of the roots.

What did he get as a gift and what does he leave behind when he leaves?

As a man, he is born with a dowry chest, that of his predecessors, stored in the 8th house. Those are the values that his ancestors left behind, the ones that they renounced.

He receives as a gift a piece of land, a house, and a family, but also a sum of unconscious structures, an emotional, behavioural and psychic storehouse, which he cannot immediately recognize. His connection with the world beyond, with what he received, is unconscious, as is his memory: where does he come from, who was he and where is he going?

The only connection with what he was, with the dimension of the unconscious world, of him, of his ancestors, of the roots created or not yet created, is the portal to the dimension that exists beyond, simultaneously, the unconscious mind, the 12th house.

In this realm, the third portal, is his last memory, the connection with what he has gathered, with the spirits nearby, with the unembodied.

*

Metaphorically, we come from the immaterial world of the 12th house, we are born into the physical world of the 4th house (also linked to the family unconscious) and we go further through the portal of the 8th house, in a permanent cycle of incarnation and disembodiment. All three houses are the gateways between worlds, between dimensions that intertwine and coexist at the same time or, at least, according to the concept of time on Earth.

The other worlds are beyond the veil, present, unseparated, though incomprehensible for the rational mind.

This is the field of quantum energy, what we call divine help, miracles, instant healings, prophetic dreams and subtle messages. Depending on the frequency they are placed, the ancestors, their spirits, live in an unconscious dimension - down, in the shadows, or are elevated masters. Behind the veil may be the magical and calm world of a fulfilled system, or it may be its horrors.

The legacy

Where do you come from, where do you draw your essence from and what lies behind your body?

Because that is what defines you.

What you are, what you receive, what you do, what you leave behind creates the chain of your life.

You are the sum of the things that were, but you become what you experience and leave behind what you have transformed!

What you receive and pass on, the way everyone gives and the value they contribute, create the entire value of the system, its path, its experiences and skills, and its wealth!

Pluto in Transgenerational Astrology

- ◊ Indicator of traumatic situations, which have become taboo
- ◊ Abuse in relationships, toxicity
- ◊ Fear, unhealthy attachments
- ◊ The depth of relationships and their intimacy, physical closeness, eroticism
- ◊ Manipulation, money and sexuality
- ◊ Recovery skills, regeneration and personal transformation
- ◊ Purgatory, rebirth, life and death
- ◊ Inner mental power
- ◊ System self-destruction
- ◊ The mental, emotional, but also physical legacy
- ◊ Death, mourning, separation by death, the dead
- ◊ Transcending and alchemizing experiences

Lilith and Chiron

Everyone carries a shadow, and the less it is embodied in the individual's conscious life, the blacker and denser it is.
Carl Gustav Jung

The shadow, the wound and the healing

A wound that does not heal and bleeds for a long time unconsciously imprints in all members of a family an emotional or psychological vulnerability, which is transmitted from parents to children and which can continue to affect several generations. It is repressed or suppressed in the shadowy part of the genealogical tree, and in order to be released, healing must occur not only on a shallow, visible level but much deeper, on a spiritual and subtle level.

The healing of an inner wound cannot happen from the outside, it doesn't come from a doctor or a medicine, but it needs a process that takes place inside, intra-psychically, that **means** self-healing.

The capacity for self-healing, employing all resources to help recover the soul, to complete the self and to dress the wound, is the process by which inner strength, power, autonomy, safety and access to inner treasures are acquired.

Inner healing takes place in the darkest realm, in the black womb of the beginnings, in a void hole, in the feminine mind, because the recovery of a part of the soul must take place in the darkness, where it was lost and only then brought up to the light.

When you heal yourself, you come to a higher understanding of the transformative experience and you have the wisdom to heal others with the same wounds, to be there for them on their journey and to light their way.

When you heal yourself, you can be a healer, because by healing yourself you also heal them, the ancestors, the victims, but also the abusers.

When you heal yourself, you forgive, you have compassion, you feel, you know, you see.

The transformation has taken place, like a rebirth, and you are ready for a new beginning.

Healing goes in all directions, and you evolve!

The Nodal Axis of the Moon

I am not what happened to me, I am what I choose to become.
Carl Gustav Jung

The Nodal Axis of the Moon is the backbone of the birth chart, the snake that crosses the lifelines and the personal contribution to the trunk of the genealogical tree. In astrology it is called the Dragon Axis, the Line of Destiny, Karma and Dharma, the axis through which karmic energy flows and is released, helping to create a new energy, enriched with experiences, adventures and emotions gathered in the current life.

The South Node, Cauda Draconis or Dragon's Tail, corresponds to the load of psychic baggage that the self has received or experienced trans-generationally, karmically, in both good and evil manner.

Here all our personal treasures, abilities, talents, and accumulated experience are found, as well as what deeply marked us, the threshold we could never cross - weaknesses and fears.

By delving deeply into this dimension one can gain wisdom, and understanding, and reveal countless explanatory meanings for the events that took place during the soul's journey, but one can also acquire all the necessary resources to move forward, towards liberation and evolution.

Planets conjunct the South Node give clues about unresolved situations, postponed things, unintegrated traumas and sufferings, which hang heavy in the present and need resolution.

The North Node, dragon's head (Caput Draconis in Latin),

by contrast, is the path that aligns the balance, that helps the growth and development of the self, but also of the entire genealogical line. Its orientation brings new possibilities of manifestation, the opportunity to advance and to overcome the comfortable, familiar zone of the pattern. It is always directed towards expansion and the future.

*

On the **Aries-Libra** axis, the soul goes in search of self-identity and love. It experiences birth, survival, pain, hunger, aggression, struggle for life, war, coldness, abandonment, defeat and victory, conquers and is defeated, defends, is victim and aggressor, falls in love, suffers, leaves and is left. It covers the distance from Me to We and vice versa, from the couple to its own person.

Psychologically, it unites the masculine and the feminine, the man-woman relationship, learning about the self and the partner's self. Spiritually, it understands the law of nature and love, goes beyond the Anima - Animus and obtains both freedom and love!

*

On the **Taurus-Scorpio** axis, the soul learns about the abundance of the Earth and the Universe, about the cycles of nature, life and death, and about ephemerality. It walks the path between needs and desires, between creation and destruction, between what it gives and what it receives in return, learning about its own worth.

It experiences desire, pleasure, innocence, conflicting feelings, sexuality, life and death, shadow, fears, addictions, loves and hates its executioner, transforms, is malefic and beneficent, builds and destroys, creates, abundance and poverty, spring and winter, dead and living!

Psychologically, it accepts death as a part of life, it accepts its sexuality, finds its personal values, the beautiful and the ugly, and is reborn from its own pain, alchemizing!

On a spiritual level, it understands the law of abundance and creation, of evolution through detachment and destruction, of having everything it needs!

*

On the third axis of evolution, **Gemini – Sagittarius**, the soul learns about the power of its mind, about intelligence, reason, intellect and truth! It advances from solving simple problems all the way to science, from being aware to knowing, from curiosity to wisdom. It experiences forms of knowledge, religions, traditions, lies and truth, gets caught in its own mind, gets lost, learns, gives up what it knows, gossips, insults, has obsessions, and is crushed so that it has brilliant ideas later!

From a psychological point of view, it frees itself from any cognitive pattern to reach the personal truth, balancing the health of the mind!

Spiritually, it understands the power of thought and speech, the way a thought/word could create or kill!

*

The **Cancer-Capricorn** axis unites the subconscious with the conscious, the roots with the present, and childhood with adulthood. The soul learns to love its father and mother, to be objective and subjective, emotional and concrete, to walk the path from child to adult and from adult to parent, from intimate to social life. It becomes father and mother, child and elder, predecessor and ancestor, root and fruit, learns empathy, detachment, forgiveness, authority, heart and hardness, is orphan or prince.

Psychologically, it learns about the family tree and its secrets, about its connection to its mother and father, and about all the beings it has inside it.

Spiritually, it learns that what is within is also without, about its energetic connection to the roots, about the world as a great human web.

*

On the **Leo-Aquarius** axis, the soul learns about the ego and its dissolution, about the individual and humanity, about power and its surrender, and about the force of a cell in a body. It is king but also nobody, becomes somebody or is laughed at by everyone, gives up its power and takes it back, laughs, loves, is young and beautiful, ugly and naked, rebellious and cheerful, mad and rebellious, strong and weak.

Psychologically, it balances the self with the ego, takes off its mask, composes itself and breaks free.

Spiritually, it learns to live in full joy and happiness!

*

The last axis of the zodiac, **Virgo – Pisces**, is the journey from the conscious to the unconscious, from the tangible to the ethereal, from science to faith, from the cleanliness of the body to that of the spirit, the journey from heaven to earth and to finding the divine in man. The soul learns about sickness and the body, about imagination, hallucination, fascination, the divine and the dust. It faces the imprisonment of the mind, soul and body, struggles between life and death, between what it sees and what it believes, between sin and guilt, between itself and God!

Psychologically, the soul unites the rational with the irrational, the chimaera with the tangible. It understands its connection with past lives, cause with effect, and what it is with what it thinks it is.

Spiritually, the soul learns to be both man and God at the same time.

Part III - The dynamics of family relationships

The greatest tragedy of the family is the unseen lives of the parents.
Carl Gustav Jung

Mars and Venus, the sons and the daughters

Harmonious aspect

We all contain multiple sides and sub-personalities, we are both water and fire, soul and spirit, yin and yang, both feminine energy, Venus and Moon, and masculine energy, Mars and Sun.

Anima is the feminine side of a man's soul (the unconscious feminine dimension), while Animus is the corresponding masculine side of a woman's soul (the unconscious masculine dimension).

A harmonious aspect between the masculine side and the feminine side creates the archetype of the androgynous, that man or woman who brings together the two sides of the self, thus feeling complete and fully satisfied with their own identity.

The men of this family system were heart-breakers and good lovers, while the women were independent, free and enterprising. Between the masculine and feminine energy, there was cooperation, union and fair distribution of forces.

The man who has connected with his Anima within is a man, but at the same time, he exhibits his tender, caring, patient, empathetic and compassionate side. He is charming, loving, a lover, but also a partner, husband or friend. He is self-sustained, knows what he wants, and is determined, but he also understands the sentimental and warm side of life, which he needs to express his love. He appreciates the fair sex, admires the woman and knows how to relate to her, how to take care of her, comfort her, or love her.

On the other side, when the relationship with the Animus is fully integrated, a woman has all the feminine qualities, being sensitive, harmonious, loving and passionate, but she also features masculine traits, being independent, strong, assertive, rational, down to earth and a fighter.

She appreciates a strong man, but also a passionate and romantic one, and is ready to open up and throw herself into his arms with sensuality, but also to take the reins, carry it off and be manly if needed.

The natives with a harmonious aspect between Mars and Venus have the ability to give and receive love, but also freedom, to maintain a correct relationship with the partner, to be natural, charming and seductive in relationships, willing to keep the flame burning and determined to show their abilities.

The two energies, Anima and Animus, work harmoniously inside them, giving them the opportunity to manifest both qualities, to rely on themselves, but also to understand, appreciate and motivate their partner in order to build a successful relationship.

They have the opportunity to reach their inner resources and distribute them constructively so that they have a lot to gain - they work hard, but also receive rewards, have patience and perseverance to advance, have a keen eye for beauty and have measure, as well as many skills or talents.

The feminine spirit seduces, creates, sustains and heals, while the masculine one conquers, acts, transforms and provides security.

Hard aspect

Depending on the historical period when one lives, and on the developmental stages of the self, on the family and on the relationship with the parents, for both a girl and a boy, the feminine or the masculine side can be repressed, badly understood or distorted.

For instance, boys are taught from a young age to become men and girls to become women. The boys have to be strong, and bellicose, to fight, and the girls have to be delicate, sensitive and loving. Boys are encouraged to develop masculine traits, while girls are encouraged to develop feminine traits, anything in between being considered inadmissible, and out of the norm.

A boy who represses his feminine side grows up to be harsh, aggressive, intolerant, misogynistic and not to hold women of much account. He simply does not know how to show such qualities, so he despises them. Conversely, a woman who represses her masculine side always needs help, is unable to manage things on her own, and is soft-spoken and very submissive.

Usually, the two are attracted to each other and form a couple!

On the other hand, a boy who represses his masculine side becomes effeminate, weak, fearful, without direction and power, feels inadequate and is dominated by those around. He attracts to him a woman with a very acute masculine side, possibly argumentative, brutal, insensitive, authoritarian and destructive.

Psychologically, in order to become fully complete, both need to go on the journey of discovering the missing energy, heal at a deep level, and release the traumatic experiences that led to the segregation of the two sides.

They must reconcile the man and woman within, accept the relationship between mother and father, between the women and men of the system, as well as the pair of forces within.

Somatization: runny nose, eczema, red skin, urinary, sexual or gynaecological dysfunctions and infections, kidney blockages, thyroid problems, kidney sand, scars in the neck area, problems with vocal cords, colds, voice change, hoarseness, laryngitis, sore throat, cervical injury

Feminity

Moon - Venus
Mother, daughters and love

Harmonious aspect

In this trans-generational system, the union between family members was valued, its main values revolving around the idea of love, harmony and security.

The maternal figure, together with the women present in the system, has played an important role over time, that of keeping the family flame burning and passing on all their emotion, care and empathy. They may have been beautiful, feminine, stylishly women with a strong aesthetic sense, who expressed both their qualities as wives and mothers. Many sisters, aunts and cousins took care of the family's well-being, of men and children, while also taking care that the houses were clean, nicely decorated and nothing was missing. It is possible that the family was not short of money, was wealthy or belonged to a high social class, of nobles, landowners, or hard-working people, who cultivated the idea of well-being, and comfort, but also cultivated work.

The aspect between the Moon and Venus is imprinted with beautiful and emotional memories, related to the intimate atmosphere of the home, to the grandmother's pantry, the mother's kitchen with her goodies, the warm kiss goodnight, hugs, large family and strong experiences. All these, later in life, awaken the most pleasant feelings and remain in the soul forever.

The child born with this aspect was fully accepted, cared for and loved by its mother, from whom it received the assurance of the right to life. It inherits the ability to give and receive love, inner harmony, artistic sense, empathy, optimism, a flair for money, but also an inclination to relaxation. It is surrounded by love, contained, protected, and in turn open to protecting others. The man with this aspect tends to look for a warm, welcoming, feminine and sensitive wife who will take care of him and recreate his home environment, while the woman with this aspect features a strong maternal sense, wanting to provide, protect and defend.

Since the feminine energy is strongly manifested, both are sensitive, emotional, tender, compassionate and very pacifistic. They seek to keep their home in balance, they don't need conflict, they value their privacy and have a strong demand for abandonment, sensuality, comfort, pleasure and convenience.

The involutory side of the aspect can create laxity, lack of action, abandonment, self-indulgence, habitualness, and the tendency to stay in the warm environment of the comfort zone.

The natives can recreate a pattern of the mother or women from the whole family system, to whom they remain loyal and carry their personality.

Hard aspect

This family system is marked by a negative maternal complex, by strained family relationships, where women were not given the right role, were rejected, disowned or did not have a good reputation, by mothers who did not know how to play the role of wife and, conversely, of wives who did not know how to be mothers, and take care of their children.

There is a discrepancy between the quality of a mother and that of a woman, of a wife - once they become mothers, women no longer have the right to be women, to dress up, to express themselves sexually or erotically, to be sensual or seduced. The mother pattern and the woman pattern are totally different, and there is a conflict between the two roles. Between the mothers of this system and their daughters, there was no strong connection, on the contrary, possible rivalry, jealousy and desire for control.

It is possible that between family members there were only meretricious relations and complacency, without a healthy attachment, where they tried to impress each other and where there were tensions, disputes or envy related to money.

The children of this family were allowed a lot, but they were not properly valued. Possibly, there were many repressed feelings, they were deprived of love or care, there were secrets related to love and money, concealed relationships, but also frivolity.

Later, in the native woman with this aspect, there is the conflict between the desire to be a mother and the abdication of womanhood. She cannot express her femininity properly, lacks empathy, is emotionally dependent or erratic, prone to strong attachments or much too independent, unable to maintain a fair emotional relationship. Not wanting to lose, she can go to extremes - she becomes a career woman but has frustrations in her private life at home, or becomes a housewife and a mother but forgets to be a woman, shrinks into herself, and becomes sad. The mother's identity is projected in relation to other women - daughters, friends, powerful women, older women, whom she will feel attracted to, disappointed by or compete with.

As a man, the relationship with the mother is projected onto the partner, who will be chosen according to a certain pattern, to reproduce childhood situations. In him there is a separation between the mother pattern and the woman pattern, therefore it is possible to be drawn into a relationship of pleasure, desire, and sexuality in the beginning, but later, after founding a family, he can no longer perceive the partner otherwise than as a mother, with whom he can no longer have the same relationship as before. In this case, possibly, his life partner would come into conflict with his mother.

In order to find themselves and be satisfied, both the woman and the man with this aspect need to reconcile the two archetypes inside, to make peace between mothers and women, to honour motherhood, and femininity with all its valences!

Somatization: digestive and weight troubles, pregnancy troubles, skin imbalance, acne, menstrual pain or irregular menstruation, nausea, vomiting, breast cysts, hormonal or menstrual imbalance, endocrine gland imbalance, problems related to thyroid, mal-absorption

Moon - Mars
Mother, Sons and Personal Independence

Harmonious aspect

In this type of family system prevailed the boys, the share of sons, cousins, uncles and brothers being higher. The attitude towards men and their role in the family was an important one and possibly marked by ancestors who fought in wars, and knights who performed many acts of bravery, evoked as heroes. The masculine spirit of freedom prevailed, as the men were heads of households, but their mothers too stood out for their bravery, inner strength, resilience and independence. Emotions, gestures of affection and candour, as well as feelings, were expressed with clarity.

The natives with this aspect have strength of character, and charisma, are attractive and always play a winning game due to their intuition. They were always encouraged by the family and felt supported in their actions, of which they are now in control. They are honest, straightforward, unpretending, and able to express their feelings without difficulty. They fight for what they want and strongly attach to whatever provides them security!

The feeling of belonging to this family, the devotion to it and the defence of its rights are a priority for the members, who throughout the generations remain loyal to it.

The downside of the aspect is that, in the absence of a war or a clear motivation for action on the part of the men, it can translate into sons wanting to stay close to their mother, not to stray too far from the core family, to remain too attached to the mother figure and to remain mama's boys, eternally pampered.

Hard aspect

The Hard aspect between the Moon and Mars contains disharmonious family relationships where fighting and aggression prevail. The ratio of maternal to male energy is neither balanced nor properly integrated, therefore out of balance. The family is not seen as a safe place, but as one where the runaway or attack feelings are very strong.

Possibly, this family's memory stores the war trauma, the pain of mothers who lost their husbands or sons in harsh circumstances, in accidents, in fights or acts of violence, or of mothers and women who were subjected to abuse, aggression or rape. The spectre of men's aggressivity, arguments, beatings, physical violence, injuries, pain, suffering, panic, battles within the family, abortions or loss of children due to bodily harm, wanders over time and demands healing.

At the other extreme, it is possible that the mother figure, in an unconscious attempt to defend herself and take revenge on the male energy, which she considers blamably, may be harsh, unapproachable, intransigent and very oppressive, and will constantly try to unman her husband or children. She keeps her men on a short leash, restricts their freedom, interferes with their business, is possessive and jealous, has frequent tantrums and terrorizes her children.

Many feelings of anger and terror, revolt and fear in the face of attack haunt this system, which will unconsciously arouse aggressive and unpredictable reactions, angry outbursts and competitive emotions in its offspring.

The turbulent home environment may cause the woman with this aspect to attract men lacking affectivity, uninvolved, or to have reactions of intolerance, demandingness and scandal. A man with this aspect can project the image of the mother onto his woman, engaging in a physically or emotionally abusive relationship with her.

They need to control their anger, filter it and make peace with their inner male energy, which they can channel into something constructive.

Somatization: emotional strain, inner and eye tension, abdominal cramps, migraines, insomnia, inflammation of the ovaries, ulcers, purulent bumps, ulcerative stomach, irritable stomach, gastritis, breast, ovarian or uterine operations, internal wounds, suppurations, discharges

Moon - Mercury
Mother's words

Harmonious aspect

The family tree of the people with this aspect has many ramifications, symbolizing an extended family, that has created many degrees of kinship, connections, relations and bonds. The family's history is known from the stories of its members, who keep documents, letters, and photos from the past and invoke them on every occasion with nostalgia.

Over time, declarations of love and promises from the bottom of the heart were made, and the words had a great emotional charge. Customs, traditions, and the memory of the ancestors are passed on by word of mouth, by expressing the emotions lived by them, and by preserving family relationships, which remain united. Family members look out for each other, advise each other, are open about the life events they are going through and always have a good word for each other. The bond between siblings is very strong, they are emotionally attached both to each other and to their families. There are no secrets between them, and the intimate side is easily settled out. The maternal figure is evoked as that of an intelligent woman, who always knew how to find the most appropriate words, how to raise questions, scold in a special way, communicate properly and encourage her children to develop, educate, socialize and learn.

Over generations, the natives with this astral aspect can easily communicate their feelings and, otherwise, they can flame spirits with their speech full of emotion and empathy. They are good psychologists, have excellent intuition, can describe many emotions in a few words, have flair, and are always spot-on! They easily understand people around them, grasp and understand information easily, and have the ability to pass it on, which comes from their hearts. They can be good traders, merchants or educators.

At the same time, they have the ability to speak very nicely, to seduce with words, to put value on their words and be good diplomats. They are charming, sociable, polite, and sophisticated, they beautifully arrange words in sentences, write beautifully and are good storytellers. Not willing to bother with their words, they are also very polite, conciliatory and careful with the terms they choose. They need people to communicate with, are attracted to intelligence and are stimulated by interesting things, that capture their attention or fascinate them. Their thinking is feminine, they have the ability to see the whole, appreciate shapes and observe symmetries. It is easy for them to imagine, think in colours, perceive intuitively and make things beautiful!

Hard aspect

The presence of a dissonant aspect between the Moon and Mercury indicates intricate family ties, lost or forgotten branches, single-parented or separated siblings, and members dispersed in all directions, who were lost track of, or no longer in touch with.

Somewhere in the past, some things were kept silent, important documents or deeds were destroyed, some matters became taboo, there were promises unkept, there were secrets, the thoughts were not expressed properly, or there were many quarrels and scandals as a result of faulty communication. Many harsh words, that left deep marks and scars were spoken, painful accusations were made, words of emotional manipulation were addressed, the verbalization was wrong, and many thoughts, emotions or ideas were repressed.

A hard aspect between the two archetypes can also symbolize a vicious relationship amongst the women in this family system, or between the mother's side and her brothers: many, but shallow, meretricious relationships, women who did not get along with each other, who addressed each other nice words, but criticized, gossiped and envied each other behind their backs, tawdry, unpolished, nagging, curious and snarky women, who maintained quarrels, scandals and discord in the family, or who contributed to the breakdown of relationships between members.

All that was passed on at a family level is naughty, malicious, venomous speech or an insulting address, not at all respectful towards people or women. At the same time, the women were not encouraged to express themselves, to learn, to speak, or the bonds between siblings were in a total imbalance.

Where the feminine component in thinking is missing or

distorted, the words used by the native with this aspect can be dirty, shameful, ostentatious and mean. They feel the need to create imbalance by the way they address themselves to others, to approach taboo subjects, but at an unconscious level they only replicate psychic experiences or memories that they have not integrated or healed.

For a woman, it can show criticism from her mother, sister, grandmother, or any important woman in the family, unexpressed feelings, unfinished statements, forbidden or shameful relationships, not talked about, unbalanced or unhealed relationships with siblings.

The natives with this aspect may feature nervous reactions, may become emotionally unstable, attached to the words spoken by others, inhibited in expressing feelings, shy, introverted or loose-spoken in an attempt to draw attention, to penalize and emphasize the nuances of the expression of others.

As long as the emotions have not been expressed correctly over the generations, many times they cannot express in words what they feel, experience a conflict between mind and soul, do not appreciate forms properly, have many slips of the tongue, use ambitious words, stutter or try to impress with vocabulary, become defensive if it seems to them that their speech is not appreciated, especially because they live with the trauma of not knowing, being stupid or having no idea.

Somatization: irregular menstrual cycle, fallopian tube problems, pulmonary oedema, varicose veins, stomach cramps, bloating, laxity or constipation, ulcers, indigestion, nausea, blood sugar problems, speech or articulation problems, stuttering

Mercury - Venus
Feminine Intelligence

Mercury and Venus cannot form an angle greater than 58 degrees - conjunct, semi-sextile, semi-square and sextile. A semi-sextile aspect, a sextile aspect or an association in a favourable sign is considered a harmonious aspect. A hard aspect can be represented by a semi-square, an association in an unfavourable sign of the two planets or an aspect stressed by a third planet.

Harmonious aspect

The human brain has two hemispheres, the left, representing the male side, the Sun and Mars, and the right one, yin, symbolized by the Moon and Venus. In general, the left side of the brain is responsible for masculine, logical, rational and analytical functions, language and mathematics, while the right, feminine side is involved in creative, artistic and spatial functions, in the perception of shapes and dimensions, in intuitive and emotional thinking.

In this type of family, there are literate or intelligent women, merchants, and people who get along with each other financially and sentimentally. For the system's members, blood ties mattered, and the relationship with the siblings was a good one, of harmony, love and understanding. Emphasis was placed on communication of feminine type, on passing on a valuable education, through beautiful speech, expressing feelings and candour.

A harmonious aspect between Mercury and Venus represents the female voice of the system, reminiscent of the social gatherings where women assembled to sew, wash or work together, while they sang, told stories, and gave each other advice on how to make the best decisions. The dialogue between them was straightforward, and the conversations carried on had great value because the power of female intelligence has the ability to weigh, discern, to bring colourful shades to thinking.

The union of the two archetypes contains love whispers, vows and declarations, love words, letters, poems, passionate or delightful descriptions, and pure and beautiful promises.

The natives with this aspect are candid in speech, appreciate intellect and conversations, are optimistic, open to socializing, but also quite volatile.

If also confirmed by other aspects, possible strong attachment between siblings.

Hard aspect

The relationships between the women of this system may have been shallow, and there may have been gossip, backbiting, arguments, pricks, tension, or possibly they did not even talk at all to each other. Possibly, there were brothers who had different values and fought over money, and wealth, they were rivals in love, or their wives fought with each other, thus breaking the bond between the brothers.

Due to conflicts and lack of harmony, the creative expression of the natives with this aspect is inhibited, and their ability to reach inner resources is hindered.

It is not easy for them to talk about their feelings, it is difficult for them to create relationships with those around them, and they lack the openness and delicacy of listening or speaking.

Many times, they won't verbalize what they feel.

Somatization: hoarseness, throat or speech problems, choking, laryngitis, papilloma, warts, bumps on the skin of the hands, arms or fingers, deformed, asymmetrical fingers, sugar problems, nephritis, renal colic.

Masculinity

Sun - Mars
Father, Sons and Masculinity

Harmonious aspect

The harmonious paternal complex of this family features a strong male spirit, of independent and brave men who fought for a cause and overcome their life hardships.

The children with this aspect describe their father as a strong, active, intelligent and liberal man who instilled in them a very high sense of autonomy. They were encouraged to act on their own, to let no grass grow under their feet, and to have freedom of movement, therefore, in adulthood they have self-confidence, vitality, and energy and can be proud of their achievements.

A man with this aspect is a warrior, has great personal power, possesses leadership streaks, is a trailblazer and a good initiator of projects. He is tenacious, focused, determined and stands out easily. He is tough, has backbone and strength of mind, is very virile and overflows with sexuality. In love, he is passionate, and likes to conquer, to make grand gestures and compete, especially if the stakes are high.

The woman with this aspect has the ability to choose a man equal to her father, but at the same time, she keeps her independence, being able to act and handle herself, being a warrior.

Both men and women seek to stand out, to come to the fore and reach the top of the ladder.

Hard aspect

Hard paternal complex, where the father's authority manifested with harshness, aggressiveness, enforcement of his own decisions, desire for control and, quite possibly, physical punishments. The father's frustration, helplessness or inadequacies are repressed by the family, wife or children who, as they grow up, will rebel against him.

It is possible that the father was jealous of his son's youth and set limits on his development and expression, which gave rise to rivalry and competition between the two. At the same time, also marked by an Oedipal complex, the son can fight against the father to remain the main hero.

Later in life, without proper detachment from the father image, the native with this aspect is full of anger, unable to control his energy well, is overzealous, fights everyone, wants validation, is always moody and restless, and lives in tension. He can be unpredictable, and due to his explosive and hasty nature, prone to accidents, injuries and dangerous situations.

If the aspect is repressed, the native has a strong inferiority complex, he feels powerless, an underdog. He interiorises, is fearful, submissive, weak, and unable to assert himself, or whenever he is on the verge of success, something happens and he misses or gets hurt.

A woman with this negative paternal complex can unconsciously enter relationships that mimic the father's masculinity, being attracted to men of two opposite typologies - either tough, aggressive, with brutal sexuality, cruel and intolerant, or men with repressed masculinity, incapable, tolerant, slack, and lacking motivation. She, in turn, may be aggressive, tawdry, authoritarian, with a great desire for revenge, or being in competition with her partner.

Both the woman and the man need the respect, validation and attention of the father, autonomy and release of aggression, otherwise, they will not have peace, they will not be able to direct themselves correctly and they will seek to impose or beg this respect from all the people they get in touch with.

Somatization: headache, inflammation, meningitis, encephalitis, fever, sunstroke, stroke, heart problems, spinal cord injury, hair loss, palpitations, angina pectoris, pericarditis, endocarditis, dental abscess, furuncle, baldness, gingivitis, inflammatory, painful diseases

Sun - Venus
Father, daughters and femininity

The two planets cannot be more than 48 degrees apart from each other, so there can only be a conjunction, semi-sextile or semi-square between them. A harmonious aspect can form in a sign favourable to the two planets, and a hard aspect can be represented by a conjunction in unfavourable signs, a semi-square aspect or Sun-Venus conjunction in a hard aspect with a malefic planet. The Sun-Venus relationship is also analysed according to the phase it is in (see "Retrograde Planets" chapter).

Harmonious aspect

The positive aspect between the Father-Sun and the feminine Venus highlights a harmonious, correctly integrated bond between the paternal spirit and the feminine side of the system, represented by the wife, daughters, daughters-in-law, and sisters-in-law, who in turn recognize, accept and validate his authority.

It is possible that the father was a charming, handsome, glamorous man who received and further developed in his children the idea of harmony, peace and balance, or it is possible that the father was surrounded by many women. He inspired love, generosity and candour, and his daughters related to him as a hero. His joyful, sociable spirit, and desire to feel comfortable and live a good life, attracted around him positive relationships and valuable connections.

As a partner, he knew how to create a healthy relationship with his wife, who was most likely married for love, to appreciate femininity and sexuality, and not to control or manipulate his daughters.

The natives with this configuration inherit valuable skills from the father's line, or even considerable wealth, which they can use to shape their destiny.

The man with this astral aspect is able to love, get pleasure, express both his masculine and feminine sides, be a talented artist or have an innate sense of money. However, he must detach himself from the image of his father, from the paternal complex, even if a positive one, and stop being his little boy (or faithful to his model of success).

The woman with this aspect can fully express herself, be creative, and have confidence in herself, but she must avoid remaining attached to the father or projecting his image onto her partner.

The man with this aspect will look for healthy relationships, vibrant, passionate, expressive and extroverted women, while the woman will want a loving, faithful and reliable man.

Hard aspect

A tense interaction between the two archetypes can show a dysfunctional relationship between the father figure and the female representatives of the family system. Maybe the father never knew how to express his love, and failed to inspire a sense of harmony and to accept his feminine side and the women around him. He may have been an authoritarian father, disturbed by the beauty of his daughters, whose sexuality he did not respect or encourage them to express. At the same time, he may have been an adventurer, in search of momentary pleasures and desires.

The natives with this aspect, both men and women, cannot easily access their inherited gifts on the paternal line, consider themselves undeserving or worthless, they always need validation and appreciation, which they constantly seek externally.

Sometimes, for fear of coming to the fore, they postpone their desires, stop pursuing their dreams and drop their bundle, other times they make a great show of zeal, and emphasize those values that don't even really matter to them.

Although they need lots of people to surround them and cannot be alone, they rarely feel they are loved and always seems to them to be missing something. To fill this void, they may compensate with expensive things, just for show relationships, or momentary pleasures. They can be reckless, indulge in parties, gambling and financial speculations, find no satisfaction or joy in anything, and therefore experience frequent moments of sadness and devitalization.

If they fail to properly integrate the aspect of the hard parental complex, they may engage in an endless chase for love or things that bring them joy, but they will not really find the peace, balance and self-esteem they need.

To break free, it is necessary to return to childhood, to understand and heal the relationship of their parents, of paternal and maternal love, to acknowledge the wounds of their inner child and the mechanisms they created to defend themselves, or not to suffer. They need a new set of values, self-confidence and much love.

Somatization: sore throat, inflammation of the vocal cords, hoarseness, polyps, nephritis, arthritis, torticollis, inflamed nodules in the neck, goitre, otitis, lack of vitality, skin eruptions

Mercury - Mars
Masculine Intelligence

Harmonious aspect

In terms of family relationship dynamics, it is possible that in this system there are many boys, brothers, cousins, uncles and plenty of male energy: enterprising people, ready for work, and action, who make decisions quickly and are always on the move, open-minded and eager to acquire knowledge. They were encouraged or forced to learn, to fend for themselves, to go out on their own and do something with their lives. Since childhood, they have been allowed to judge independently, to decide, to have autonomy, and to be free to explore, move away, leave, socialize and train! There may have been intellectually powerful men who contributed through their actions or thinking to important cultural, social, and political moments of their time.

The natives with this astral aspect have great mental focus, distributive attention, being great speakers. They are able to nail their colours to the mast, they can duel with words, and always have a winning speech, because they rely on their knowledge and intelligence. They have a sharp mind, fast thinking, don't miss a thing, and make connections very quickly.

Since they put so much sentiment in what they say, their

words have the ability to penetrate, inspire and inflame. They are not the kind of people who ruminate about what happened in the past, but are rather focused on what they are doing now. If they are provoked to enter into debates, they cross the t's and dot the i's, are sarcastic or acid, and drive those they catch off guard into a corner. They talk much, fast, and loudly, give a lot of information or have a very convincing logic.

Inasmuch as they were systematically encouraged to express themselves, there is harmony between what they think, say and do, they have the ability to succeed in what they set out to do, and cannot be forced to do something they wouldn't do. They always have something to learn, being both curious and eager to pass on and teach those who are at the beginning of their journey. Able for a great deal of movability, they always move forward, never stopping, because they are tireless.

Most of the time, they maintain a relationship with their relatives and are ready to do a lot for their siblings, whom they support to a great extent. Since they need mental stimulation, movement, and intelligent conversation, the natives seek partners with whom they can have a dialogue, who would stimulate them mentally, whom they can consult, and with whom they would constantly have something to talk or do.

Hard aspect

Possible situations in the family past - rivalry, fight or rift between siblings or other family members, hard sibling complex, insults, slander, bad, hurtful or fight-inducing words, threats, provocation, instigation, quarrels and tensions, scandals, screams, howls, psychological abuse, destruction of information, intrigue, conspiracy, defamation, enforcing certain reasoning in thinking, mental torture, verbal aggression, punishment, possible accidents in travel - car, train, bicycle accidents, the loss of relatives in accidents, battles or war.

What has been transmitted in this system causes a strong intra-psychic conflict to the natives, who become argumentative and ready to start a fight if you do not agree with them. They are verbally aggressive because they, in turn, have recorded in their structure words that hurt - swearing, curses, and insults.

To defend themselves or to win, they put words in other people's mouths, seize upon any mistake, are hectic in speech, act like tittle-tattlers, have fits of anger and nervous bursts, always being in tension. Sometimes they keep their negative opinions to themselves, pile them up without expressing them, and then they erupt like a volcano.

Deep down there is a lot of strife that hasn't been consumed, repressed anger, that's why they also harbour thoughts of revenge. Always sure they are right, tend to silence those they interact with, are impatient, jump to conclusions, and find it extremely difficult to admit when they are wrong, even if they know they are wrong.

Their nervous system is stretched to the limit, so they need to unwind, calm down, allow themselves to relax and make peace with themselves. They need to forgive and dissociate themselves from what hurt them, to learn to be gentle and to use words properly, without rushing. At the same time, they need to rest, to learn to stay, or walk in the right direction, not astray.

If they have siblings, they may have a loss, there may be conflicts, arguments, competition, rivalry, or there may be a lot of unexpressed tension. The system needs justice, peace and balance, and reconciliation. Any of those involved needs freedom, self-identity and, above all, authenticity in finding personal truth.

Somatization: stuttering, speech disorders, nervous tension, migraines, brain disorders, hand and finger injuries, nerve damage, lung inflammation, acute pneumonia, lack of coordination and orientation in space, limb fractures, impairment of senses, pancreatitis, inflammation of the spleen or liver, peritonitis, hernia, accidents in travel or in means of transportation, ADHD, nervous breakdowns, choleric temperament

Part IV - Patterns

Those who learn nothing from the unpleasant facts of life force cosmic consciousness to reproduce them as many times as necessary to learn what the drama of what happened teaches. What you deny submits you; what you accept transforms you.
Carl Gustav Jung

Aspects of the planet Jupiter

Jupiter - Sun

Harmonious aspect

When a harmonious aspect links the Sun and Jupiter, the thinking patterns, ideals, moral values and education were received from the father or, trans-generationally, down his line.

Possibly, the father was a good teacher, an educator, an erudite person, with high ideals or strong faith, had another nationality, was a traveller or a philosopher, and wanted to pass on a valuable cultural or educational heritage to his children.

In such cases, the children perceive their father as an important, generous, altruistic person, full of optimism and enthusiasm, which helps them grow and develop, opening or smoothing their path with opportunities and chances. The father inoculates the children a desire for growth, for knowledge, for freedom or for overcoming their own limits.

The natives are eager for knowledge, personal development and ascension. Life is regarded with optimism, confidence and joy. They want to travel, to learn, to research, to understand the answers to the questions they ask themselves. They are confident in their strengths, they know they can rely on themselves, and their image about themselves is confident, if not grandiose!

Possibly they have ideals, principles and values that they respect in life and that they pass on to their descendants. Life is seen with optimism, with openness, and there are no limits they cannot overcome.

The people with this aspect are extroverted, very good-humoured, adventurous, and particularly imperturbable. Although they are idealistic and often set their bar too high, thanks to their pleasant presence, they always have open doors and luck. They enjoy going outdoors, to sports and interacting with people as diverse as possible, from whom they know they have something to learn. In turn, they can be good teachers, writers or intellectuals, as well as good parents or mentors.

Due to their philosophical air and knowledge, they can become great personalities, imposing, demonstrative, declarative and very passionate about their visions. Most likely, they enjoy standing out, being in the spotlight, showing off and being proud of themselves, often even in an imposing, haughty, grandiose or narcissistic manner.

They have a tendency to place themselves first, but also to be generous, to offer or take under their wing those whom theybelieve they can help.

They are good storytellers and comedians, they like to tell anecdotes and put the people around them in a good mood. When they laugh, they laugh lustily, when they fall in love they burn like a flame, and when they have their heart in what they do, they go to the bitter end.

Since their family memory stores the image of royal times, ballrooms, opulence and grandeur, they like to surround themselves with beautiful, shiny, luxurious things in their everyday life. They like to have fun, eat and drink, and often go overboard with the pleasures they offer themselves.

The Jupiterian archetype expands and magnifies, therefore the ego can be very exacerbated, the desires very strong and vivid, and the expectations they have both of themselves and of those around them, very high. They usually do not give up, and always go on, chiefly because they draw a great deal of vital energies from their family tree, that are sustained. They have a mentor, a spiritual guide, and a fatherly figure they believe in and follow. The bond with the father is strong, and his image gives momentum.

Principles and moral and ethical laws are coded in their DNA, which they are very particular about. They have a strong sense of justice and are ready to rule, direct and do justice.

They are charming, pleasant, warm, loving, and very passionate, but also adventurous in relationships. They like games, love to seduce, flirt, make grandiloquent gestures to impress, and maybe even dramatize or romanticize their experiences. They are open-minded and have no problem marrying people of another religion or nationality, especially when in their family tree such a pattern of mixed marriages may have existed before.

It is possible that the native was given a lot of credit in childhood, was encouraged, very loved, adored, educated, allowed a lot of freedom, or the male figures of the system were prominent people.

◊ **Famous people with a harmonious aspect between Jupiter and the Sun:**
◊ Thomas Mann, Mick Jagger, Jennifer Aniston

Hard aspect

This family system's standard of living was either too high or too low positioned by the parental figures - a parent of easy virtue, a traveller, adventurer, exaggerated in gestures and attitude or hyperbolized as a hero, whose image produces in the child's mind a desire for fame, success and popularity, but also competition and eagerness for revolution. To that effect, there is an unconscious desire to belong to a certain social class despite one's capabilities, talents or values, possibly imposed by the father or inherited down the paternal line. At the same time, what was transmitted at the educational level does not let the child be himself, and limiting beliefs or dogmas suffocate the authenticity of the self.

Other possible situations: the child was left on its own, in a loose leash, praised excessively, flattered, placed on a pedestal, and things came very easily to them in life; the father always on the move, distant from the family clan; attraction to a certain religious cult; slander, failure, defamation, loss of reputation; troubles with the law enforcement bodies, different ideologies within the family, social class discrepancy; amusements, games, parties, disorganized family life, not offering children a healthy growth structure; immoral, exuberant, loose, gaudy, opulent, but worthless environment.

In an attempt to live up to expectations that it perceives as very high from the very beginning, the child always tends to do more than they can, exaggerates, tries to stand out, wants to be noticed, impresses, is boastful, strident, grandiose or obviously too potent in the qualities it ascribes to itself.

In adulthood, they live beyond their means, suffer from a strong ego, and think they know everything or they are perfect. They brag about their knowledge, but they have no sound knowledge. They may have a false ideal, a desire for growth, but without relying on something concrete, education or knowledge. Their appearance is of intellectuals, but they have many gaps in their knowledge, they speak by the book without understanding the content, and boast about concepts they did not comprehend.

At the same time, due to their tendency to get things very easily, they can also resort to less orthodox ways to make money, to obtain a position, or to acquire a certain honour! They can end up in frivolous, contested situations, draw attention through a scandal or through their new, strange concepts, that go beyond normal horizons.

Their view of the world is nevertheless grandiose, optimistic, fiery and often much more positive than it actually should be! Since they need to be loved and given a place, to be praised and appreciated, they put themselves in situations where they are particularly generous, jump to everyone's help, and make grand or bravado gestures.

If the aspect is unintegrated and pushed to the extreme, the natives may end up with psychological disorders characterized by a persistent delusion of grandeur, believing themselves to be superior, self-sufficient and worthy to be put upon a pedestal. They put far too much emphasis on the importance of their own person, are overconfident, and when they leave the stage or are no longer seen, they panic, cool down, lose confidence in themselves, and are fearful and nervous.

Due to their vibration, they attract social circles that promote a materialistic and self-centred style, which - in an effort to be trendy - they want to keep up with, or to be recognized by. In such cases, they become arrogant with the excluded, those who do not have the same importance.

Their need is to break free in a healthy way, to be authentic, but also to receive the father's approval. If the father fails to understand their desire and to give them his blessing, if they do not feel they are seen and accepted, they will always seek to draw his attention, exceed their limits and initiate a conflict with him. At the same time, they will tend to copy their fathers' failure or immerse in indulgence, gambling, frivolity, reluctance to take any responsibility, and inconsistency.

Somatization: heart or spine troubles, fever, enlargement of the heart, convulsions, palpitations, hypertension, lung infections, hot flashes, fatigue with exertion, lack of stamina, back pain, heart attack, obesity, sometimes an excess of energy - other times lack of energy, mood swings - great joy followed by bitter sadness, heartburn, acidity, baldness, inner turmoil, tremors

Stages of awareness and healing phrases

◊ I honour my father and my paternal line
◊ I accept my father's beliefs and free myself from them
◊ I see and accept myself as I am, I have nothing to prove
◊ Joy, love and acceptance are inside me
◊ I have the right to be authentic
◊ I happily open myself to life
◊ I am on the verge of discovering the virtues that define me
◊ I build the faith that represents me and I follow the ideals in which I believe
◊ Everyone has the right to be as they want, as long as they do not interfere with the freedom of the other
◊ I am free to get the education I need to evolve
◊ I am my own mentor, whom I trust
◊ I see myself, respect myself and give myself the rightful place in the system

Transgenerational transmission

Unintegrated experiences related to this aspect can occur in offsprings who have the Sun in Sagittarius, the Sun in the 9th house, Jupiter in 5th or 10th house, as well as the Sun in hard aspect to Jupiter. Repetitive or revelatory experiences can take place during Jupiter's transit to the Sun or during Jupiter's transit through the 5th and 10th houses.

◊ **Famous people with a hard aspect between Jupiter and the Sun:**
◊ Edgar Cayce, George Lucas, Oscar Wilde, Monica Lewinsky

Jupiter - Moon

Harmonious aspect

In this family system, no resentments and secrets were kept, there were no emotional blockages, and life events were passed easily. Cheerfulness and open spirit prevailed inside, and the feelings between the members were very strong. Quite possibly, an extensive family tree, multicultural, of a special provenance, from a good social class or with well-established principles of life.

The aspect symbolizes a family environment open to culture, education, knowledge, philosophy, studies and spirituality, where emphasis was placed on the development of healthy, social, moral or religious principles. Possibly, the maternal figures of this system focused on the children's education, or they were good teachers, storytellers, and very brave women, who instilled optimism and a strong ideal in the heart of the family.

The natives with this aspect grow up with a very strong sense of belonging, being deeply attached to their birthplace, family, parents or their mother, whom they portray very beautifully, like an icon. The bond between them is strong, fiery, driven by a great ideal.

In turn, they have great maternal qualities, they are compassionate, forgiving, gentle, and capable of very strong feelings. They love to give, care for others, be surrounded by love and form deep intimate relationships.

As parents, they care a lot about their children, to whom they become mentors, but they are also very attached and dependent on them. They value very much their children's education but also tend to be very emotionally vulnerable if others do not reciprocate.

They get involved in acts of charity, jump in to help, are ardent about their passions, and listen to the voice of an unwritten law that whispers to them from backstage. Due to her tolerance and desire to protect, a woman with this aspect has the ability to be a mother even to children who are not hers, providing for them all equally. Their ideal is that of a large family, a community, and a world where moral values matter and are implemented by everybody.

The people with this aspect feel comfortable travelling, can easily move to another country, are tolerant of other religions or cultures, and more than that, they are very eager to explore them.

◊ **Famous people with a harmonious aspect between Jupiter and the Moon:**
◊ Angelina Jolie, Charles Darwin, Wolfgang Mozart

Hard aspect

It is possible that this aspect was transmitted trans-generationally as a result of some families that, disadvantaged or even very well positioned, did not encourage their children towards a sound education, based on clear or correct principles. At the same time, it is possible that there were repressed, unfulfilled ideals, or people who did not belong to a certain culture were rejected. For example, children who were raised by indulgent bohemian families or mothers, children who were given the freedom to do whatever they wanted, or who were pampered and overestimated, will later, in adult life, also exhibit a self-indulgent or permissive approach towards their own person.

The natives with this aspect contain an intra-psychic conflict between their need for belonging and the emotional unavailability of their mother, who is: on the move; absorbed by the lecture; on the wrong side of the law; or far away.

Due to a history of the genealogical tree where families were separated by social class and spread around the globe by relationships with other nationalities, the natives may not find their place and may have to split themselves or fight to feel integrated into the family.

The alternation between ambition and abandonment, between pleasure and disgust, between high standards and very low ones, is frequent, and the oscillation between the contrasting emotions they feel is very deep. Due to their inner lability, they make hasty decisions, get angry, are choleric, exaggerate their feelings, draw attention through emotional dramas or outbursts, and then become exhausted and do not know how to correct their mistakes. They live at the extremes and need to learn moderation because this attitude can lead to mistrust on the part of others, who will ultimately reject them.

To compensate for the voids they feel, they adopt a philosophy of life with distorted beliefs, in which they are overly generous, spend excessively, eat compulsively and erratically, build opulent houses for themselves and fabricate a false ideal related to the family.

The natives with this aspect unconsciously view life without too many challenges, want it to be easy and do not get involved in actions that would take them out of their comfort zone. Even if they are resourceful and talented, since they do not put enough effort into potentiating their strengths and lack patience, focus or determination, they get wasted and limited along the way. They may be idealistic, aspirational, and quick to fire up a desire, but they cannot organize themselves to complete it, and at the slightest impediment or difficulty they encounter, they lose motivation, cool down, and give up.

On the other hand, they can get excited easily, they can fall in love suddenly, they can relocate, all on impulse, and then all of a sudden they may become sad and nothing satisfies them anymore.

Another variant of the past can be of those families where the children were not given any chance for education, where nobody took an interest in them, who come from families parted by distance or different cultures, who were left alone at home, where the messages received were inconsistent. They were underestimated, labelled as incompetent, and humiliated for their ignorance. Later, this wave of shame is transmitted as distrust of their own intellect, as impostor syndrome, as some unconscious desires to impress or to prove themselves. Indoctrination, fanaticism and attachment to a particular faith are all born out of the desperate desire to belong, to be right, to prove the possession of ultimate knowledge.

The natives with this aspect project the image of their mother in their ideals and conversely search for ideals to please their mother. It is very likely that their mothers tried to emotionally manipulate them in their beliefs, to blackmail them based on certain principles or false morals.

Somatization: overeating, increased weight, enlarged stomach, indigestion, hiatal hernia, water retention, gout, nervous disorders, enlarged glands, heavy or absent menstrual cycle, fertility problems, inability to maintain pregnancy, ovarian problems, retroverted uterus, oedema, mastitis, obesity, inflammation of mucous membranes and cavities, flatulence, hormonal disorders, excess of some hormones

Stages of awareness and healing phrases

◊   I honour my mother and my maternal line
◊   I understand my mother, her ideals and beliefs
◊   I recognize the family blazonry, I accept it, but I forge my own
◊   My place is where I feel good
◊   Justice needs to be restored in the family
◊   My soul is at peace and content with what it has got
◊   I am allowed to build a family where I can enjoy my loved ones

◊ There is security in relationships, and I can maintain harmonious relationships
◊ I find my place in the world and become what I want to become

Transgenerational transmission

Unintegrated experiences related to this aspect can occur in offsprings who have Moon in Sagittarius, Moon in the 9th house, Jupiter in the 4th house, or Moon in hard aspect to Jupiter. At the same time, repetitive or revelatory experiences can take place during Jupiter's transit to the Moon or during Jupiter's transit through the 4th house.

◊ **Famous people with a hard aspect between Jupiter and the Moon:**
◊ Adolf Hitler, Johnny Depp, Jean-Claude Van Damme, Glenn Close, Jodie Foster

Jupiter - Mars

Harmonious aspect

A harmonious aspect between the two archetypes symbolizes a family history of fierce fight for a noble cause, for justice, rightfulness and truth, of dynamic investment in the education of their children, for a better chance, for their progress, for the evolution of future generations or of the community.

The expansiveness, passion and spirit for adventure characterize the men of this family tree, who were encouraged to express themselves, to act with courage and bravery, to push their limits further and further, to conquer the world and be daredevils, physically or intellectually.

The masculine energy flows harmoniously, and the natives with this aspect manage to quickly achieve their goals, applying what they learn, they always move forward and love competition.

Gifted for sports, they are agile, and fast, they want to be always the first, to discover new horizons and to go as far as possible. They have strong instincts, are ardent, and feature a great desire for conquest, both in relational and social life. They feel they have a mission, have grand plans and aim high, targeting a high social standing. Although they are very capable of multitasking, have so many skills and are good at so many things, they raise the bar so high and have so much energy that nothing seems impossible to them. At an ever-alert pace, driven by instinct and impulse, they work to complete exhaustion.

They enjoy travelling, and outdoor activities, to provide people with and invest time in their own education, by which they plan to rise to great heights. Thus, they can contribute to the education or development of others, becoming their guide.

In life, due to their heritage, they are righteous, principled, sincere, direct, honest and straight to the point, head-on. As an unconscious ideal, they feel that they can be part of or contribute to society's advancement, so they have no time to rest, and when they set out on the road, they know they go a long way.

Since they have great self-confidence, they know who they are and their identity is strong, they feel they can enter any competition, can move mountains, and can be the first. Pioneers, groundbreakers, the others have to make an effort to keep up with them. Fearless, they take risks, throw themselves into battles, fight for their causes and march forward unhindered, ignoring the problems.

Thanks to their charm, they have the ability to open many doors, to be the right people at the right moment and to have a chance. They always have a tailwind, extensive and multiple plans, and work on far-reaching or high-scale projects. They have many inner resources, positivism and will, their weapons are knowledge, experience and the ability to stand out.

Their enthusiasm for travel makes them be on the move whenever they have an opportunity, venturing to faraway places and making a lot of connections.

Being always alert and on guard, the inner turmoil and the desire to get to the end is great, they tend to burn incessantly, and their involvement in too many things at once alternates with long periods of relaxation and rest.

Since there is an open channel between intellect and physical strength, it seems that the natives are always followed by luck, that they always have the stars on their side, or that they know what and how to do to attract success. Good tacticians, translate in practice everything they learn, catch things on the fly, and can become very good professionals!

◊ **Famous people with harmonious aspects between Jupiter and Mars:**
◊ Angelina Jolie, Charles Darwin, Wolfgang Mozart

Hard aspect

In this genealogical tree, there is a conflict between the desire for personal freedom and the restrictions enforced by law, morality, times, society or system. The natives feel a desire for freedom, for personal space, forging a path and an ideal of their own, but they miss a set of values or a benchmark to go by.

Possible situations: misunderstandings and quarrels within the family regarding personal ideals and beliefs, fanaticism, imprudence, anger, authoritarianism, indoctrination, men of easy virtue or on the wrong side of the law, illegality, loss of freedom, waste, losses, lack of direction or guidance, wandering, grossness, distortion of identity, wrongful assessment of potency or potential. Because in the past their wings were clipped or they were let down, didn't get where they wanted, or their actions were not recognized, the natives feel they have to prove themselves, to fight and find their way. They are explorers and adventurers, they wouldn't stay put, confined, deprived of the chance to experience or taste the cakes and ale.

A lot of anger or repressed energy needs to surface, and the people who inherit the aspect can become hot-tempered, stormy, impulsive, and uncontrollable. They are in pursuit of a personal identity, which is not well defined, or it is a distorted self-image. Although the aspect implies a lot of masculine energy and the belief that mountains can be moved, it takes control and focus to manage this burst of enthusiasm, which they do not know how to tame or manage properly.

In everyday life, they are fidgety, always on the move, they sense a lot of adrenaline, are tensed, under pressure, would always do something, cannot rest and rush in all directions.

Because they tend to take many tasks on their shoulders, start many actions at a time and multitask, they may become overwhelmed, overworked, out of control, and only manage to complete what they set out to do at the last minute.

They often rush headlong without any sense, take risks with

no stake, gather life's roses, are not able to control themselves and give in to impulses and momentary pleasures.

In relationships, the native can be a conqueror, but also an adventurer, a perfect yet fickle lover, overflowing with sexuality. They often engage in vainglorious acts, try to impress with their actions and gestures, react impulsively, lack tact and good manners, or kick the can in the most important moments.

They enjoy drinking, eating, and living well and are prone to excesses. They would like their identity to be appreciated, but they don't identify it well either - sometimes they trust themselves and know who they are, other times pretend to be more than they really are so that in the end they don't know anything about themselves!

In their inconstancy and ambivalence, they swing from one concept to another, swim between two waters, today they are ardent believers, and the next day they are atheists, they would like to leave, but also to stay. Since they are not patient enough to see things through and get bored, they procrastinate, postpone, cancel, escape, run away, and may seem very unreliable. Sometimes, getting rid of any trace of morality, they indulge in scandalous, inappropriate, easy virtue relationships, even playing at multiple ends. For them, the game is enjoyable until it becomes too serious or too thorough until they are asked to really get involved. From that point on, they once again need something to make them happy and give them some excitement.

It is possible that in his system there are men condemned by their times, excluded from society, who were exiled, or who have been convicted for their acts.

Therefore, the descendants have in their blood the desire for competition, for justice, for repairing the injustice. They are searching for a truth, a lost cause, but it is not their cause, and the harder they look for it, the more incomplete will they feel.

In order to find a balance, they need to temper themselves and understand why are they running, what are they fighting for, and where are they going, to stop excesses and find themselves!

Somatization: intracranial tension, aneurysm, poor blood circulation, headache, stroke, blows to the head or face, inflammation of the face, vertigo, hypertension, deficient release of neurotransmitters and stress or male hormones, commotion, anxiety, panic, inflammation, deep bloody wounds, fever, ulcers, painful growths, blisters, liver or blood troubles

Stages of awareness and healing phrases

◊   I honour my system's male line
◊   I am free to find my own way
◊   I know who I am and I value myself correctly
◊   I am driven by high ideals and know my direction
◊   I create my own set of values and act according to them
◊   Everyone is free to have their opinion, to develop and act according to their own beliefs
◊   I accept myself as I am
◊   I channel my energy properly; I measure my time correctly and I won't waste myself
◊   I channel myself and focus in the direction needed for my harmonious evolution
◊   I release my inner tension in a constructive and healthy way

Transgenerational transmission

Unintegrated experiences related to this aspect can occur in offsprings who have Mars in Sagittarius, Mars in the 9th house, Jupiter in the 1st house, or Mars in a hard aspect to Jupiter. At the same time, repetitive or revelatory experiences can take place during Jupiter's transit to Mars or during Jupiter's transit through the 1st house.

◊ **Famous people with a hard aspect between Jupiter and Mars:**
◊ Paul Walker, Elon Musk, Bono, Brad Pitt

Jupiter - Venus

Harmonious aspect

In this family system, feminine energy predominated, women or their existence were valued, respected and honoured, and love relationships were free, pure and unmarred. The favourable aspect between the two archetypes is transmitted further in the genealogical tree by families where marriage and kinship relations were a beautiful experience, based on love, trust, devotion, fidelity and sincerity, where emphasis was placed on value, beauty and true feelings.

Thus, the following generations inherit trust in love, the capacity to give and receive, as well as a positive, optimistic, open and flexible personality.

The natives with this configuration are multitalented and resourceful, the embodiment of love and joy in life, and as a result of their good energy they attract opportunities, receive gifts from all over the place, have open doors everywhere, and are lucky people.

Since they are peaceful and pacifist, they want to have harmony and relaxation, to fulfil their desires and feel pleasure. Prone to luxury, wealth, and high financial gains, they are true self-respecting people. They love art, and culture, are surrounded by beautiful things, are fashionable and make much account of value.

Creativity and artistic sense are very strong, and the desire to have an achievement is very powerful. It is possible to attend high circles and benefit from relationships that help them succeed in what they set out to do. They have a great inner vision, thanks to which they can describe scenes, scenarios and entire stories, and at the same time, they can materialize and stage their image. They have a great capacity for love and are fiery, passionate and charming when they get involved.

Since there is a great love in the memory of their family tree, they have a strong ideal to that end, they breathe and live to be in love, put a lot of soul into it and are the perfect romantics. More than likely, they will marry for love and will seek to make the most of the relationship with their partners. They have much to offer and are willing to, but they need a great partner.

They enjoy being sexy, catching eyes, and making graphic gestures, but once they get what they want, they are likely to sink into relaxation, convenience and indulgence.

Money comes easy to them, possibly from inheritances, business or good pay, they get what they want, and that's why they can be very indulgent.

◊ **Famous people with harmonious aspects between Jupiter and Venus:**
◊ Drew Barrymore, Paul Newman, Roman Polanski, Steven Spielberg

Hard aspect

The hard aspect between Jupiter and Venus is transmitted from times when love was restricted by social and moral rules, dogma or family, ending up being experienced and understood distortedly over the generations. Possibly, in this genealogical tree there were also love stories where the partners belonged to different social classes, so the unions could not be truly consummated or certified, leaving deep marks. For example, women or men who loved passionately outside of marriage, repressed loves due to family rules and principles, restrictions and lack of freedom, alcove or slum loves. Also: relationships or marriages to obtain a social rank or material favours, debauchery, multiple relationships, disorganized relationships, multiple partners, unsuitable, hastily made marriages.

The natives with this aspect may not find their place in love. They have chaotic, changing relationships, and fall in love quickly, but just as quickly get over it if they no longer find things interesting and exciting with the other. To feel good, they need challenges, petty thefts, small scandals, and even several partners at the same time. They are attracted to people who do not always honour them or have a different standing. Love is never guaranteed or stable, both on their part and on the part of the people they appeal to.

They may be surrounded by unfaithful people or may show little loyalty, have low standards in relationships and have questionable moral qualities. They feel good among mediocre people, without many ideals, principles or moral values, following a pattern of laxity and decay.

They wish to be appealing, liked, to love and be loved, but their concept of love is not clearly outlined. Sexual promiscuity, no-strings-attached relationships, idylls, affairs, gambling and life games, amusement, financial speculation and lotteries are far more attractive to them than the prospect of a settled life, which they would consider trivial.

They don't enjoy hard work, but rather have fun or make a quick penny, which makes them opportunists. They are often extravagant, ostentatious, tawdry, spend a lot of money on things of no value, are greedy and quickly become addicted to whatever gives them pleasure. They have a large circle of friends, like to be in the spotlight and are charming, but if they have to take responsibility or make a commitment, they would rather run as far as possible.

They need moderation because they tend to make many excesses - clothing, culinary, relational and sensory, to constantly seek to fill a void, which they do not understand.

What they saw in their parents' relationship may have affected them. They actually need acceptance and love, they need to feel they are worthy, but for that, they must value themselves first.

In terms of values, it is possible that on a trans-generational line, abuses have been committed related to money or fixed assets, or someone's property, a financial injustice has been done, or a fraud has been committed.

The natives with this aspect tend to make money but do not value themselves properly, spend too much, let opportunities slip through their fingers, put a price on invaluable things, or disregard themselves.

Somatization: sore throat, enlarged thyroid, hoarse voice, polyps, enlarged tonsils, inflammation of the vocal cords, liver problems, liver enlargement, blood sugar problems, diabetes, urinary incontinence, flatulence, weight gain, goitre, blocked nasal passages, pus in the throat, thrombosis, fat deposits, hormonal imbalance, cysts or tumours of the fallopian tubes

Stages of awareness and healing phrases

◊   I honour my system's female line
◊   I love and respect myself
◊   My value lies in who I am
◊   I value and valorise myself correctly
◊   I deserve the most beautiful love relationship
◊   I deserve respect
◊   I create my own set of values and act according to them
◊   I accept myself as I am
◊   Love relationships provide me with security
◊   I can have relationships based on truth and trustworthiness
◊   I am allowed to be in a lasting relationship and enjoy life with a partner
◊   I use my skills to create something of value

◊   I easily access the treasures and values that belong to me by divine right
◊   I have the right to love and be loved

Transgenerational transmission

Unintegrated experiences related to this aspect can occur in offsprings who have Venus in Sagittarius, Venus in the 9th house, Jupiter in the 2nd or 7th house, or Venus in a hard aspect to Jupiter. At the same, repetitive or revelatory experiences can take place during Jupiter's transit to Venus or during Jupiter's transit through the 2nd and 6th houses.

◊   **Famous people with a hard aspect between Jupiter and Venus:**
◊   Britney Spears, Tina Turner, Jon Voight

Jupiter - Mercury

Harmonious aspect

In this family system, there are no loopholes, lies or secrets, so the mental space is fluent. They communicated, placed emphasis on understanding, disclosure and fairness, and information was correctly transmitted from one generation to another. People maintained family ties and had the flexibility to learn from each other, to be permissive, and fair. There may have been a desire for elevation, strong ideals and encouragement towards education, towards moral, financial and social growth.

A family system with many branches, many relatives, cousins, brothers, and uncles, spread over many lands - an older brother may have occupied a special position in the system, may have been more lettered or distinguished by his ideas full of inspiration, groundbreaking, or even innovative.

The natives with this aspect are good visionaries, optimistic, confident about their knowledge, with a wide openness to life and a strong intellect. Faced with the new they get excited very quickly, in particular because they are very curious and always eager to learn new things.

They have many ideas, fluency in speech and writing, are good storytellers and care to carry forward their sound principles. Open-minded, they can accept many different opinions and have the ability to make quick connections.

They can have very prominent voices, are able to cover the noise of crowds of people, and have very sharp senses. Due to their ability to learn new things quickly, they may speak several foreign languages fluently, and thanks to their reason, of how they express themselves and their broad knowledge, they conclude many relationships and have many friends, acquaintances, and admirers.

They feel the need to write, tell stories, to teach others, and their genetic heritage is an intellectual one. They have a good memory, and imagination, and get fired up quickly, but if you don't stir up their interest, they get bored just as quickly.

They can be people with special mental skills, which they must channel into something constructive, otherwise, they would waste them on many opinions, ideas and ideals. However, when used correctly, they have the ability to philosophize, to question the information, to ask questions and quickly understand the answer, and to contribute to the development of new concepts!

Because their family tree is very extensive, with many arms or branches, they also tend to hit the road, to be on the move, to travel on and on. They need to see the world, socialize, learn as many things as possible, and share with others everything they learn. They are good marketers, and have a flair for persuading others, seducing them through their vocabulary or high verbal ability.

◊ **Famous people with harmonious aspects between Jupiter and Mercury:**
◊ Oprah Winfrey, Marilyn Manson, Jim Morrison, Jack Nicholson, Diana Ross, Yves Saint-Laurent

Hard aspect

In this family system, no solid structures related to education and learning were created, ties were broken due to ideology of life, members were excluded due to their way of living or morality, and education was not encouraged for all, but maybe rather for one of the several children, or there were many restrictive beliefs and dogmas, which were enforced without people feeling it. Possibly, a branch of this family were intellectuals, cultivated and interested in culture, but there were also members who might have been dishonest, might have abused the good faith of others, had no ethics and morality, kept no promises, might have violated the law or rebelled against it.

A family system with many scattered branches, superficial connections, different doctrines, and intellectual discrepancies. The aspect shows many connections, relationships, and acquaintances, possibly with ill-famed people, or people with questionable social standing. Many branches, scattered in many corners of the world, gossip, quarrels, love affairs, comings and goings, instability and turmoil at the inner level.

At another extreme, injustices may have been committed in this system, immoral situations may have existed, someone may have abused the law or committed illegalities, distorted the truth or transmitted information in bad faith. In turn, the natives with this aspect have no scruples when they want to persuade people, therefore the lie can be perpetuated.

The natives deal with an intra-psychic conflict between what they consider to be true and what they were taught to be true, between what is imposed on them as morality and the inner resentment they feel.

They need to come to a new set of beliefs, not from books, copied or told by others, but based on their own judgment and certainty! They have great mental capacities, but they should no longer compare themselves to others, feel judged, examined, and punished if they did not learn the lesson. At the same time, they need to detach themselves from their family's set of ideas, not fight them, but to form their own opinions.

Because they feel revolt inside or need to release the anger of the lack of freedom, they are able to get into frivolous scandals, lacking in tact and refinement, can quickly get fired up, say things they don't really mean, judge and throw bitter words. They may lack common sense, may speak dirty, shrill or vulgar, without tact or refinement in speech, but at the same time discriminate against others, consider themselves superior, and take an intellectual face.

Many times, they promise more than they can deliver, they

rush to judge or give their opinion, they talk too much, too loudly, and they don't have the patience to learn and fathom, especially because they either think they know enough or don't think they know anything. In an attempt to attach greater meaning to their thoughts and ideas, they might frequently overstate or overestimate, bending the truth. They are joyful, clever, funny, and make connections very quickly, but at the same time they can become arrogant, sarcastic and very acid. Sometimes they lose their sense of reality, get excited with ideals and raise the bar, before becoming hectic and no longer able to support all the mental pressure.

Actually, they are angry with the past, as they have not integrated the trauma of having been told what they must think or say. Also, perhaps because they have been shamed, they are concerned about what others think of them and feel the need to prove themselves, to impress, to show what they are capable of.

Somatization: pulmonary haemorrhage, arterial problems, haematological disorders, poor blood circulation, pancreatitis, inflammation of the spleen or liver, peritonitis, hernia, pain in the hips and thighs, sciatica, hypertension, pulmonary embolism, nervousness, lung tumours, anorexia or bulimia, nervous disorders, insomnia, mental restlessness, ADHD, deformity of fingers or arms

Stages of awareness and healing phrases

◊ I honour the intellectual lineage of my family tree
◊ I respect my ancestors' beliefs, values and principles, but I have the right to form my own
◊ Truth is my ultimate value
◊ I have the right to think freely and create my own set of

beliefs
◊ I free myself from the unconscious promises I made
◊ I have the right to study, educate myself and learn what I want
◊ I try to express high values, learn and educate myself permanently, according to my visions and desires

Transgenerational transmission

Unintegrated experiences related to this aspect can occur in offsprings who have Mercury in Sagittarius, Mercury in the 9th house, Jupiter in the 3rd house, or Mercury in a hard aspect to Jupiter. At the same time, repetitive or revelatory experiences can take place during Jupiter's transit to Mercury or during Jupiter's transit through the 3rd house.

◊ **Famous people with a hard aspect between Jupiter and Mercury:**
◊ Kevin Spacey, Jamie Foxx, Chris Tucker

Aspects of planet Saturn

Saturn - Sun

Harmonious aspect

When the Sun and Saturn are connected by a positive aspect, the father's line is prominent and strong in the native family system. The paternal figure is evoked as that of a responsible, serious, determined, hard-working man, who tried to pass on to his children solid rules to guide them in life.

Although not expansive, rather traditionalist and conservative, he may have represented a pillar for his family, a manful and just leader, the decision-maker, on whom the members could always rely. Even if he controlled the steps of those around him firmly, without bending the rules, he knew how to convey paternal security and love in his own way. Assertive, attentive, and involved, but also harsh, he was there when he had to be and stood out, imposing his status. Possibly due to his inner structure and the hardships he experienced himself, he wanted his children to be organized, and to have a routine, and gave them responsibilities in a good way, assigning them tasks in the house, but also rewarding them plentifully. He also kept his promises, and his words were carved in stone!

The native with this aspect is proud of his father, and respects and trusts him, thanking him for the wisdom with which he raised him. The connection with him is a solid one, based on a long-lasting construction.

Since they have confidence in their strengths, roots and inner structure, they in turn become people capable of overcoming many impediments successfully. They are patient, determined and persevering, they get things done - reliable persons.

Many times, due to their serious demeanour and the status they enforce, they can appear cold, tough or distant, but they have a special maturity, and the older they get, the more elegant and refined they become. Their jokes are wise, they have a fatherly air, and they win through seriousness.

They are good professionals, do things by the book, observe the rules, and stick to the schedule. They have a special routine, very well laid out, and they respect not only themselves but also others, which makes them good professionals.

Because their heritage is deeply rooted, they can carry a lot on their shoulders, have endurance, are strong and resilient, in very good health. However, driven by a special fidelity and loyalty, they tend to continue the father's line, to be very long-lived, to seek status and not deviate from the inherited pattern.

A man with this aspect wants to be a career man, seeks to strike out on his own feet and manages to achieve honours throughout his life. They are able to support their clan, therefore they become the head of the family or take over the leadership.

A woman, serious, with strong self-control is attracted to a mature, responsible man, with a certain status, or an older man. She needs to feel she has someone to rely on, that she can build with someone, or thanks to her man she can benefit from a certain social status or esteem.

Both carry on their father's line, which they preserve and perpetuate in a traditionalist spirit.

◊ **Famous people with a harmonious aspect between Saturn and the Sun:**
◊ Winston Churchill, Robert DeNiro, Leonardo DiCaprio, Elton John, Catherine Deneuve, Meryl Streep

Hard aspect

A tense aspect between Saturn and the Sun indicates a sense of paternal abandonment, an unintegrated trauma related to it, or a blockage in his line. The family relations on the father's line are austere, oppressive, without joy and brilliance, full of responsibilities and debts, which the following generations must submit to in self-punishment.

Possible situations: missing father due to an early death, a divorce, rejection by the family, a relationship where he does not assume paternity or has no knowledge of the existence of his child; absent or sick father, or with a tyrannical, authoritarian and emasculating personality, who demolishes his children; unavailable father, who works too much, or who has too narrow views and does not give freedom to his children; introverted, internalized, frustrated father who lacks the joy of living; authoritative figure with very clear demands, claims or rules regarding discipline.

When the father is absent, unreliable, fails to keep his promises, is not around when needed and would not take any responsibility, or is a sad, uncommunicative or insipid man, the child is at sea, it misses the guidance it needs to grow and to develop, and feels there is nobody it can rely on. It lacks the backbone, the pillar on which it can lean and the paternal figure it needs to form its structure. The sun does not shine for it, there is no hero or mentor, and a huge void is created in the child, that of paternal abandonment.

The young man has no one to follow, and his Self remains introverted, his power of expression blocked. In order to make his way in the world, he needs to know who he is, manifest his identity, take heart and go forward alone, even if at first without vitality, gloomy and restrained.

He needs to understand his longing and his emptiness, and then to fill himself with himself.

If the father exists, but has a narrow view of life, frustrations and unfulfillments, if he is introverted and fearful, the child takes on his sadness, becoming, in turn, pessimistic and dark, without joy and zest for life.

A lacklustre father, jealous and threatened by the child's youth, becomes tyrannical and authoritarian. He tries to inhibit his child, reduce its will and trust in itself, confines it and does not let it be. Since he criticizes, comments, judges and reacts harshly to any attempt at disobedience, the child feels limited, cannot express itself as it wants, fears and closes itself in, blocking its true personality. The paternal figure is felt to be dull, boring, nagging, too severe and outdated, incapable of love.

In turn, projecting the image of the father, the child may become just as severe, both with itself and with those it cares about. They refrain from pleasures, cancel themselves, fail to follow their true path, sabotage themselves, and end up being sad and unhappy.

When you deny a young man's right to life and throw a wet blanket over him, you close the wave of vital energy that flows through him and restrain his autonomy. The inner child is locked in a prison, its childhood is lost, and it is forced to grow up far too early. The man with this aspect may be introverted, have inhibitions, find it difficult to find motivation and be gloomy or depressed. Having a program of limitation in their subconscious, when the chance of success arises, they postpone or sabotage themselves, punishing themselves. He is not programmed for success, therefore he may remain single, alone and without any personal success.

Projecting the image of the father to heal herself, the woman with this aspect attracts mature men, possibly older, with many responsibilities or demands, who are harsh, cold, absent, busy, domineering or tyrannical. She does not feel love, she is mostly alone, as misunderstood or unappreciated as she was in her childhood, locked in a relationship that won't give her satisfaction.

The natives need to change the pattern, to break out of it, to reinvent themselves on an inner level, disassociating themselves from the paternal complex. They need self-esteem, appreciation and love, which they alone can give themselves! They vainly beg from others, because what they will receive will only satisfy them temporarily, momentarily and not deeply. With small but sure steps, they have to come out from behind the shield where they are hiding and find their motivation to exist, the joy of playing and the optimism to go out into the world with all their confidence.

The inner child, alone and repressed, fearful and sad, begs to be seen and appreciated by the now grown-up self, to gain trust that the world can also be a good, safe place for it, where there is joy, and where the sun shines for everybody. The more security it will have, the more joy it will be filled with, and the more it will let go of the complicated and unhappy situations in its life, the more complete it will be and the higher will rise with pride.

They are capable of great creation, of building their own kingdom, but in order to reach it and master it, they must first give themselves permission - to love, be happy, live and enjoy everything that they are and they have!

At the same time, they need to know who they are, not to fit into what others want for them, not to copy patterns that don't represent them, and to follow a career of their choice. They need to discover themselves and be genuine, choose the path that makes them happy and represents them the most.

Somatization: back, heart and immune problems; thickening of the arteries, atrophy, cardiac arrhythmia, non-assimilation of vitamins, malformations of the spine or pain in the lumbar area, lack of radiance of the face, pallor, vitamin D deficiency, calcium deficiency, sadness, apathy, scoliosis, herniated disc, dehydration, fainting, weak immunity, lack of energy

Stages of awareness and healing phrases

◊ I see, accept, recognize and honour my father
◊ I accept the choices he has made in his own life and allow myself to be me
◊ I understand that whatever life my father had, he gave me life and is the right father for me
◊ Even though he is gone, a part of my father is in me
◊ I see myself and I recognize myself
◊ I respect my existence and my right to life
◊ I am confident in my strength and I am proud of myself
◊ I am free to become who I want to be
◊ I have the right to shine, to be and to show my true nature
◊ I unleash my creative abilities and enjoy life
◊ I can be a loving parent to my children
◊ I am the divine child who has grown up and I am on the path to becoming myself
◊ I express love, first of all for myself

Transgenerational transmission

Unintegrated experiences related to this aspect can occur in offsprings who have Saturn in Leo or in the 5th house, Sun in the 10th house, or Sun in a hard aspect to Saturn. At the same time, repetitive or revelatory experiences can take place during Saturn's transit to the Sun or during a Saturn's transit through the 5th house.

◊ **Famous People with a harmonious aspect between Saturn and the Sun:**
◊ Salvador Dali, Jim Morrison

Saturn - Moon

Harmonious aspect

The harmonious combination of the two archetypes - Moon and Saturn - indicates a family tree with strong traditions and stability in the family space. The maternal figures, mothers or grandmothers, were outstanding personalities, with strength of character. The sense of security that souls need to grow has been transmitted through the family, women, or through the maternal line. The family created the basis that supports the future adults.

Might be a family respected due to some members who held important positions, and had a certain status or reputation.

The family of the native with this aspect may not have been emotional, or sensitive in nature, but its members have taken up the household and domestic responsibilities that fell to them, treating them seriously. Hard-working, rigorous, self-possessed mothers provided their children and elders with everything they needed - support, a hot meal, a tidy home, clean clothes and emotional security.

The home reminds us of a space where traditions, holidays, and age hierarchy were respected, where members showed respect for each other, where very old grandparents had grandchildren around them and where many traditions, emotions, feelings and memories were preserved.

Might not be a family with many members, but the family ties are durable, enduring, and have a long history together. The traumas and sufferings of the past were overcome with resignation, fortitude and self-control. Although not easy, they managed to build a family with strong trunk and roots, anchored deep in time, by hard work and determination.

The people with this aspect receive a legacy of correctness, seriousness, inner stability and fidelity to where they belong, which they stick to all their lives and pass on to their children.

The natives respect their roots, which they feel very connected to, are emotionally mature, are certain of their feelings, have self-control and can lay the foundations of an equally stable family.

Due to the memory of their past, they are conservative in relationships, hard to get attached, but when they do it they do it for a long time. They need things to be clear, stable and secure, they don't like complications, and that's why they choose the path that seems to offer the longest perspective - long-term, mature, serious and hard-working partners.

Their home is tidy, clean, and simple, with small decorations from the life of the village, of the ancestors, or meant to honour them. Because their presence is still strongly imprinted, and the past lives in the present for them, they are attracted to things that evoke the old days: attics, basements, antique shops, history, vestiges or architecture.

As a man, the native chooses a partner whom he can build a family with, who inspires in him the safe environment at home, perhaps an older or very homely, hard-working partner. The bond with the parent is strong, based on devotion - perhaps they rely on each other, live or work together, even at a very old age.

As a woman, the native surrounds herself with female friends who are older or of a certain function, prestige and stability, with whom she creates a narrow community. She is very conservative, has clear principles and is very much like her mother or grandmother, from whom she takes her attitude or inner structure. Their circle of friends is small, but it breathes respect, sustainability and longevity.

◊   **Famous people with a harmonious aspect between Saturn and the Moon:**
◊   Prince Charles, Harry Belafonte, Oscar Wilde

Hard aspect

Due to the life events experienced by the family, mother or people in her system, there are many repressed emotions, pain, sadness and suffering in this genealogical tree. The aspect indicates a burdensome family environment, weighed down by many responsibilities and troubles, lacking love and affection, restrictive and austere, where the warm, intimate energy of the home or mother is stalled.

Perhaps the family endured illnesses, poverty, separations, deaths, shortages, experienced social traumas, such as economic crises, bankruptcy, war, natural cataclysms, or was established on considerations other than love. It is possible that the mother was absent from the family, passed away, was emotionally unavailable, or treated her children with stiffness and apathy. Due to restrictions, helplessness, life situations or conditions of past times, family members have been deprived of emotional expression, being forced to endure, resist, refrain from crying, and keep any kind of pain or suffering inside.

Other situations and possibilities: mothers who lost their children, children who lost their mothers, or mothers who emotionally abandoned and physically rejected their children; mothers who were deprived of their children for various reasons; mothers removed from the system, or who have left the system; reversed roles between parents and children, parentification; the children get to take care of the parents at a young age; children who do not marry or start families in order to take care of their parents' household and care for the sick; women who raise their younger sisters and devote themselves to them, children who grew up in very austere, rigid, confining environments; sad, unhappy, emotionally blocked mothers; the mother's relationship with the children is blocked or discontinued; difficult childhood; parental relationship that does not inspire love, children growing up with a single parent, divided families, and so on.

In any of these situations, the domestic or emotional

unhappiness, sadness, and suffering were repressed and family duties and responsibilities were carried forward by its members.

Due to the shattered relationship with the mother and the maternal figure of the system, there is immense inner pain in the native with this aspect, which leads to great sadness, depression, melancholy and an inability to let go of the past. The absence of their mother in their life creates a huge void in them, the feeling of abandonment, rejection and lack of food!

Due to the deprivation of their first relationship, the relationship with their mother, of intimacy and hugs, in their adulthood they become introverted, depressed, anxious, and fearful, building a thick wall in front of their soul and many protective barriers against the fear of suffering. Apathetic, lifeless, lack enthusiasm, feel dissatisfaction with everything, are drastic and self-disciplined, put a lot of pressure on their own feelings, restrict their own pleasures and have a pessimistic, melancholic attitude.

For a woman, if the wound is not healed, due to the blocked maternal energy and the unconscious painful feeling induced by the idea of being a mother, she may encounter difficulties in becoming a parent, as this aspect translates, in the worst cases, into infertility. To integrate the experience of the past, she may attract heavy family circumstances, go through divorce, separations and losses, may raise the children alone, deprive herself of feelings by internalising the same, or, due to the fear of being alone, may become emotionally dependent. She needs to take care of her soul, to open up and release the pain, to accept her mother and understand her pain, and to let herself feel, thus becoming vulnerable to emotions.

The man with this aspect can exhibit the pattern as an act of emotional closure, refusal to make a family, fear of intimacy, as well as hardness, severity and coldness with the fair sex. Looking for a mother, he projects the pattern on his partners, attracting women who are older or affected by health troubles, who come from families with many difficulties in everyday life and who beg to be rescued.

The descendants of this system are bound to it by responsibility, debts they feel they must pay, loyalty to pain and hardships to deal with. They unconsciously carry a deep mourning, which they need to release.

Although emotions are associated with something painful that they often move away from, they must approach the feeling, and come into contact with their wounded soul. They need to receive, but also to offer love, warmth, and comfort. They need forgiveness and empathy towards their own person, whom the mother was unable to take care of, acceptance and reconnection to the sense of belonging of the whole family.

Whatever emotions they feel, they must step into every chamber of their soul and go deep into the feeling, embrace the suffering, the pain, the loss, the sacrifice, the humiliation of the past, offering forgiveness, understanding and love to their predecessors. In this way, they will be able to free themselves and heal emotionally, they will regenerate spiritually and become full adults, parents who can continue to support life, since they have made peace with their past.

Somatization: slow digestive process, weight gain/weight loss, stomach pain, dysfunction of the ovaries, and uterus; infertility; lack of water in the body, dehydration, dryness, absence of forms, poor assimilation of nutrients, starvation, refusal of food, stomach cancer, stomach laceration, hormonal imbalance, menstrual pain, early menopause, cysts or tumours in the ovaries or breasts, endocrine problems, oestrogen/progesterone imbalance, small uterus, nodules, calcifications, obstructions, impossibility of maintaining pregnancy, pelvic deformity, hysterectomy, depression, addiction to drugs or sedatives

Stages of awareness and healing phrases

◊ I accept and honour my entire family tree
◊ I connect to my birthplace, family, the source of my life, my roots
◊ I recognize my roots and feel the energy I draw through them
◊ I respect my ancestors and honour my family, with all their experiences
◊ I accept my history, my nation, and my homeland and I honour them in my soul
◊ I understand and accept the pain of my mother and all mothers in this system
◊ I honour my mother and thank her for the life I received
◊ I am an open channel through which love, femininity and maternal energy flow
◊ I release my emotions and agree to cry
◊ I let myself feel
◊ I accept my ancestors' pain, but I allow myself to have my own way
◊ My life is a link on the timeline
◊ I am the link between ancestors and descendants and belong to a whole family system, to which I am consciously and unconsciously connected
◊ I go further
◊ I honour my right to be a parent
◊ I choose to keep life going

Transgenerational transmission

Unintegrated experiences related to this aspect can occur in offsprings who have Saturn in Cancer or in the 4th house, the

Moon in the 10th house, or the Moon in a hard aspect to Saturn. Repetitive or revelatory experiences can take place during a Saturn transit to the Moon or during a Saturn's transit through the 4th and 10th houses.

◊ **Famous people with a hard aspect between Saturn and Moon:**
◊ Hermann Hesse, Mata Hari, Ivana Trump

Saturn - Venus

Harmonious aspect

The harmonious aspect between the old Saturn and beautiful Venus invokes the picture of grandparent couples still walking hand in hand in the park, who have loved each other since they were young, have married and lived next to each other throughout their lives, to the end. After all these years, besides their love, that burned brightly at the beginning, they gained many other values - devotion, respect, and fidelity. They overcame hardships, built together from scratch, fought and won, and their patience, determination and sure steps in life brought them wisdom and strength to their relationship. They made a team, they always relied on each other and had the power to go all the way.

It is possible that the women of this system were brought up with a certain discipline, had a special status or were respected as authoritative, prominent figures of the system. They knew how to keep their men at home, be true wives for them and keep the prestige of their relationship unblemished. This family system had good financial status, money was secure, they were fond of wealth, and inheritances, the values and assets were preserved trans-generationally - possibly land, houses, art objects, paintings, stylish furniture, books or things that hang heavy, loaded with history.

At the same time, the traditions, moral values, talents and skills were passed on and maintained, due to the respect shown to the elders of the family.

What the children with this aspect witness in their parents' relationship is stability, devoted love, longevity, and clear values related to marriage. In adulthood, they valorise themselves correctly, have self-esteem, love themselves, appreciate relationships, are down-to-earth, practical and pragmatic.

They become traditionalists, therefore they need serious life-long commitments. They do not play around with multiple partners, they keep to the straight and narrow path and stay with the other even in less than favourable conditions. They have the capacity to maintain long-lasting relationships, to give respect to their partner and to go with him/her all the way.

Their pattern is that of hard-working, disciplined and serious people, who attach themselves to and value their status. They want to preserve their memory, to accumulate, to tidy away, and also to build. In the memory of their ancestors, they keep their values intact and carry them forward.

Aesthetically, their legacy is a mature sense of form and architecture, by which they can create something of value and long-lasting, especially in the second part of their life.

◊ **Famous people with a harmonious aspect between Saturn and Venus:**
◊ Grace Princess of Monaco, Agatha Christie, Albert Camus

Hard aspect

In this family system, there is a self-love blockage, a wound of unhappiness and loneliness in the couple, a trauma related to a conditional marriage, divorce, separation, abandonment or death of the partner, and absence or loss of the loved one. It is possible that due to the family's rigidity, love was repressed, carnal desires were considered sins, women were blamed, disrespected, driven into a corner, and removed from the family for their sexuality.

Possible past experiences: divorces, separations, loveless, unhappy marriages; partners unconsciously attracted as a true copy of one of the parents or with whose union a past relationship is mirrored, especially the parents' relationship; coldness in relationships, the absence of joy and harmony in the couple, remoteness; relationships affected by many hardships - illness of one of the partners, commitments made as prerequisites for marriage; financial difficulties, disinheritance as a result of a marriage; lack of intimacy and sexual pleasure in the couple; mismatch, lack of respect, lack of values in marriage, lack of attachment or a wrong view of what love means; the role of women in the union seen as a bargaining chip, as an object, femininity devalued; women who have stalled in unhappy relationships due to restrictions, powerlessness, circumstances, or lack of money.

At the same time, from a financial and material point of view: unkept promises related to money, unpaid debts, poverty, financial restrictions, prohibition of being rich or exceeding the financial condition of the family, avarice, alienation of assets or confiscation thereof; problems with authorities or authoritarian figures who are stingy, greedy, reluctant to give further, or who created relationships based on wealth exclusively; part of wealth was not shared correctly or by right, alienated assets, loss or dispossession of goods, disinheritance, bankruptcy, damage, injustice committed for money or enrichment; partitioning, wrongly divided lands; dispute over inheritances, money, goods, land or property.

*

Marriages conditioned by life, family or pattern are from the very beginning unconscious statements by which the entry into unhappy relationships is signed.

What are the chances of really falling in love, being a match or having a fulfilled union and not seeing marriage as a contract that must be complied with and carried out through, if you only see your partner for the first time at the altar, or your marriage is a covenant made from your birth by your parents?

When a marriage is arranged to gain an advantage - status, property, reputation, political alliances, to respect a tradition - those who marry are just a bargaining chip, have a price, and their value is measured according to their benefit.

In the case of these out-of-necessity or conditional marriages, there is no love, understanding, or harmony, and those married against their will have the feeling that they are not worth more, they do not deserve more, love must be hard and bring no fulfilment.

A woman who has to submit to a man without wanting him, to offer herself to him when he desires, who has to bear with a husband who does not honour her, who does not treat her honourably and whom she does not love, lives a life full of frustrations, regrets, repressions, and her anger, hatred and sadness pass through the next generations of daughters and women, who feel her pain.

Femininity, sexuality, and love are not encouraged, and womanhood is repressed. The consequences are sexual inhibition, frigidity, pudicity, inability to honour her body and feel good in it, and low self-esteem.

*

In memory of their past, the natives with this aspect refuse to be touched, hate intimacy and open up very hard, after long penances and sufferings. May not be open to marriage, sexuality, relationships or partnerships, be hard to satisfy and prefer celibacy, or attract relationships where the partner is hard to please, austere and cold.

They enter into difficult, loveless or very conditional unions, which involve many difficulties, responsibilities and challenges, which block them emotionally and in which they risk turning on themselves. They don't receive or give love, they don't feel they are valued, and in turn, they despise the other.

Having such low self-esteem, they believe they are less than they are, do not value themselves correctly and enter into relationships with people who are lesser than them. Therefore, they are frustrated, suffer in relationships, are inhibited and do not allow themselves to be happy. Unconsciously, they feel they need value, but they look for it in others, in work or in money, to which they devote themselves very much! Their inner resources are vast, but they cannot reach them, they do not recognize them easily, and their legacies are blocked.

In order to heal themselves, they need to let go of the old contracts made by their ancestors, get rid of mourning and demand their right to love, creativity, prosperity and fulfilment in relationships!

Even if the native did not witness the love between his/her parents if they separated or were not compatible, he/she is the sum of the union between them, so he/she needs to understand them, honour them and recompose them inside him/her!

In order to do that, they must first return to themselves, love themselves, remove from their environment any relationship that does not bring them joy and love, reject hardships, and choose the easy way, the straight and smooth path.

Their relationship should not be like their parents' or ancestors', they do not need suffering, but to value themselves. Regardless of their past situation, they are allowed to flourish, express themselves, create, show love and fulfilment, to have a happy marriage and life, without limits.

They are allowed to relax, enjoy what they have and correctly value their priorities, placing themselves first.

Somatization: dry, irritating cough, slow thyroid function, loss of voice, choking, suffocation, lump in the throat, lack of appetite, sore throat, skin problems, dry skin, darkening of face or skin - hyperpigmentation, urinary retention, kidney stones or sand, haematological problems, bursitis, gout, skin diseases, infertility, accumulation of toxins in the body, frigidity, rheumatism, lack of pleasure, inhibition, depression, inhibition of the senses, dysfunctions of endocrine glands and the genital, reproductive system

Stages of awareness and healing phrases

- ◊ I honour and respect my parents
- ◊ I accept my parents' relationship, which is how I received life
- ◊ I accept and honour the female line of my entire family tree
- ◊ I understand and accept the pain of all women in this system
- ◊ I understand and accept all past unhappy relationships
- ◊ I release myself from the conscious or unconscious mourning carried by my predecessors
- ◊ I am an open channel, through which love, femininity and feminine energy flow
- ◊ I love myself, value myself and accept myself as a unique, wonderful being
- ◊ I have the right to be loved, to love and to have a fulfilled love relationship
- ◊ To love is to be happy
- ◊ I gladly receive all the riches and values of this system
- ◊ I happily display my skills and talents
- ◊ I am fair and true to my values
- ◊ I appreciate love fairly and hold precious values in feelings, experiences and inner treasures
- ◊ My earnings are a reflection of the value I give to my own person
- ◊ I have the right to earn money, live in prosperity and abundance without making sacrifices and working hard
- ◊ I have the right to enjoy what I have, to relax and give myself pleasure

Transgenerational transmission

Unintegrated experiences related to this aspect can occur in offsprings who have Saturn in Taurus, Saturn in Libra or in the 2nd and 7th houses, Venus in the 10th house, or Venus in a hard aspect to Saturn. At the same time, repetitive or revelatory experiences can take place during Saturn's transit to Venus or during Saturn's transit through the 2nd and 7th houses.

◊ **Famous people with a hard aspect between Saturn and Venus:**
◊ Adolf Hitler, Lisa Marie Presley, Luciano Pavarotti,
◊ Jacqueline Kennedy Onassis, Frank Sinatra

Saturn - Mars

Harmonious aspect

Since the boys, men and elders of this family system played an important role, plenty of masculine energy flows through its branches. The aspect reminds us of times when stamina, power and strength were life prerequisites. Hard labour, war, cold, stone, mountain, construction, major impediments and hardships are the keywords of this combination of archetypes, which gave men to the family in the true meaning of the word. They are warriors, leaders, rulers, and heads of families, who execute everything with precision and with a heavy hand, being in control of power, inner discipline and resilience. Talented athletes, good handlers of arms and weapons, tools or instruments, with a great capacity for work, don't shy away from anything, are very organized and get things done. They don't waste their energy unnecessarily, are long-distance runners, and you can count on them. Good all-rounders, perseverant, and talented, they are builders, craftsmen, soldiers, hunters, riflemen, defenders, fathers and husbands.

The descendants of the system inherit energy in abundance, which they know how to dose. In turn, they have courage, self-control, fortitude when dealing with hurdles, and great confidence in their actions and powers!

Thanks to a highly developed sense of identity, they climb the social and professional ladder in small and sure steps, and in adulthood they can enjoy a good status, and respect from those around them, which they acquire through concrete and tangible performances!

They are loyal to the path taken by their predecessors, they feel a need to get involved in something serious, to do things well and to see them through. Keeping the flag flying and being useful until old age, they acquire a well-established social and family role.

A man with this aspect overflows with masculinity, is virile, sexually potent and confident, takes difficult challenges and overcomes them with discipline, endurance and self-organization. With the pattern of his predecessors in mind, to get his share of effort and work, he often chooses a well-trodden path, or chooses the hardest way, but has the ability to get things done. He doesn't jump into relationships head-on, he chooses carefully, he wouldn't get involved with just anyone, and when he does, he likes it to be long-term.

A woman with a favourable combination between Mars and Saturn is self-possessed, libertine, independent and has the ability to attract a stable and emotionally mature man to her side. In the absence of such a man, she is quite well on her own, or enters a relationship only in the second part of her life, when she is already financially and professionally stable.

◊ **Famous people with a harmonious aspect between Saturn and Mars:**
◊ Rudolph Steiner, Leonardo Da Vinci, Denzel Washington

Hard aspect

In this family system, masculine energy is blocked as a result of experiences such as men being removed, excluded or accused, driven into a corner; men undermined, driven out, deserters, who were not present or did not act; lack of identity or masculinity; men who were emasculated by mothers, fathers or partners, had their manhood taken away and were limited in expressing themselves or acting freely; aggressive parents, terrorized, abused children, deprived of freedom and the right to be; children whose freedom was restricted, who were forbidden to do, to act, to get involved, who were treated with force, beatings, with fear, or who were much too pampered; inhibition of self-confidence with phrases like - you're good for nothing, you're incompetent, don't put your hands on it, you're screwing it up, let me do it for you, you can't handle it, you're not able to, or in situations where the children were locked up in the houses, punished, not allowed to experience life; authoritarian parents, restrictive family relationships, difficult conditions, helplessness, procrastination and resignation; harsh parental laws, prohibitions; abandonment, giving up as a result of historical times, laws, leadership, social or political structure, financial power - it's better this way, that's it, you can't help it, it's impossible, stop fighting, nothing can be done, stop trying, anyway you can't, we're not allowed, it's not appropriate, you can't, you're not enough; incarceration, imprisonment; the sense of defeat and surrender of arms; the absence of male energy, confidence in life, and a mentor.

The natives with this aspect inherit strong feelings of inferiority, lack of ambition and determination, always ready to back down or retreat. They cannot trust their own strength, they do not react constructively, lose their energy or exhaust it with too much effort, and they start something and never finish it, especially since everything seems more difficult to them and they experience blockages more than others. Often, they hide behind a thick wall, or create a shell around them, have deep fears and lack identity.

Due to their unconscious memory, when they enter a competition, they have to work harder, try harder, come up with something at the last minute, make things difficult and struggle, or throw sand in the wheels, in self-sabotage.

As a man, he may have a blockage in the manifestation of his sexuality, fears of expression and fear of his masculinity, a blocked and difficult-to-access identity. Due to inner anger or unreleased energy, he can become cruel, violent, aggressive, but also impassive and reckless. Although he has some power of action, this cannot be easily managed. He isolates himself, denies himself, restricts himself, locks himself in a self-imposed limitation, does not allow himself to be free, then projects his anger onto any form of authority. Due to his harsh upbringing, military spirit and lack of love, he tends to get into wars, fight and be a vigilante.

A woman with this pattern attracts the type of man described above, an inhibited, impotent, uninvolved, harsh partner, a frustrating relationship, or rejects the man from the very beginning, considering them something useless or something that causes her suffering. In this pose, she would rather be alone.

Because their self-identity is blocked and the natives do not know who they really are, what is their capacity and fighting strength, they accept to obey, to be submissive, to sit in the shadows and not assert themselves, to stand at the courtesy of somebody or, on the contrary, they are aggressive, harsh, cold, distant, hostile, authoritarian and commanding.

That is until the day when their frustration with failures, tensions, unfulfilled relationships and their potency becomes too much to bear and they step on the path of realizing what is happening to them, forgiving and breaking free.

They have to break through the fences they inherited, step beyond the system and allow themselves to move forward with confidence, releasing their anger or repressed energy.

The journey for the discovery of the self and personal identity can be long, dotted with many trials, but if they man up and direct themselves towards this goal, they have great chances to reach stability and success in their personal life!

Somatization: sinusitis, deafness, earache, inner ear troubles; facial deformity, scar on the face or scalp, darkening of the face, stroke, headache, brain tumour, intracranial circulation problems; knee strikes, joint locking, spine or skull injury; toothache, jaw pain, vision problems; degeneration of the locomotor nerves, inhibition of some reflexes or some neurotransmitters, inhibition of the secretion of adrenaline, testosterone, lack of energy, sleep disorders; cuts, wounds, fractures, surgical interventions, accidents; psoriasis, bedsores, skin diseases; sexual dysfunction, prostate problems, poor erection or poor functioning of the reproductive system, genital problems, infertility; constipation, malabsorption of iron, clavuses; and apathy.

Stages of awareness and healing phrases

◊ I accept and honour the entire male line of my family tree
◊ I see, honour and respect all the men of my family tree
◊ I understand and accept the pain of all blown ambitions in this system
◊ I understand and accept all the blockages, struggles, and failures of my ancestors
◊ I gladly receive all the riches and values they have acquired
◊ I am a channel through which the energy of will flows easily
◊ I release the anger of unfulfillment and allow the masculine energy to flow easily and come to the surface
◊ I have the right to be free, act and express myself according to my unique identity
◊ I have the right to fight for my ambitions
◊ I accept the relationship of my parents, which is how I received life
◊ I honour and respect my parents
◊ I know who I am and who I want to become
◊ I move on and accept that life continues through me

Transgenerational transmission

Unintegrated experiences related to this aspect can occur in offsprings who have Saturn in Aries or in the 1st house, Mars in the 10th house, or Mars in hard aspect to Saturn. At the same time, repetitive or revelatory experiences can take place during

Saturn's transit to Mars or during Saturn's transit through the 1st house.

◊ **Famous people with a hard aspect between Saturn and Mars:**
◊ Julius Caesar, Jean-Claude Van Damme

Saturn - Mercury

Harmonious aspect

This family system has a very powerful Psyche, where much information of value, wisdom and knowledge is gathered, as in a very old archive, a storehouse, which has collected, sorted and classified all the transgenerational information in very accurate, clear and durable patterns. The aspect between Mercury and Saturn reminds us of a council of the elders and wise, which the whole system esteemed, of strong authoritarian figures - righteous people, soldiers or generals, teachers or prosecutors - who implemented in the family a certain conduct in relationships, thinking and manifestation. The relationship between brothers, uncles, and cousins, if any, is one of hierarchical respect, help, fairness and support. For instance, an older brother takes on the responsibility of raising younger siblings or supporting the family and thus becomes a paternal figure himself. Later, the tree develops branches as strong as the trunk. For the family members, what matters is the word given, the promise kept, the inner laws of the system, the value of communication, clear and accurate situations, fidelity to blood ties and the created order. The family's history is known to the descendants, the words of the past remain anchored in the present, and the memory of the predecessors is preserved in letters, photographs, diaries, notes, facts of life, clearly endorsed by them.

The descendants of this system feel they have to take the plan further, to build on it too, or even to develop it further. Their connection with the past is very extensive, that's why they can memorize many things, and remember very accurate data, facts and experiences, which helps them to be constantly organized in their ideas. Their thinking is practical, they know what to rely on, have clear opinions and are very rigorous. They keep to the logarithms they run in their heads, they are logical, mentally sound, intellectually mature and serious. They rarely change their minds, are quite inflexible and need solid arguments to change. Things are black or white for them, they don't have time for nonsense. Prudent with their words, they own what they say and always know what they mean. Conservative, they adhere to the advice they received in childhood, which they integrated, understood and respected and which, over time, became their way of life.

Their views - although may seem old-fashioned to many - are sound, they weigh correctly, think lucidly and objectively and do not get involved in silly discussions. Many times, they use heavy words or regionalisms, and if they report something or tell a story, they do it seriously, documented, based on real facts, technically, exactly as it happened. When they are focused, their mind works like a computer, making connections and developing circuits to solve the problem at hand.

Thoroughly thinking and taciturn, they can deepen in their thoughts, observe, contemplate, sink into themselves, philosophize and theorize, and then thoroughly teach everything they have learned.

◊ **Famous people with harmonious aspects between Saturn and Mercury:**
◊ Paul Newman, Olivia Newton-John

Hard aspect

In this family system, there were very clear rules and boundaries about what to say and what not to say. It is possible that a piece of information has been blocked, a truth of which nothing is known has been buried deep, an important deed destroyed, or the word given was broken. Members were forbidden to talk about or remember a situation, experience or person, or who was removed altogether.

At the same time, due to the rigidity of the authoritarian figures, intra-family laws, or the possibilities and life circumstances, the children of this system were not given the right to speak, their opinion did not matter, they were not allowed to learn, they did not have access to school, or they were constantly told that they are stupid, slow-minded, speak nonsense, are not right. Outdated, limiting, strict patterns of thinking were implemented, which created pressure, frustration, helplessness and a lot of pain.

Other past situations that can contribute to the development of this aspect: are broken promises, messages not reaching the recipient, torn up contracts, destroyed information, stolen letters; ban on speaking or moving; the impossibility of free expression or thought; blocked flow of information; separation of siblings, hidden or adopted sibling, sibling feud, authoritarian brother or forbidden relations between relatives; untreaded paths, unspoken conversations, quarrels, scandals, insults; restricted, unpromising life system; not communicating, not knowing, cutting ties, blocking roads; stuck relationship with the neighbours.

The ban on telling, the trauma or blockage suffered as a result of the refusal to communicate, creates the pressure over generations that the truth must be found, told, restored, and the gaps filled.

The natives with this astral aspect need to unstick themselves from patterns, to heal and set free their minds, otherwise, they tend to project their anger onto themselves and others around them.

Failing to free themselves, they become angry with people, especially with the system and the authorities, and they judge blame, are gloomy, inflexible, oldish in thinking, and behave like resentful old people or inquisitors.

Many times, their judgment is clouded, they have dark thoughts, are pessimistic, get sad fall into depression easily, or see no solution to their problems. Because they are narrow-minded and place many mental barriers in their ways, are inflexible, reluctant to take advice, reject information, are superstitious, and have a permanent desire to be right.

If they fall prey to their complexes and frustrations, they can close themselves in, becoming introverted, shy, and slow in thinking and expression. Because they do not trust the reasoning of their mind, or because they are afraid to speak their mind, they tend not to speak, not to interfere, not to say what hurts them or what they think, remaining with unsaid things, non-involvement and frustration.

Due to their distrust and need for stability, they may attract harsh teachers or mentors, who limit them even more. Feeling unintegrated or rejected by those around them, they have a tendency to remain on the sidelines, but to stay vigil, watchful, strict on details and punish any kind of mistake. In the pursuit of justice, they can become prosecutors, judges or executioners, and in solitude, they can dive into intellectual work, in the study of very deep, existentialist life themes.

Many painful memories are repressed in their Psyche, creating voids in their memory, or on the contrary, maintaining a separate, lucid, painful memory, that they cannot let go of.

The rigidity of this system, where authoritarian figures have limited the possibility of expression, free-thinking and communication of the members, creates an intra-psychic tension in the following generations, who must find their own truth, make peace with their own people and those around, free themselves from the burden of unsaid things and outdated mentality, as well as broaden their horizons, become flexible, finding their unique way of expression. To the same extent, the natives need to reconcile with relatives, neighbours, people around and with their children, with the memory of the past and with the facts of the present, to restore the natural order in the system, speaking, but also listening to the others, leaving the truth, knowledge or information to come to light and giving up the grudge.

Somatization: calcifications, deposits, stones, obstructions of channels or blood vessels, rheumatism, arthritis, fractures of the arms and fingers, blocked joints; chronic bronchitis, pneumonia, pulmonary emphysema, lung tumours, pulmonary congestion, TB, asphyxia, breathing problems, suffocation, apnoea; nervous tremor, lack of nutrients in the body, nodules on fingers, inflexible fingers or toes, paralysis, inability to move arms, fingers or legs; intestinal occlusion, hepatitis, colitis, duodenal ulcer, large/small intestine dysfunction; speech or articulation defects; deafness, muteness; intellectual inhibition; accidents while travelling, inability to orient in space or drive vehicles.

Stages of awareness and healing phrases

◊ I accept and honour my entire family tree, with all its branches

◊ I see, honour and respect all the brothers, cousins and uncles of my family tree

◊ I understand and accept the mentality of my ancestors, the way they thought and acted

◊ I understand and accept the hurtful things they didn't want to say, the arguments they had and how they chose to express themselves or remain silent

◊ I understand how my parents or ancestors understood to educate their children and how they acquired knowledge or education

◊ I am a channel through which the information flows easily

◊ I free myself from the anger of unsaid things and the weight of heavy words that remained in the memory of this system

◊ I have the right to think freely, express myself and maintain what I feel and think

◊ I replace negative thoughts with a new, authentic view of life, based on my own experiences and reason

◊ I accept the relationship of my parents, which is how I

received life
◊   I honour and respect my parents
◊   I allow myself to think and learn
◊   I allow myself to have fulfilling and harmonious relationships
    with all the people in my life

Transgenerational transmission

Unintegrated experiences related to this aspect can occur in offsprings who have Saturn in Gemini or in the 3rd house, Mercury in the 10th house, or Mercury in a hard aspect to Saturn. At the same time, repetitive or revelatory experiences can take place during Saturn's transit to Mercury or during Saturn's transit through the 3rd house.

◊   **Famous people with a hard aspect between Saturn and Mercury:**
◊   Vin Diesel, Steven Seagal, Tiger Woods

Aspects of the planet Uranus

Uranus - Sun

Harmonious aspect

The paternal figure of this system is evoked as that of a modern man, a friend of his child, who understands the new generation or keeps step with it. The father preserves his youth or free spirit, understands the child's needs of the new, supports its initiative to be different, inspires its ability to differentiate itself, free itself from the tutelage of the system, and conquer new horizons. He comes from times when modernism, liberalism and independence were encouraged, when family members were allowed to be authentic and truly express their creativity, to be reformers of their times, and to evolve and adapt to new demands: technological, cultural, social, philosophical or idealistic!

The natives with this astral aspect have the ability to break away from the system with ease and be on their own, without rules, dogmas or impediments, or to carry on their father's pattern of freedom. They are visionaries, brave and genuine people and like to be different because their view of life goes far. They want to contribute through their personality to the evolution of their collectivity, society or humanity as a whole and see the broad picture, and far into the future. They can be good, generous and charismatic yet very original leaders.

As traits of the self, they fascinate with their vibration, electrify with their presence, and there is a note of discord about them, as if they come from another world, from the future. They are eccentric, forward-thinking, progressive, always on the move and highly confident in themselves. They need innovation, adrenaline, exciting situations and adventure, to keep their spirit young. They enjoy socializing and being among people, and they quickly gain popularity, even notoriety.

In relationships, they tend to be good fellows but choose partners as easy-going and fashionable as they are. Their goal is freedom in all its forms, and this is exactly what they express. In lack of serious commitments, they can value their image and development, which if well directed can be fulminant. Doors open easily for them, they have protectors and supporters, are vibrant in expression and very charming.

Ostensive, often explosive, full of energy and adrenaline, enthusiastic about their projects and always eager for adventure, sensation, pleasure and ecstasy, they seem to have climbed into a roller coaster where life is an unpredictable series of tumultuous experiences.

They need to release whatever they mean and feel and turn them into something great, to leave something behind, to create, to assert themselves or to become famous.

◊   **Famous people with harmonious aspects between Uranus and the Sun:**
◊   Isaac Newton

Hard aspect

In this family system it is possible that the paternal figure suddenly disappeared, was not prepared for a true, serious relationship, was not involved in the child's education, or what was received from him and on his line was inconsistent, random.

The tense aspect between the Sun, as the Self, and the surprising Uranus may represent situations such as: sudden separation from the father, unstable relationship with him, or unexpected situations in relation to the paternal figure, with his libertine, detached, uninvolved, random, out-of-the-ordinary personality; turbulent childhood, with many turns of the wheel; unbalanced, disorderly environment, lacking a structure or foundation; personality defragmentation by receiving conflicting education - one member says something but acts contrary to expectations, another member maintains something else, one parent is permissive, the other is restrictive; multiple growing environments, several types of education or personalities that have prevailed in the upbringing of a child, multiple parents or fathers, inconstancy in finding a mentor or tutor; sudden loss of a family member, of freedom, or enjoyment; the splitting of the self as a result of uncontrollable events that suddenly appeared; tense environment of revolt, struggle and revolution; unstable family relationships; events that led to the feeling of loss of authority, disrepute, defamation, lack of honour of the paternal figure; defeat, depersonalization, scandals, denial, flight, rebellion, blame, lack of attachment or involvement.

This energy destabilizes the child who lives with it, who is not sure how to behave or react, and what to believe. It suffers from the insecurity of its own personality, which as an adult, in turn, passes on. Although they desperately want to fill the void and draw attention, to stabilize or create something, they will not be satisfied until they learn to balance themselves and relate to something consistent until they find their own authenticity.

In their quest for a relationship with the father, in order to understand and integrate it, they show an oscillating personality, get into borderline, under-pressure situations, cause chaos and are extravagant. They need risk in their life, live to the fullest and want freedom, but then they don't know what to do with it. Sometimes they throw themselves into a void, put all their eggs in one basket, then get scared, suddenly abandon and leave. They have many innovative ideas, and are spontaneous, creative and pleasant, but due to their choleric, volcanic or unpredictable temperament, are qualified as unstable and unreliable.

They often make grandiloquent gestures, are boastful, eager to stand out, promise a lot, get fired up, dramatize, and cry nervously, but their enthusiasm is doomed to disappear as suddenly as it appears, the natives being prone to last-minute self-sabotaging.

There are multiple personalities inside them, that's why they are also very restless, rebellious, revolted, and in many situations, when faced with themselves, they feel the urge to run away. When bullied, hampered and threatened, they become violent, and aggressive and lose their self-control, only to erupt like a volcano!

With this unconscious and unbalanced inner content, the natives can become temperamental, choleric, narcissistic, disorderly, distracted, with a great potential to destabilize the environment, and with a persistent desire to be free, not commanded, not told what to do, to occupy the central place in their life. For this reason, they can show an antisocial attitude, refusing to align themselves with the system. In order to be clearly distinguished from others, they can take refuge in groups or entourages that have a common interest, and develop a cult together.

As a man, the native cannot stay in relationships for long, and cannot take responsibility for and maintain serious conduct, because he too cannot find his place or his true nature - he quickly gets bored of a particular role, wants to change the character, lights up and falls in love in a flash, wants adventure, instant passion, adrenaline. He has no plans or long-term perspectives, he lives in the present and for what the moment brings, and any form of coercion irritates him.

As a woman, she enters unstable relationships with indecisive, uninvolved or adventurous men, develops strange unions with younger people with no perspective, or people with controversial and contested personalities.

Both men and women need inner peace by assuming their own personalities, by finding stability in everyday life, and by developing long-term plans to create and evolve around. They need a centre, centralization and wholeness of self, regathering of the scattered pieces and balance.

Somatization: spasms, tremors, tics, electrocution, shocks, palpitations, arrhythmia, fainting, fever, rashes, heart pain, heart attacks, anaemias, autoimmune diseases, degenerative diseases, sudden decreases in immunity, malabsorption of vitamins and nutrients, deficiencies, blood circulation problems, toxins in the blood, seizures causing hypertension, angina pectoris, hair loss, epilepsy

Stages of awareness and healing phrases

◊   I see, recognize and honour my rightful genitor
◊   I see, honour and acknowledge my fathers who have protected me, guided me, or been a part of my life
◊   I accept the choices my fathers made and their personalities
◊   I understand that whatever life my father had, I was born thanks to him
◊   Even though he is gone, a part of my father is in me
◊   I see myself and I fully recognize myself
◊   I am the divine child who has grown up and I am on the path to becoming myself
◊   I recompose myself from the thousand pieces it dissipated

into

◊   I find my inner peace and I am happy with myself
◊   I am perfectly centred
◊   I express love, first of all for myself

Transgenerational transmission

Unintegrated experiences related to this aspect can occur in offsprings who have Uranus in Leo or in the 5th house, Sun in the 11th house, or Sun in a hard aspect to Uranus. At the same time, repetitive or revelatory experiences can take place during Uranus's transit to Saturn or during Uranus's transit through the 5th house.

◊   **Famous people with a hard aspect between Uranus and the Sun:**
◊   Stephen King, Oliver Stone, George Washington

Uranus - Moon

Harmonious aspect

The positive aspect between the two archetypes suggests family emancipation, progress and openness to the new - families who moved from the village to the city, who got out of the social structure they were in and progressed, who kept up with the times and gave the children the freedom to choose whatever they want, who have adopted a much more modern lifestyle compared to their parents. It is possible that the discrepancy between parents and children is large - parents with no education, but multi-graduate children and very successful in life, parents who grew up rudimentary, but with children who are very advanced in understanding the technology, and very up-to-date.

This type of family encouraged libertine relationships, personal freedom and emotional expression. Ideas such as mothers raising their children alone, cohabitation without marriage, marriage without virginity, moving to another country, marrying a younger partner, not following some traditions, etc., were accepted and unjudged. The connection with the mother or the maternal line is seen as one of friendship, understanding and acceptance, possibly due to age, or generations close in mentality.

Even if there are no strong attachments in the family and the members are allowed freedom, they feel that they belong to something, that they identify themselves with their family, or the process of separation from it is done harmoniously, without hard feelings and obligations.

In their turn, the natives with this aspect need freedom, and open family relationships, where they won't feel trapped - they may be attracted to non-conformist relationships, choose a partner who already has children, remain single or have a loose, modern relationship and many friends.

Their entourage can be large, in particular, due to the fact that they feel good when integrated into something more comprehensive, help with projects related to society, humanity and the environment, or get involved in acts of charity.

Therefore, they feel attracted to groups with the same ideals as theirs, they associate and fraternize, are good mates, make their contribution, and are involved, but also want to progress. When they can no longer find their place, they are ready to move on!

Since they inherited a great intuition, have the ability to see into the future, to predict or feel how some situations will unfold, sometimes due to glimpses that they strongly feel inside. They are visionaries, have flair, and what they feel guides them in many life situations, like a spotlight.

Emotionally, with a legacy of relaxed or self-controlled mothers, they have the ability to reset quickly, overcome challenges, and not get crushed inside. Uninhibited, casual, able to clarify emotions and pass them through the filter of reason, they won't sit still and break away quickly if necessary. Their vision is progressive, flexible, understanding and broad - they quickly adjust to any environment, but avoid limitation or routine.

As parents, they encourage their children to stand out, be independent, accept their evolution and their right to change, and they even keep their spirits young.

◊ **Famous people with harmonious aspects between Uranus and Moon:**
◊ Kirk Douglas, Larry King, Gwyneth Paltrow

Hard aspect

The hard aspect between the two archetypes suggests a totally unbalanced family life, unaligned with the classical archetype, which failed to provide the natives with the emotional security they needed to develop harmoniously in childhood.

Possible past situations: disorganized environment, without rules, where everyone comes and goes as they wish, where the family members do not have meals together, where no one really takes care of the home, because they are busy at work; possible tense space, frequent moves, scandals at home, fickle relationship of parents, sudden disappearance of a member, suddenly broken relationships, unexpected incidents that destroy the harmony in the family and the inner and emotional stability of its members; children who no longer know where they belong and what are their roots; the feeling of disintegration and coldness between family members, remoteness, indifference; loss of home or mother, which led to uprooting and separation of members; unpredictable situations that led to a break in family ties; loss of traditions, comfort zone, safety; families whose members have departed and emancipated, and the affection between them has been lost; unstable, insecure, inconstant relationship with the maternal figure of the system, with the collectivity, the family or the country, frequent crises, changes or interruptions; deportation, flight from the country, escape, wandering, collectivization, bomb, explosion, abandonment.

In the natives with this aspect lie the feeling of anger and rebellion, the trauma of disappearance and the fear of separation. They are like volcanos, many fickle emotions lie in them. As a result of their breaking up with the system and their internal explosion, they feel tension, turmoil, and anxiety, and their inner environment is chaotic and full of inconsistencies. They cannot feel happy without adrenaline, something is always pushing them from behind, and when deprived of family protection, or with the memory of a disturbed mother, they often burst into emotional crises.

Due to their inner instability, they constantly need risk and adventure, they do not know how to calm down and how to give up fickleness, how to settle down, and what really means to be well.

They plunge into the void only to release emotional content far too laden with anxiety, they are full of emotion but do not know how to apportion it, they are rebels without a cause, they are like revolvers ready to fire, but they can't see the target!

Relationally, they tend to have an unbalanced emotional life, where they are overwhelmed by many stormy emotions, a changeable temper, irritability, inconstancy, and many out-of-the-ordinary events. Unforeseen situations may occur in the couple's relationship: sudden separations, reconciliations and separations again. They tend to marry, then divorce. This minute they are happy and joyful, only to cry and be angry the next minute!

The natives mistake the abnormality for normality, and even end up behaving deviantly or suspiciously. They subconsciously try to recreate an unstable environment that shakes them to the core, and where they project their needs onto those around them until they understand that the need for care and stability they seek is found inside them and not outside.

When it's too quiet, they tend to hit, start fights, reenact chaos and defeat, leave home, drive or chase away their loved ones, destroy what they have created, give up relationships and abandon everything!

The way for them to heal is the acceptance, an anchor and the disclosure of their inner balance - in love, attachment, sensitivity, empathy and in creating relationships based on intimacy, depth and love. They need to find their roots, release themselves emotionally and anchor themselves, making peace with the past, family and mother. The fear they feel inside and the desire to run away from suffering make them wanderers, while what they actually need is to sit still, cry, understand and heal from abandonment.

Somatization: stomach spasms, nausea, vomiting, gastric reflux, regurgitation, eructation, digestive problems, bloating, food allergies; uterine contractions, risk of spontaneous abortion, abdominal spasms and menstrual cramps, irregular menstrual cycle, unwanted pregnancy, hormonal disturbances, early menopause, swelling of the breasts, disturbances in pregnancy and breastfeeding - milk rage, mastitis, sudden loss of milk, blockage of mammary ducts; emotional crises, hysteria, depression, anxiety, panic; ankle swelling, dehydration or water retention, anaphylactic shock.

Stages of awareness and healing phrases

◊ I see, recognize and honour my family
◊ I accept the choices my ancestors made
◊ I understand that whatever life they lived, thanks to them I was born and received the right to life
◊ To have stability in my existence, I need an anchor, and roots and to acknowledge where I belong
◊ Peace is in my soul
◊ I have the security of a quiet life, and what I cannot control is in the nature of life
◊ I release myself of the fear of loss and allow myself to love
◊ I am the divine child who has grown up and I am on the path to becoming myself
◊ I find my inner peace and I am happy with myself
◊ I express sensitivity and compassion, both for my ancestors and for myself
◊ Life is a safe place and family is a place of love, soul and privacy
◊ I have the right to establish a happy, stable and long-lived family where I can be fulfilled
◊ I allow life to move on through me

Transgenerational transmission

Unintegrated experiences related to this aspect can occur in offsprings who have Uranus in Cancer or in the 4th house, Moon in the 11th house, or Moon in hard aspect to Uranus. At the same time, repetitive or revelatory experiences can take place during Uranus's transit to the Moon or during Uranus's transit through the 4th house.

◊ **Famous people with a hard aspect between Uranus and Moon:**
◊ Lisa Marie Presley, Donald Trump, Fred Astaire

Uranus - Mars

Harmonious aspect

Individual freedom, overcoming one's own limits and boundaries, conquering new horizons and advancing rapidly are the key terms describing this aspect. It is transmitted from times when the desire for progress, change and collective help was very great - men who stood up and fought for progress, for overcoming limits, for a common ideal of the masses and all humanity.

The natives inherit a lot of originality, enthusiasm and boundless energy to explore and research, to be free to discover new ways of dealing with life, of doing things and evolving. They have a broad spectrum of interests, a large entourage of supportive people, work well in teams and tend to serve large masses of people through their actions.

They are very inventive and creative, having a unique way of doing things. They change whatever they lay their hands on, have artistic talent and are able of multitasking. They are good wielders of utensils, devices, knives, tools, and gadgets, are very accurate in their actions, and are also groundbreakers and pioneers.

In what sports are concerned, they have strength and power, enjoy taking risks, going to extremes, or getting involved in activities that require the mastery of multiple skills and talents.

Just like their ancestors, they fight for identity, justice, equality, rights, and ideals they believe in, sometimes letting go of themselves and investing in others, or in causes and concepts. Since they enjoy getting involved, they can be part of associations, organizations, and groups of people with the same interests as theirs, where they stand out as ardent activists and good fellows.

They are attracted to technology, are great with modern devices and can understand complicated mechanisms. The speed and momentum they use at work keep them connected and powered, so that they consume, but also release a lot of energy. They work well in spurts, where they alternate hard work - which leaves them totally exhausted - with periods of total rest.

Since they are true mentalists, who quickly see and understand complex structures and connections, they can invent new things, take concepts out of boxes and innovate them, and inspire and breathe new life into their environment.

Relationally, they are seducers and need flirting, stimulation, play, experimentation, and exciting relationships on the verge of non-conformism, otherwise, they get bored and need something else. Although they like to take risks and be surprised, they are honest, and libertine and have their own way of getting involved. They need to be stimulated, their interest kept alive, to be walked and to be in motion, not kept in captivity, and thus they can go far, where they have dreamed.

◊ **Famous people with harmonious aspects between Uranus and Mars:**
◊ Marlon Brando, Emily Dickinson, Andre Agassi

Hard aspect

The energy expressed by the aspect between the two archetypes is very volcanic and heated, reminding of a battlefield. In the turmoil of the battle, the danger is so great, that life can be lost at any time, that all that matters is that very moment, radical, possibly the last one, where you strike with all your might, or you run away!

In this system, there is a lot of negative masculine energy, uncontrolled anger, aggression, and desire to rebel against any form of control, an energy that has not been properly integrated and released.

In the family's unconscious can be the memories of a terrible period, of flogging and suffering, or a brutal, premature death that happened suddenly.

Possible situations - accidents, explosions, death by electrocution or as a result of an unpredictable, shocking situation; bodily harm, quarrels, scandals, fights, tension, rivalry and fighting in the family, especially between men; the sudden interruption of some important events; the death of a man; ruined plans; sudden deviation of the course of life, skidding, loss of direction and identity; a man who is infamous or who becomes the black sheep of the family; violation of personal freedom, intimate space, repression of sexuality, rape, erotic-sexual abuse; struggle for life and identity; aggression, tyranny, control, rejection; identity taken.

This bubble of past trauma generates hatred against authority figures, nervous outbursts of rebellion, anxiety and fear of losing control, of being hit again, or being in danger. What the natives with this aspect feel inside creates a lot of tension and pressure, which can only be released in mighty explosions. They reject any form of limitation, attack or hostility, and lose their temper very easily. When they react and work themselves into a rage, they won't think about the repercussions, they would rush head first to strike, or to do justice to themselves. They are righteous, rebellious, but also intolerant heretics, often aggressive, unruly and stormy, revolted and ready for war at any moment.

In order to feel good, they need situations on the border between life and death, they put themselves in danger, they live at risk, and anything that floods their body with adrenaline becomes a drug for them. It is possible to be prone to accidents, injuries, hitting, cutting, and also have the tendency to get involved in sports that satisfy their need for release.

Since they hardly adjust to the demands of life, they have aggressive, choleric, unpredictable behaviour, rejecting the routine and emotional relationships that require long-lasting involvement. Now they're here, then they're there, they leave, they turn, they run away, they're in no mood, one moment they get involved, the other they give up, they're convinced they know what they want, and where they are heading to, then all of the sudden change tune. Their direction is never nailed, the day of tomorrow is uncharted, and the future can be rewritten at any time.

Due to the unintegrated trauma and the projections they make, their intimate relationships are strange, they do not trust the intention of the other, nor their own, they show a desire to explore their sexuality in unconventional ways, or often oscillate between being, or not being submissive.

As a man, he cannot maintain his path straight, he is fickle and indecisive, fierce, hard and cold, and he does not know what he wants, or what he is looking for. His relationships, if any, are not lasting, and subsist with a lot of tension, separations, breakups and inconstancy. As a woman, she attracts men who are not willing to get involved, who frequently change their minds, who cannot be relied on and who do not provide her with the stability and peace of mind she needs to function.

In order to get healed, the natives need to release their anger, channel their energy into something constructive, trust themselves and their actions, correctly define their identity and find their right place. They have the right to freedom, individuality and life, peace and longevity, and no longer need to wage war to succeed.

Somatization: throbbing, sharp and intense headaches, apoplexy blows to the head, accidents, cuts, injuries, fractures, spasms of blood vessels in the eyes, intracranial tension, stroke, brain operations, epilepsy, paresis, loss of teeth, intracranial bleeding, hyperactivity, meningitis, sudden loss of identity, paralysis, sexual dysfunction, abortion, chills, sprains and strains, adrenaline and testosterone problems, restlessness, insomnia, senility, ADHD (Attention Deficit Hyperactivity Disorder)

Stages of awareness and healing phrases

◊ I see, recognize and honour the male line of my entire family system

◊ I honour the battles my ancestors fought, their victories and their defeats

◊ Their wars are not mine

◊ I have full power of action and am free to channel my energy constructively for my best interest

◊ I know who I am and who I want to become

◊ I have the ability to go all the way in fulfilling my desires

◊ I have the right to a peaceful and fulfilling life and understand that what I cannot control is part of the natural cycle of the world

◊ I release the fear of loss and stabilize myself, gathering the energy wasted needlessly

◊ I express independence, but also stability, volition or inner peace

◊ I am ready to fight for myself, to defend myself, but at the same time to respect peace and the right of every individual to freedom, life and own identity

Transgenerational transmission

Unintegrated experiences related to this aspect can occur in offsprings who have Uranus in Aries or in the 1st house, Mars in the 11th house, or Mars in a hard aspect to Uranus. At the same time, repetitive or revelatory experiences can take place during Uranus's transit to Mars or during Uranus's transit through the 1st house.

◊ **Famous people with a hard aspect between Uranus and Mars:**

◊ Roman Polanski, Patrick Duffy, Johannes Kepler

Uranus - Venus

Harmonious aspect

Trans-generationally, the positive aspect between the beautiful Venus and the electric Uranus is transmitted from a time when women were allowed to experience, to love, to express their authentic femininity, a time when female energy and feminism were in expansion. Possibly, in this family there were women who fought for their rights, who achieved independence and broke out of patterns, in whose lives art, fashion, intellect, principles, love, relationships and values went through a period of modernization very fast.

The natives with this aspect saw attractiveness, freedom, friendship, non-conventionalism and power of expression in the relationship between their parents, therefore they are conciliatory, reluctant to commit to problems or responsibilities, hate scandal and war and have their unique way of avoiding conflict. They can adopt a flower-power type of personality, are open to love, extroverted and very expressive. They like to experiment in relationships, thanks to which they make great progress. Their presence is charismatic and charming, and their appearance delightful - an explosion of beauty. In relationships, they easily seduce and let themselves be easily seduced by novelty, but to stay in a relationship they need more values.

Because feminine energy flows rapidly in this system, women pave the way for the natives and protect them, so they have a large circle of girlfriends or many unconventional ties. They love to be surrounded by people, are easygoing and sociable, and appreciate the connections they can gain. They are inspired by art and modern, minimalist or very airy, large places, where there is plenty of room to move, not feeling confined.

They want everything to happen now, have an innate flair

for money and can earn easily and quickly, taking advantage of many opportunities that appear when they are least expected.

While this is a favourable aspect, due to their unpredictable nature, the natives can be subdued by lightning passions, attracted by infidelity, by the taste of the new, and of the relationships that unfold and are consumed quickly, stealthily, suddenly, or against the clock.

◊ **Famous people with harmonious aspects between Uranus and Venus:**
◊ Carmen Electra, Marlene Dietrich, Gene Hackman,
◊ William Blake

Hard aspect

In the memory of this system, there is the remembrance of periods when there were disinheritances, when people were suddenly dispossessed of what they heaped in a lifetime, or when they lost everything in extreme situations - explosion, earthquake, fire, landslide, war, demolition, partition, bankruptcy, stock market crash, or devaluation of money as a result of social and economic changes, or high-risk investments. From a relational point of view: fugitive affairs, multiple partners, couple scandals, mismatch, unavailability for marriage, sudden break-ups, divorces, turbulence that shook relationships, controversies, atypical, unnatural relationships, against natural evolution, inconstancy in feelings, exclusive sex-based relationships, swift exchange of partners, relationships without conduct, without impositions, without attachments, without expectations; sudden loss of partner or relationship, divorce, lack of values related to marriage; revolt against forbidden, despotic marriages, obeying the rules or fitting the patterns; discharges of unhappiness; non-acceptance of a love relationship by the family, family intervention in a relationship, ruining it; women expelled from the family system, or fugitive women.

The memory of the unpredictable loss of a life partner, of relational instability and the trauma left by separations, leaves an unconscious imprint that creates in the natives the fear of emotional attachment, the feeling that they cannot be loved, are worthless and do not deserve to be happy.

What the natives saw in their families and in their parents' relationship provided them no security or comfort, so they are in a perpetual search for lost peace, which they are not sure how to evaluate or capitalize on. Actually, they don't trust themselves, they don't know what they deserve and what their value is, and they want to be loved but don't really know what that means. Under no circumstances would they obey traditions, they would seek to stun or draw attention through their relationships, to shake up and revolutionize the system, to lay the axe to the root of the tree. They project the need for friendship, understanding and detachment in their love relationships, but also vice versa, they project on their friends the need to be loved. They can fall in love at first sight, as well as seduce instantly, but their passions do not last long, something happens and they disappear. On the other hand, they have unbalanced partners, who are either as unstable as they are, or very dependent and attached.

Because they feel they don't want to fully commit, to avoid suffering later, they tend to be attracted to people who are just as unwilling to commit as they are. If the relationship becomes serious or they feel they are getting too attached, a crisis situation on an unconscious level occurs, which would break them and move them away from their comfort zone.

Without realizing why, they can get married and then divorce on impulse, have unpredictable, short and flashy extramarital affairs, and are dominated by erratic feelings, that not even they are able to understand, entanglements, overturnings, reconciliations and separations.

In protest, their clothing style is avant-garde, shabby, gaudy or slangy, they appreciate a type of art that few understand, have strange tastes, and their aesthetic sense, or the way they decorate their homes is innovative, but often chaotic, messy and ever-changing.

Their revolt is for the absence of love and the fear of being abandoned, which ultimately makes them never truly fall in love and be eternally restless.

They are rebellious, misunderstood, excluded or unseen children who need appreciation, acceptance and blessing.

Due to the unintegrated property-related trauma, the fear of losing again is transmitted trans-generationally and creates the tendency to build a protection mechanism against unforeseen events, manifested by a compulsive acquiring pattern, and attachment to property and possessions. At the same time, there is a spirit of justice raised in the following generations, who tend to balance the injustices done and revolt against similar situations during their existence.

The natives with this aspect need to change their entire set of values, redefine themselves as identities, free themselves from what they are tied to, and what fails to confer them authenticity and heal the wound.

They have to recede from everything they valued in the past, things that brought them stability and security, and redefine the concept of good, beauty, wealth and personal worth.

Somatization: thyroid dysfunction, sudden loss of voice, spasms, urinary incontinence, kidney or bladder problems, back pain, tractions and spasms, ankle deformity or pain, panic attacks, anxiety, facial tremors, tics, Tourette syndrome, ADHD

Stages of awareness and healing phrases

◊   I see, recognize and honour the unions in my family system

◊ I accept the love, marriages and separations that have occurred between my family members
◊ I accept and honour my parents' relationship
◊ Thanks to the encounter between my parents, I came to life
◊ Regardless of past experiences, I have the right to safety, love and happiness in relationships
◊ I value myself fairly, I know how much I deserve and how much I have to offer/receive
◊ Relationships can be happy as long as you first value and love yourself
◊ I free myself from the fear of loss and let myself love
◊ I deserve to be loved
◊ I express independence, but also stability; love, but also control of my feelings
◊ To love is wonderful
◊ I happily receive, respect and honour all the treasures of my family tree
◊ I happily enjoy and pass on what I have
◊ Life is a wonderful exchange of gifts

Transgenerational transmission

Unintegrated experiences related to this aspect can occur in offsprings who have Uranus in Taurus or Libra, Uranus in the 2nd or 7th house, Venus in the 11th house, or Venus in a hard aspect to Uranus. At the same time, repetitive or revelatory experiences can take place during Uranus's transit to Venus or during Uranus's transit through the 2nd or 7th house.

Famous people with a hard aspect between Uranus and Venus:
◊ Johnny Depp, Angelina Jolie, Diana Princess of Wales

Uranus - Mercury

Harmonious aspect

This family system encouraged the right to free expression, satisfying curiosities, the development of concepts and the expansion of visions.

It is possible that some members were part of liberal, progressive circles, which cultivated in them a sense of innovation, and gave birth to new currents of thought. They happily accepted and integrated the change, modern times and the right to be unique, not to be limited to a single concept.

The natives see things differently than those around them because they can look from other perspectives, understanding new, complicated or abstract concepts. They are highly creative and ingenious, having a great mental capacity. They are able to see the whole picture, on a grand scale, far into the future, being good visionaries and forecasters.

Since they are always watchful, they think and speak very quickly, always have an explanation, come up with a solution, find the answer to a problem or invent something that most people wouldn't even think of! Without patterns, templates, limits, or faith in limiting theories or beliefs, they have access to a system where information and knowledge flow very quickly, and they capture it very easily. They have flexible and curious minds, are constantly open to new opportunities, always trying to see what lies beyond. They are able to make associations and draw new neural tracks, they can read patterns and see beyond the symbol, as well as understand the most complicated mechanisms.

They have a fertile imagination and are unique and original, but also fiery and passionate with their reasoning. Attracted by everything that is new, the state-of-the-art technology, they are looking to implement their ideas on a larger, social or collective scale. Due to their reasoning and extended vision, they are also often frightened or shocked by what they see, feeling like they are losing their mind or going crazy.

In conversations, they love to exchange opinions, to be updated with other people's way of thinking, to startle with their capabilities and to shock with their way of expression.

They are intellectually competitive and attracted to intelligence, able to multitask, and to write or talk much, being excellent communicators, teachers or mentors.

◊ **Famous people with harmonious aspects between Uranus and Mercury:**
◊ John Steinbeck, Leonardo DiCaprio, Keanu Reeves

Hard aspect

In this family system, there was a lot of contradictory information, inconsistency in learning or in teaching some notions, and sudden interruption of some relationships, which led to major turbulence among the members.

Transgenerational trauma can occur as a result of scandalous, tense family relationships, yelling, shouting, verbal violence, threats, insults, mental pressure, nervous tension, and increased anxiety; members who rebelled against the family system; siblings who suddenly disappeared - accident, escape, departure, riot or sudden separation of siblings; family members who suffered accidents; quarrel between brothers, relatives and neighbors; unnatural relations between family members - relations outside the natural order; controversy, tension, change of power hierarchy between brothers or cousins; promises cancelled at the last moment, lack of understanding or vision, cancellation of some documents; lack of consistency in communication or relationships, contradictory information; overturnings as a result of narrow judgment; different opinions, desire for control, or change of thinking; truths or words that destroyed relationships and overturned plans; cancellations of some agreements, or the violent exclusion of some members from the system; fight for justice, equality and fraternity; separation of the family clan into several groups; children who have been indoctrinated; intolerance of avant-garde thinking; sudden interruption of studies or education, deprivation of liberty or truth; intellectual groups banned for their thinking; organizations, groups, parties of which the family members were part, but whose membership produced schism, or heretical actions; disturbance of the psyche and mind by violent outbursts; psychic attacks, riot of mind, hysteria.

The next generations feel this unintegrated conflict as a pressure to break away from the system, to erupt violently, and to rebel against it. The intensity of confrontations of opinion and vision between generations creates the desire to reconfigure old mental constructions, in order to create a new pattern of thinking, ideas and ideals.

Something has to be changed, but this is not easy, because the differences between the old way and the new way are very big, even antagonistic. The separation has to be sudden and radical.

The natives with this aspect have a special, new vision, often misunderstood by those around them, whom they fight to receive approval. Mentally, they feature chaos and instability, due to which they are hectic and indecisive, and change their minds easily.

They are contradiction maniacs, and conflict maniacs, they feel outraged easily and get angry quickly, are choleric, and angry, have a high verbal rate and speak quickly, but they are quick to hit, attack and fight those who do not see things the way they do. With their temperament, they can become outsiders, persons you cannot rely on, who create madness and who, due to their mental instability, have no credibility.

They cause trouble in discussions, seek discord, quarrel, scandal and cannot help being sarcastic or incendiary. They row against the tide, give no approval or validation to anyone, are inconsistent in decision-making and verbally or nervously unstable.

They think about several things at once, have a lot of ideas, but are not organized, have no patience to read, or listen, and their minds run in all directions. They jump to conclusions, tremble if don't have anything to do, move chaotically in all directions and cannot calm down easily. Their ways are always messy, they change circumstances easily and are troubled at all times.

Because their psyche is dissociated and shattered into many pieces, their main goal is to give up fighting, to keep calm and to make peace between contradictions. Their healing comes through inner peace, balance in thoughts, and opinions and release from tension. They have to understand that everyone's truth is personal, they do not have to be always right, and they are entitled to think freely, as are the others.

The rebellious part of their mind needs to realize that they are the only ones responsible for their own person, that they don't have to hit anyone to fulfil themselves, and that they can always decide for themselves.

The revolution lies in their own mind and in their own system, not in the world outside.

Somatization: muscle contractions; contractions of the fallopian tubes, spasms and cramps of the hands and fingers; hand tremors, electrocution; dislocations, fractures, accidents of hands and fingers; anxiety, nervousness, nervous breakdowns, insomnia, panic attacks, nervous tics, neurological disorders, hysteria, ADHD, loss of concentration; circulatory disorders, colics, intestinal occlusion, bloating; asthma attacks, drowning, suffocation; stuttering, verbal tics; accidents with car/ bike/ roller skate/ instruments/ tools; psychic attacks.

Stages of awareness and healing phrases

◊ I see, recognize and honour the relationships in my whole family system
◊ I accept the arguments, scandals and misunderstandings between my family members as an integral part of life
◊ Their reasoning, thinking and words are not mine
◊ I have the right to the truth, lasting relationships and free expression/thinking
◊ I have the right to an opinion, but I also respect the opinion of others - everyone has their own cause
◊ I express independence - but also stability in thinking, and truth - but also control of my ideas
◊ I make peace with my thoughts and all parts of me
◊ My mind recomposes in a righteous vision of the truth
◊ The relationship with my brothers is stable - everyone is where they need to be, and the order is restored

Transgenerational transmission

Unintegrated experiences related to this aspect can occur in offsprings who have Uranus in Gemini or in the 3rd house, Mercury in the 11th house, or Mercury in a hard aspect to Uranus. At the same time, repetitive or revelatory experiences can take place during Uranus's transit to Mercury or during Uranus's transit through the 3rd house.

◊ **Famous people with a hard aspect between Uranus and Mercury:**
◊ Bjork, Voltaire, Charles Chaplin

Aspects of the planet Neptune

Neptune - Sun

Harmonious aspect

The paternal figures of this system played an important role in family life, which they led on a subtle, spiritual level, or in a way that helped shape an idealized portrait of them over time.

They were people totally dedicated to a vision, inclined to dreaming, contemplation, art, and painting, but also clairvoyants, healers, shamans, and people with certain extra-sensory abilities, which they expressed and practised with devotion.

This family perpetuated anyone's belief in their own person, but also in a higher power, which is imagined as something wonderful, miraculous, spectacular, a superhuman figure. The environment where the family was built is a warm, sensitive, pleasant place, and the children see in their father a tolerant and compassionate man, mysterious in his own way, possibly a believer, a pious man, or a man with a special ideal. For them, he is a source of inspiration, providing confidence, harmony and inner peace.

The natives with this aspect are connected to the unconscious of their family tree and to another dimension, which they subtly perceive and from which they draw their entire essence and rationale. They have the ability to see beyond, to let themselves be carried away by intuition and imagination, to create wonderful things and to see the world in vivid colours.

Dreamers, idealists, often with a utopian vision of the world, have the ability to see the good in people, to be inspired by any situation, and to emanate their mystical air wherever they go. They may have the gift of healing, to see into the energy structure of the other, read between the lines and see in images, or sense what is in someone else's soul. They have a desire to help, the power to understand anyone, the ability to forgive and a great intuition.

Many times, due to their connection to the subtle world, they let themselves be guided by signs, communicate with elements invisible to those around them, have visions, merge with the universe and fall into a dream, in a very vivid inner world.

Their bohemian, artist-like nature can make them carefree, homelike or lazy, but when they truly want something and believe in it, they have all the ability to bring that thing to life.

Inspired, creative, with a very fertile imagination, generous, compassionate, as if landed from another world, they are attracted to mysteries, to occult, mystical things, to experiences meant to take them out of the physical world and transport them to a wonderland.

Their self-expression is drawn from a larger world, that belongs to a space beyond the physical world, of a special essence. With their vision of the world, combining the conscious with the imagination, they can become poets, philosophers, artists, healers, painters, writers, clerics, directors or actors.

They easily absorb the energy of those around them, which they feel like vibrations, but they also have the ability to dissolve, burn and pulverize it. They are often naive, get delighted easily, believe in people, abandon themselves and trust people who let them down later, but their power of forgiveness is great, so they let the supreme justice have its say.

◊ **Famous people with a harmonious aspect between Neptune and the Sun:**

◊   Priscilla Presley Diana, Princess of Wales,
◊   Friedrich Nietzsche, Michelangelo

Hard aspect

The absence of information about the life of the parents, the secrets about them, and what is hidden from the offspring remains imprinted as a hunger to find the missing person or situation, which the native cannot explain. What remains unsaid, the voluntary absence of transmission and the missing information deprive the descendants of the family tree of the elements necessary to develop a real, true identity.

Possible past situations: illegitimate children, unclear parentage, lack of genitors, a woman raising another woman's child as if it were her own (the child was adopted, or is her sister's, daughter's, son's, etc.), children conceived in extramarital relationships, lies or secrets related to paternity, missing or hidden children, children unattended, left out, with uncertain identity; children lied to, deluded, whose life was presented or whose identity was painted in wrong colours; witchcraft, curses, dirty dealings, complications, theft of identity or life on the father's line.

The idea of identity has been mistakenly transmitted across the generations, people have identified themselves with distorted roles, or there have been many secrets, hiding places, unknown things, voids, betrayals and lies. The parental image is fuzzy, unknown or false, and theft, stealing, cheating have existed in one form or another. There is something missing, a void that leaves room for interpretations, or that has confused multiple existences. Since the lie or illusion was perpetuated, the secret is still around and misguides all the family members.

The child with this aspect expects his father to be the ideal hero, but during his life or in adulthood he ends up being disappointed, realizing that the image he created of his father is not the real one. In an attempt to make themselves wanted, they project their desires onto other parental figures, whose company indulge or whom they obey, but by whom they ultimately feel betrayed, lied to, used or humiliated.

They have a very distorted self-image - seeing themselves as much more than they truly are, putting themselves onto a pedestal, or they have no clear image at all, considering themselves very weak, dull and unimportant.

Since nothing is clear to them, they have fears and frights, hide behind their fingers, dissimulate, lie, imagine things, and sell an image of themselves created by themselves. Although they feel inside the untruth and that they miss something, they are caught between worlds, not knowing what they are looking for, their reality distorted by many chimaeras: they do not see the world as it is, do not know the exact facts, are misled and pretend to be other people than they really are. Sometimes, even if their intentions are sincere, what they convey can be perceived by others as false, ambiguous or pretentious. Being accused and driven into a corner, they become even more confused.

In this chain, they attract people who betray them and make them feel guilty or unworthy. The need to escape reality is great, and if they cannot find ways to do it through their profession, they tend to live a double life and dissimulate, wasting themselves in virtual worlds, games, alcohol, drugs and very insecure situations.

Since they fail to see their true selves, they are pretenders, searching for themselves and playing several roles to find their own - they duplicate easily in a chameleonic style, sometimes uncertain or ambivalent, hidden behind masks, or roles they use as protective shields.

Both what they see of themselves and what others see of themselves is fake, and disappointment and shock occur after a rude awakening, when their position is not validated when they are exposed as being other people than they wanted to appear, or when their world falls apart like a sandcastle.

They can choose to fight and show their true identity and shine, or they can fall prey to victimization, in which case they beg for attention, complain, are fearful, hypochondriac, fragile, sickly, shy, with many personality problems. Although idealistic, compassionate, visionary and good artists, they carry within themselves a sense of insecurity about how will be they received by people.

The image of themselves must be aligned to what they really are, otherwise, they develop multiple personalities, which would confuse both themselves and those they relate with.

The first step towards healing is self-acceptance and activation of their own potential, recomposing themselves and getting out of the shadows.

They need to be seen, to be integrated, but first of all, they must see themselves! All the circumstances they are caught in, and all the untruths they face reveal the secrets hidden in their unconscious.

At the same time, the relationship with and the correct definition of the father are important.

Somatization: low blood pressure, heart disease, autoimmune disease, back problems, deformed lumbar spine, herniated disc, lymphatic problems, swollen lymph nodes, poor blood circulation, hypochondria, phobia, panic attacks, obesity, weak immunity, dysregulation of vitamin and nutrient absorption, depression, hair loss, strange childhood illnesses, or childhood illnesses manifested in adulthood, introversion, autism, vitamin D deficiency, hyper-pigmentation, or skin discolouration

Stages of awareness and healing phrases

◊   I honour my birth father and my adoptive father
◊   I accept the choices my parents made and I respect their personality

◊ I understand that whatever life my father had, I was born thanks to him
◊ Even though he is gone, a part of my father is in me
◊ I am ready to learn the truth and discover my purpose
◊ I am ready to reveal my true personality
◊ I am aware of myself as something real
◊ I have a right to clarity, life, joy and light
◊ I find my inner peace and I am happy with myself
◊ I express love, forgiveness and compassion, first of all for myself

Transgenerational transmission

Unintegrated experiences related to this aspect can occur in offsprings who have Neptune in the 5th house, the Sun in the 12th house, or the Sun in a hard aspect to Neptune. At the same time, repetitive or revelatory experiences can take place during Neptune's transit to the Sun or during Neptune's transit through the 5th house.

◊ **Famous people with a hard aspect between Uranus and the Sun:**
◊ Lady Gaga, Angela Merkel

Neptune - Moon

Harmonious aspect

The natives with this aspect have a family memory as taken from fairy tales: an idyllic, picturesque space, where love and devotion for God, people, country, birthplace, home and family is the central theme.

The memory of the past stores hospitable, compassionate, good people who helped heal others, women who fed the needy or people in distress, people who honoured places of worship or prayer, who built shelters for the homeless, merciful people who took everyone under their wings, no matter who they were, who had their heart in their mission to contribute, protect and heal with love everything on Earth.

The natives with this aspect are connected to the unconscious space of their families, from whom they receive messages in dreams and visions.

Structurally, they feel, scent, and perceive the emotions and states of those around them, always knowing how to soothe, how to comfort and how to nourish them on an inner level. They have a great ability to heal and provide protection and support to others.

Since their image of the world is that of a home, where all people are contained by Mother Nature and Father Universe, their plan is to integrate themselves into this greatness, to preach peace, harmony and love between people - it is the typology of the universal mother, who cares for all, with compassion, candour, and kindness.

In life choices and experiences, they let themselves be guided by intuition and what they feel, and are inspired by beauty - music, nature, art, poetry - and everything that moves their souls. They live in verses, see in vivid colours, and feel inside the harmonics of the world, and before such greatness, they can sink into themselves, in deep meditation, contemplation and abandonment.

Although they are perfectly fine living in solitude, in their intimate space, they need relationships, close ties, family and roots. They have a very sensitive nature, and attach themselves to those around them, to the past and to their loved ones, and the feelings they have for them are very deep. Although vulnerable, melancholic, romantic, sensitive and fragile, they are able to sacrifice themselves, being ready at any time for a great sacrifice.

Since they are open to love and ready to embrace anyone at any time, they may give too much, they can offer themselves and compromise themselves, having great satisfactions, wonderful loves, as well as very deep disappointments and disillusions.

As a woman, she is very fertile and wants a large, close-knit family, and as a man, he tends to attract a woman with deep maternal traits to protect, comfort and support him.

In order to fulfil the role of mother they feel inside and since in their memory dwells an ideal figure with whom they identify, the natives may illustrate this aspect by choosing a career of a doctor, psychotherapist, healer, medium, caretaker, or by offering protection, food and help to those in need.

◊ **Famous people with a harmonious aspect between Neptune and Moon:**
◊ Queen Latifah, Matt LeBlanc, Catherine Zeta-Jones

Hard aspect

In this system, there are unknown facts related to origins, family, mother, close ties or belonging. Concepts such as family, union, and maternal protection are distorted, and many mixed feelings have been perpetuated among the members.

Possible situations: lies, secrets, voids, entanglements

between families and trees, hidden motherhood (mother raises daughter's child because she gave birth too young, children mistaking parents for grandparents, adoptions kept secret), abandoned children, families left in the lap of the gods and scattered, the absence of the mother, illness, hospitalization, imprisonment of some members of the family.

We may also deal with a dysfunctional family, with many hidden ties, secrets, false emotions and feelings, pretence, betrayal between members, duality, dissimulation, unhealthy attachments, violation of intimate space, love or marriage relationships with many deviations from normal or taking place behind closed doors - sisters living with the same man or, conversely, brothers sharing the same woman; mothers and children developing intimate relationships, swings between family members - exchange of partners, homes, roles and places. Possible curses, insults, unclean, mysterious affairs, tangled threads or spells.

On a transgenerational line, traumas of this kind are inherited and further translate into disruptive emotional patterns, discomfort and chaos regarding one's own feelings related to childhood and relationships, inconsistency that leads to the loss of the family, abandonment, insecurity in concluding a marriage and unhealthy attachments.

The children's relationship with the mother figure or with the family is one of sacrifice and unhealthy compromise, of dependence at an emotional level and helplessness, which causes deviant emotions and behaviours.

The natives with this aspect are very vulnerable to the conditions of those around them, people they live for and who they want to comfort, and any imbalance they feel in connection to those people turns them upside down, leaving them prey to fears and anxiety.

They dream of an ideal family, a house with many children, and pure love between its members, and this image is projected on everyone. Since they fear family challenges and won't get involved in a conflict, they have the talent of pretending that they did not notice any trouble, they keep it to themselves, very easily forgive the mistakes committed against them, repress painful emotions, only to explode later into bouts of depression, sadness, deep melancholy, frustration, somatizations and regrets.

Thanks to the protective mechanism that they activate to avoid pain, they would project their maternal ideal onto the world, considering that the world is a good, warm, welcoming and harmonious place, where they feel safe.

They feel compassion and understanding for people, want to heal them emotionally, take care of those in pain, and assume the role of mother to everybody. They refuse to see the ugly side of things, the shadows and weaknesses, showing tolerance even to the most horrible human deeds. They are sensitive, very fragile emotionally and get involved with all their heart in what they do. They tend to attract people who abuse their feelings and idealism, their kindness and bubble of sensitivity, to take advantage of them and reject them after they get what they want. Being very easily manipulated and emotionally blackmailed, in permanent search for affection and protection, they become eternal victims of their boundless kindness and sensitivity.

Their inner world, of dreams and ideals, is very deep and vivid, but also volatile, and often reality intertwines with imagination, creating a distorted perception. It is difficult for them to ruminate and release their emotions, especially those related to their loved ones, placing themselves in the background most of the time.

They keep inside many secrets and traumas, pain and fears related to loss, death and abandonment, which they need to become aware of, to heal and release.

They need to take care first of all of their soul, which is disintegrated into a total mess of emotions, illusions and strong disappointments, to gather the scattered pieces and give them a concrete shape, otherwise, they will tend to become eternal victims - both their own's and their family's or people's around.

They have to understand their nature, set sound barriers, stop being emotionally abused and invaded, create a safe inner space and be emotionally independent.

At the same time, they need to cut unhealthy attachments to the family, if any, to find their own place in the world, to build a home for themselves and stop sacrificing for anyone - father, mother, brothers, sisters, partner or children. They need to live their own life, stop playing the saviour roles, get rid of complications and vain ideals and recognize/satisfy their own needs and feelings.

The help won't come from outside, from a higher power or God, in whose hands they leave themselves, but from the capacity to be the masters of their own decisions and to act according to their inner integrity. Their need to be with their parents, the loved ones, comes from the need to save them, but the real persons they need to save are themselves.

Somatization: digestive problems, stomach and gastric juice problems, fertility disorders, breast oedema, malformations of the ovaries, uterus or breasts; retroverted womb; depression, melancholia, addiction to alcohol, cigarettes, drugs, pain relievers or medicines; digestive intoxication, gas, bloating, false pregnancy, ectopic pregnancy; mental or emotional problems, obesity, problems with the circulation of water in the body, problems with swallowing, dehydration or water retention, problems in pregnancy and breastfeeding, rare diseases of the stomach, deviations - pelvis, uterus, digestive tract, basin, vagina, breasts, retracted nipples; the absence of an organ.

Stages of awareness and healing phrases

◊ I honour my whole family tree
◊ I accept the choices my parents made and I respect everyone's personality
◊ I understand that some things, life experiences or people

have been hidden over time, due to the times and the family context

◊ I am open to the release of the truth
◊ I'm ready to learn the truth and discover where I belong
◊ I am aware of my right to life as something real
◊ I find my inner peace and I am happy with myself
◊ I express love, forgiveness and compassion, primarily for myself
◊ I free myself from the unhealthy attachments and duplicitous, hidden, uncertain relationships I am a part of
◊ I release myself from the lie, falsehood, repressed emotions, from everything that I have hidden
◊ I can be vulnerable and I can show my true nature
◊ The truth sets me free and releases my soul from burdens
◊ I allow myself to maintain life, to move on and to procreate safely
◊ I have the right to a safe family and visible, concrete and stable relationships
◊ I have the right to be born and to give birth

Transgenerational transmission

Unintegrated experiences related to this aspect can occur in offsprings who have Neptune in the 4th house, the Moon in the 12th house, or the Moon in a hard aspect to Neptune. At the same time, repetitive or revelatory experiences can take place during Neptune's transit to the Moon or during Neptune's transit through the 4th house.

◊ **Famous people with a hard aspect between Neptune and Moon:**
◊ Al Pacino, Sigmund Freud, Martha Stewart, Bruce Willis, Marilyn Monroe

Neptune - Venus

Harmonious aspect

The harmonious aspect between Venus and Neptune contains within itself the memory of the space where deep, intense, romantic, idyllic, fabulous loves took place, which transcended human boundaries and powers, crossed time, space and death and demolished physical space to unite in the heart, in the dream, in the unconscious.

The feeling of love bound the partners in a subtle, eternal, all-encompassing union, in a common consciousness, which made them one single person. They only had eyes for each other, they dived in and fully tasted the magic of love, and the reality of one took shape and made sense only around the existence of the other. They were magnetically attracted to each other, they were connected and felt as if they were one, they always breathed on the same frequency and portrayed each other in the most sublime way.

In this family system, love, beauty, peace and harmony were elevated to the height of an ideal, and beautiful values, precious things, pure feelings and experiences were offered as a gift.

The women of this system left behind a valuable legacy - love of God, creativity, capacity for seduction, beautifying places, relationships and feelings, understanding and forgiveness, union between family members, and unconditional support.

The native with this aspect is very pacifist, eternally in love with love, with an amazing ability to make a love story out of any situation, very romantic, with an innate artistic sense and great creative power.

They are very loving, but often live outside reality, are looking for the ideal partner, the muse able to inspire them, eternal love and everlasting youth, which they can quickly project onto an ideal.

Their capacity for abandonment, faith and sacrifice make them compassionate, forgiving, empathetic, sensual, and romantic, but also easily hurt and vulnerable.

Graceful, loving, warm, sensitive, affectionate, with a high ideal projected on relationships and partners, in the absence of someone who truly understands them and protects their delicacy, they can immediately shatter. In terms of skills, they have a special aesthetic sense, are inspired, graceful, and delicate, have a beautiful, warm or calm voice, and have a very rich imagination, which helps them create mystery, enchantment and stories. Money comes easily to them, they have a chance, luck, help and support to dedicate themselves to their exquisite ideals.

◊ **Famous people with harmonious aspects between Neptune and Venus:**
◊ Nick Nolte, Ivana Trump

Hard aspect

The aspect brings to mind times when something was stolen or substituted, or a person was cheated on, or robbed of possessions, love, the most valuable assets. Possible situations: lies, hidden loves or marriages, infidelity between parents or family members, love secrets, duality, entanglements on the female line or exchanges of relationships and partners, which led to duplicity, tangled family trees, incest and brain fog; betrayal, parallel lives; deviant, out of the ordinary relationships; marriages or relationships between relatives; stealing the partner by occult means; the distortion and desecration of love; lies in the desire to be loved or liked; false love, the appearance of love, disappointing, changing relationships; mistresses, lovers, women who tempt or steal the partners of the people around; perjury and misstatements; captive relationships, manipulation, forgery, theft, fraud; relationships built on covert interests - theft of property, obtaining goods or valuables; absconding of a member with the family fortune; distorted, deformed moral or aesthetic values; questionable values; relationships that were not supposed to take place; abandonment, disappearance of the partner; unexplained or strange ruptures, followed by curses; spells cast for love and welfare. The sense of personal worth and self-love is distorted, and the persons under the influence of this pattern tend to deceive themselves in relationships, reconstruct a hidden secret, to relive an untold story from long ago! They have the patience to find forgiveness, healing, and understanding in relationships, but they attract people with deep wounds and complicated lives, and they mess up things even more.

Because there is an idealistic expectation about giving and taking, being worth or having value, there is a predisposition for the natives to abandon themselves, to give all, to forget themselves for the other's sake, or, conversely, there is the expectation that the other will be the saviour, a certain imagined character, who would express, be and do according to the duplicated image. For this reason, they become the victims of their own projections, surrendering to the hands of others or playing their healers.

In an effort to have the perfect relationship, the natives lend their partner an ideal image, qualities and traits and a noble personality, and if the partner goes wrong, rather than admitting they were hurt, dishonoured or disrespected, they tend not to start a conflict, to be passive, find excuses, beautify reality, and lie to themselves. When they can't stand anymore, they blame their partner for not being what they were supposed to be, victimize, complain and humiliate themselves, and if the other is no longer with the living or is far away, they still see themselves next to him/her, imagine they are in a relationship and live in his/her world.

At the same time, they can have imbalances, strange passions and tastes, fall strangely in love with the most unsuitable people, wish to try and experience unusual things, fall prey to momentary pleasures and vices, and then feel guilty and disappointed in themselves.

On an unconscious level, they tend to identify with the other, to depersonalize themselves, to abandon everything to be one with the other, and when the other is no longer there, realize that they offered and lost everything just for an illusion. Due to the confusion in feelings, they can be dual, have several relationships at the same time, hide what they feel or indulge in confusing situations, where they accept to stay in the shadow, be just a lover or play the role the other would like them to play.

If they land in a relationship only for the sake of a habitude or an uncertain memory, a dream that is not theirs, they will feel sad, and disappointed, will realize that they do not really love the other, before they will want to run away, to find something else that would bring them satisfaction.

They lie, hide, and betray, so they live in a world that will become increasingly difficult for them to master - if they lie, are lied to, if they steal, others would steal from them, and so on, in a chain of disrupted values, business, relationships and feelings, where really nobody has anything to gain.

They need clarity in their feelings, valorization of their own person, new values in everyday life, honouring their own relationship and sexuality and a healthy expression of their own personality.

Their ideal of harmony and beauty can also sublimate into attraction for art, design, cosmetics, pleasure, relaxation, luxury, music, and beautiful and elegant places.

Somatization: thyroid dysfunction, voice change, vocal cord problems, lethargy, apathy, sexual deviance, bunions, gout, leg tenderness, clumsy gait, varicose ulcers, glandular disorders, lymphatic system problems, weight problems, increased blood sugar, diabetes, glaucoma, cataracts, problems with the sense of touch, anaemia, kidney disease, body asymmetries, skin problems, kidney and urethral dysfunction

Stages of awareness and healing phrases

◊ I honour my whole family tree
◊ I accept the choices my parents made and I respect their personality
◊ I accept the love stories of the past and whatever could not be said
◊ I am open to the release of the truth
◊ I am aware of my worth and my right to a happy relationship
◊ I find my inner peace and I am happy with myself
◊ I express love, forgiveness and compassion, first of all for myself
◊ I see my relationships clearly and am ready to value myself properly
◊ I deserve to be valued, seen and appreciated
◊ Money is an important resource for me and I earn it honestly

Transgenerational transmission

Unintegrated experiences related to this aspect can occur in offsprings who have Neptune in the 2nd and 4th houses, Venus in the 12th house, or Venus in a hard aspect to Neptune. At the same time, repetitive or revelatory experiences can take place during Neptune's transit to Venus or during Neptune's transit through the 2nd and 7th houses.

◊ **Famous people with a hard aspect between Neptune and Venus:**
◊ Pamela Anderson, Prince Charles

Neptune - Mars

Harmonious aspect

Throughout these generations, masculine energy has been transformed into compassion, sensitivity, charitable and benevolent actions, with a focus on spirituality. Men of this system had uplifting visions, and healing abilities, or worked with energy on a subtle level.

Being very good advocates, the next generations will feel the need to reach out to those in need, those with troubles.

The native with this astral aspect has inherited the ability to act from behind a veil, operate with subtle messages, manipulate and activate energy without being seen. Used correctly, the aspect helps dilute and integrate their inner aggression and transform it into art, and also helps them receive guidance on an unconscious level, and create based on their gifts. They can immerse in meditation to obtain amazing inner resources, guided by a hidden sense and a special compass. They have healing, and shamanic skills, feel the vibration and energy, and react very easily.

Conversely, if the moral aspects are not soundly developed, they can use their abilities to manipulate or control other people, to hide and steal, to swindle and cast spells.

Their magnetism is great, they have power of attraction and absorption, which can make them leaders or courtly partners. They have the ability to walk on secluded, hidden paths that not many would tread, are drawn to mystery and fairy tales, and to the realm where they can create the world as they wish!

Their creative capacity is immense, being a master in translating the image in their mind into reality, in expressing their dreams, painting or drawing what they see, turning into art their mind and experience.

Since they keep the family flag flying, they can build a mission they truly believe in, are devoted to, and constantly dream about. However, they need to avoid immersing themselves in imaginary spaces and dimensions for too long, identify their ideals properly, avoid stalling for too long and go all the way or, conversely, stop if they find that the road would not get them anywhere.

◊ **Famous people with a harmonious aspect between Neptune and Mars:**
◊ Pablo Picasso, Pharrell Williams, Jackie Chan

Hard aspect

The aspect suggests that in this system something has been distorted, the will has been disintegrated, the manhood has been annulled; certain actions were repressed, cancelled, distorted by occult causes and have not ever taken place; a man was hidden, concealed, unfaithful or duplicitous; someone was pushed to do thoughtless or unwilling acts; a situation or a person was manipulated to obtain an asset, an advantage or to win a competition; actions carried out on the back; spells, charms, unclean affairs; uncertain or hidden sexuality; actions kept secret or concealed; imprisonment, deprivation of liberty; a member whose identity has not been recognized or stolen; false ideals, repressed struggles, abandonment, flight, abduction, evaporation, mist related to events and actions; acts in ignorance, wrongdoing, recklessness, unconscious fighting, unlawful acts or activities, unclean war; a man who messed up many destinies.

Being driven by a vision, phantasma or spell, the natives with this aspect indulge in activities that are deceptive even for them, where they get lost in a labyrinth, postpone what is important, get lazy, and excited, and then they are not in the mood for anything anymore. Hell breaks loose when it comes for them to make a choice and adopting a position of control over their own person, they get involved in many unrealistic actions, especially those coming from an inner impulse, when they completely ignore reality.

Like the donkey driven by the ever-unattainable carrot, they tend to work very hard, to the point of exhaustion, for the particular mission they have set for themselves. What they feel is possibly beyond the normal limits and boundaries of reality, because they let themselves be inspired by a high ideal, that makes them always move forward, that makes them act and fight. They have high expectations of themselves, and of their capabilities, which is why they raise the bar higher and higher.

Many inner, compulsive tensions lay in them, which are difficult to perceive, often pushing them to do something, before they suddenly change their minds, withdraw, abandon everything, rest in isolation and dream, directionless.

They may have a strange functioning pattern, deviant behaviour, obsessions, vices and addictions, which affect both them and those whom they relate with. There is a higher power that makes them act, sometimes to the point of abandonment, that lead them into a circle which they can hardly get out from.

Unintegrated, this aspect can make them act behind masks, pretend, pose as victims, act without good intentions and perpetuate what they receive, or attract partners of this kind. They become dependent on their imagination, parallel worlds, alcohol or drugs, they have the illusion of a mission or an ideal, think they are chosen and glorify themselves, only to give up later for lack of substance.

To heal themselves, they need to get out of the illusion, fight against it, regain their personal identity and find out who they are! They need to take on the situations they got into, face reality and find the way to the light. At the same time, they need to identify their dark, hidden side, which they have repressed for too long, and to recognize themselves!

Somatization: adrenal gland dysfunction, cerebral oedema, face oedema, meningitis, allergies, rhinosinusitis, herpes, autoimmune diseases, sexual deviance, impotence, sexually transmitted diseases, discharges, non-healing wounds, falls or inexplicable symptoms, without physical, medical causes, arthritis, alcohol, drug or medication addictions, autoimmune diseases, metabolic and fat burning disorders, disorders of nutrient absorption and transformation processes, injuries in strange circumstances

Stages of awareness and healing phrases

◊   I honour the masculine line of my family tree
◊   I accept the choices my parents made and I respect their personality
◊   I accept the love stories of the past and whatever could not be said or shown
◊   I am open to the release of the truth
◊   I am aware of my identity and the right to a real, genuine life
◊   I find my inner peace and act according to my ideals
◊   I express love, forgiveness and compassion for the men around me
◊   I see my relationships clearly and am ready to engage properly
◊   I deserve to be free and go in the direction of my choice
◊   I free myself from unhealthy attachments and have clarity of my actions and their consequences in the physical and spiritual plane

Transgenerational transmission

Unintegrated experiences related to this aspect can occur in offsprings who have Neptune in the 1st house, Mars in the 12th house, or Mars in a hard aspect to Neptune. At the same time, repetitive or revelatory experiences can take place during Neptune's transit to Mars or during Neptune's transit through the 1st house.

◊ **Famous people with a hard aspect between Neptune and Mars:**
◊ Tommy Hilfiger, Jimmy Hoffa, Steve McQueen

Neptune - Mercury

Harmonious aspect

Between present and past, between now and then, between the conscious and the unconscious of this family tree, there is a channel of communication, which can be either a plus or a great imbalance. Trans-generationally, there may have been prophets, clairvoyants, mediums or people who encouraged openness to spirituality, art, creation and idealism in this family. The bond between its members was extremely strong, and telepathic, and was maintained beyond space and time in a separate dimension. They were bound together in a connection that transcends the five senses and goes far beyond and deeper, in a subtle complicity.

The natives who inherit this aspect have a very vivid imagination and can create with great ease, have tremendous mental receptivity, spontaneity, artistic and writing talent, and a very vivid vision of reality.

Their contracts are soulful and spiritual, they know no grudge and want to live in a poem, in a verse or in a world where magic and mystery still exist on earth.

They may know information or answers to questions intuitively without any logic to back them. They have sensitivity, receptivity, many prophetic dreams and can be in two worlds at the same time. Due to their vision, they can be very successful in art, music, literary creations, poetry, film, photography, painting or fashion. At the same time, they can be good therapists, healers, clairvoyants or doctors.

They have the help of their ancestors on their side, are connected to the system, guided and tutored, with an amazing ability to read behind, in the shadows, in people, to communicate with those beyond, whom they feel connected and bound to.

Often, they live too much in their mind, where they imagine, build, dream, fly away with their thoughts and pay no attention to the details of the mundane world. They hear the whispers of those beyond, see or sense their presence, and can pass beyond very easily.

When they speak or tell a story, they capture attention at once, due to their gift of rendering wonderful worlds, describing them in the thousands of details and images that they can see.

◊ **Famous people with harmonious aspects between Neptune and Mercury:**
◊ Michael J. Fox, Oscar Wilde, Shirley Temple Black, Robb Thomas, Mia Farrow, Meryl Streep

Hard aspect

To escape punishment, to face the cruel reality, to make their way in life or not to be seen, judged, put against the wall, humiliated or held responsible for their own mistakes, these people can fabricate facts, experiences, excuses, reasons or arguments, which they report as the interlocutor needs to hear them in order to see the expected image. They put things in a different light and context, stretch the truth, and add or omit information, precisely to remove themselves from the landscape and victimize themselves, or to create a false identity of themselves. As time goes by, truth evaporates, dissipates, is forgotten or misinterpreted, and people's opinions and actions are based on something that is not accurate. Many chimaeras or much mystery surround the whole family system, which is lost in an illusory past and vanity.

Possible past situations: broken promises, postponed, unfinished things, unrealistic wishes; information is missing from the family system, something was hidden, kept secret or omitted; a brother is hidden or his existence is not known, he was given, abandoned, adopted, has a different origin than the one declared; a lie perpetuated over several generations; betrayal, omission, relationships left to chance, hidden contracts or documents, gaps in information, disappearances of persons of whom nothing is known, distortion of the truth in all its forms; complications, unclean affairs, incest between siblings, deceitful, illicit exchanges or transactions done behind someone's back; theft, spell, mystery, occult forces; distortion, deviation from normal, family environment vitiated by alcohol, drugs, immoral, illicit situations.

It is something more than it appears, it is something beyond this reality, and the natives with this aspect feel the call to go beyond in search of the truth, to receive the subtle messages that pervade time. Their reality may be inexplicable to others, or they may look mad because they know, feel, see, but cannot express in words what they cannot fully explain to themselves. Because they constantly feel that something is hidden, they suffer from conspiracy theory syndrome, and they suspect everyone, projecting their insecurities onto others, whom they see as different from they are.

Unconsciously, to avoid being discovered, prevent suffering and turn things to their own advantage, they have a permanent tendency to dissemble or escape reality and juggle it.

Reason intertwines with imagination, especially when they do not want to face something that would cause them suffering or destroy the ideas and vision they have formed about a person or a situation.

They often invent, hide, fabricate a scenario, add details, and can't help using twisting words to their advantage.

In his world, dreams intertwine with dreams, illusion with desire, paranoia with reality, and the ideals and stories they would like to tell themselves, they recreate again and again from nothing. They are prone to lie, but also to be lied to, are very naive, hallucinate or bend the truth, and they also end up believing their version. They have hallucinations, are not always conscious, get involved in stories that do not concern them, assign themselves roles that should not be theirs, and have no concrete moral or spiritual qualities.

What they received from their family or what they saw in their parents is false, hidden, deceitful or dual, and they must understand themselves, leave the brain fog and see or accept things as they really are.

Mentally distorted images of childhood related to their own identity, the flawed environment, and the unreal that stood in the way of logic and reason need to be revealed and recognized.

Although this is a challenging aspect, because reality interferes with imagination, they need to find out the truth, break the spell that has surrounded them all their life and get rid of the masks.

*

When somebody does not know that they have another brother or sister, an entire branch of a system lives apart from another, with a thick fog between them. The voice of the blood, of the tree and of the system may call them close to each other, but even if they happen to meet on the street or make acquaintance at a juncture of life, they will not recognize each other as relatives, they will not really know of the other's existence. Over time, the members of the systems may even come together, fall in love, and form relationships with each other, which would unconsciously complicate things even further.

Somatization: poor lung oxygenation, pulmonary emphysema, intoxication, smoking, impaired speech or thinking, aphasia, poor orientation in space, poor coordination of hands and fingers, deformed fingers, the sensitivity of the soles, scar on the foot or on the toes, tuberculosis, pneumonia, senility, amnesia, Alzheimer's, hallucinations, autism, confusion, mythomania, toxaemia, alcoholism, drug or medicine intoxication, poor peripheral circulation, occlusion, dizziness, internal ear disorders, forgetfulness, dementia

Stages of awareness and healing phrases

◊ I honour my entire family system, with all its branches
◊ I accept the choices my parents made and I respect their personality
◊ I am open to the release of the truth
◊ I demand the right to a real and truthful life
◊ I see and accept reality as it is
◊ I give up ideals that no longer conform to current reality
◊ I see my relationships clearly and am ready to engage in them properly
◊ I speak the truth and I don't shy away from it
◊ I am freed from unhealthy attachments and have clarity in my words and thoughts
◊ I call and honour my brothers, unknown relatives and blood members I never knew anything about
◊ I am ready to remove the fog and bring light to the whole system of my family tree
◊ I accept the consequences of my words and thoughts because I am aware of and clearly see their importance

Transgenerational transmission

Unintegrated experiences related to this aspect can occur in offsprings who have Neptune in the 3rd house, Mercury in the 12th house, or Mercury in a hard aspect to Neptune. At the same time, repetitive or revelatory experiences can take place during Neptune's transit to Mercury or during Neptune's transit through the 3rd house.

◊ **Famous people with a hard aspect between Neptune and Mercury:**
◊ Bob Dylan, Jim Morrison, Donald Trump, Marlene Dietrich

Aspects of the planet Pluto

Pluto - Sun

Harmonious aspect

Due to the transformative role he played in the family or in society, the paternal figure of this system is perceived as very intense and profound. The father imprinted his will, personality and deep character on those who surrounded him, being an influential person with a strong personal magnetism. In life, he managed to overcome extremely painful, difficult, perhaps traumatic experiences, and move on with dignity, power and inner strength. As a parent, he wanted to firmly draw the lifeline of his children, inspiring strong life principles in them.

The natives with this aspect inherit a great power of regeneration, power of expression and great personal magnetism. The male sexual energy is very strong in this system, and they feel it to the full. The physical needs, instincts, sense of survival and sense of identity are intense, creating a very potent personality in many ways.

When they make their entrance, they have the ability to magnetize the audience. They are able to see into people, but also to manoeuvre things from the shadows. They have great self-control, are able to manage their reactions, change their personality, and easily overcome difficulties.

Intense desires, great creativity and capacity for expression, regeneration, and depth, all are part of their structure. They are attracted to mysteries, to everything that is hidden, and their light can penetrate deep. They have the capacity to fight great forces and defeat them, becoming a colossus of energy and gaining power.

It is possible that the legacy passed on by his system is also a financial one. The natives are visionary, able to manage large amounts of money or wealth and have the ability to fructify and build as well as develop further. They have a particularly powerful engine inside, always energized.

The man with this aspect is very virile, sexually potent, attracted to carnal pleasures, but also a great seducer. The woman has strong masculine traits, she is seductive, but very capable, bellicose and sexual, looking for a man who can support this devouring energy of her.

◊ **Famous people with a harmonious aspect between Pluto and the Sun:**
◊ Nicolas Cage

Hard aspect

The hard aspect between the two planets indicates a trauma suffered on the paternal line, unfinished mourning, a major wound yet unhealed, the death of the father, the abusive, domineering character of the same, or fights for power related to him. Ambition, force, desire for dominance and control, aggression and extremism are the main tendencies to be integrated. What has been passed down through the generations is intense, deep, because it has to do with death, with the secrets that surround it and with taboo topics, such as abuse (physical, emotional, mental), murder, rape or aggression.

Transgenerational situations - premature death of the head

of the family: the father, an authoritative figure, or a person with leadership/power attributes; manipulation or abuse to obtain paternity or disposal of the father/ breaking the relationship with him; terror, dread of the father or of his loss; unintegrated paternal trauma; abuse of power, torture, envy, jealousy, conspiracy on the paternal line or against the father; murder on father or his personality, child abuse, self-persuasion; poisoning; destruction of joy; fight with abusive, aggressive, domineering persons; struggle for survival, or power; death of a child, abortion; taboo sexuality; child resulting from an abusive or toxic relationship; destruction of autonomy in childhood, dominance over a child, abusive and power relations directed at self or a child; external pressure on a single person; imposing another personality; destruction of personality; abuse, insult, manipulation, obsession, control, enemy lurking in the shadows, coercion to do something against one's will; demonic persons who destroy childhood.

The natives with this aspect have many inner fears, which they do not understand, especially the fear of being destroyed, of not being or of losing the other, which is implemented at a subconscious level.

There is an ocean of feelings, emotions and experiences inside them, which they have to externalize, but the fear of revealing themselves, becoming intimate and losing control is very strong. In response they withdraw from the conflict, are not willing to be in the middle, are afraid of life and do not manage to find themselves, or, in turn, become cold, harsh, manipulative, and hidden.

There is a pressure to be what others want, to be someone else, or to do more than their shoulders can take, and they no longer know how to behave, or who they really are. Unlike what they exteriorize, they have a very intense dark side locked up inside them, which erupts in borderline situations or which they keep repressed, but due to this, they can become self-destructive or addicted to a certain state.

The attitude towards authority is ambivalent - on the one hand, they want to stay in control and others to obey them, on the other hand may have a desire to be subjugated, dominated and tormented. Their fears are projected onto the people they interact with and come into conflict with for dominance, control and manipulation. In a desire to feel that they are strong and that others are weak, they can be uncompromising, harsh, domineering, despotic or tyrannical - but also secretive, fearful, treacherous, dissimulating. Seeking to be healed, they can be vengeful, fierce, and ready for war, but also fear-ridden, scared and self-destructive!

They attract toxic relationships, where others try to dominate them, destroy their personality and kill their creativity, undermine their self-confidence and brilliance, which can bring out the worst in them, but also a fierce desire for death and rebirth, regeneration and transformation.

The others want to chain them, or they want the power, but more than anything they want not to suffer, to be protected and safe.

Because everything comes from themselves, they need a deep transformation, releasing the energy of insecurity and suffering, gaining confidence in themselves and their potential, rebuilding the structure of the Self, and forgiving. They have to cut all the unhealthy strings around them, show themselves as they are and get freedom.

At the same time, it is necessary to heal the wound of the father, of the relationship with him, and to find the peace, security, acceptance, and strength they need to believe in themselves.

Somatization: spine surgery, heart disease and attacks, cardiac arrhythmia, heart surgery, reproductive system disease, infection, sexually transmitted disease, fibroma, ulceration, painful boil, agony, split personality, phobias, allergies, low immunity, autoimmune diseases, scalp ulcers, burns, solar plexus pain, panic attack, anxiety, paralysis, paresis, blood vessels trauma, cardiac arrest, blisters, herpes

Stages of awareness and healing phrases

◊ I honour my father, no matter his personality
◊ I honour all the authoritative figures of this system
◊ I understand the trauma, violence and abuse my ancestors went through
◊ I understand their unexpressed pain, fear and helplessness, and how the experiences they have gone through have prompted them to act in a certain way
◊ I understand that no matter what life my parents and grandparents had, thanks to them I was born
◊ Even though they are gone, a part of them is in me
◊ I am ready to release all the pain gathered inside me and discover my purpose
◊ I rise from my own ashes in my best version
◊ I find my inner peace by forgiving the evil that was in the past
◊ I express love, forgiveness and compassion, first of all for myself
◊ I allow myself to exist, to shine, to express myself genuinely, and to be successful
◊ I allow myself to be who I want to be and let life continue to flow through me

Transgenerational transmission

Unintegrated experiences related to this aspect can occur in offsprings who have Pluto in the 5th house, the Sun in the 8th house, or the Sun in hard aspect to Pluto. At the same time, repetitive or revelatory experiences can take place during Pluto's transit to the Sun or during Pluto's transit through the 5th house.

◊ **Famous people with a hard aspect between Pluto and the
Sun:**
◊ Elvis Presley, Margaret Thatcher

Pluto - Moon

Harmonious aspect

In this family system, many pains were overcome, and traumas were processed very well on an emotional level. The maternal figures were strong women with special mental and financial abilities - they had to quickly release the pain of any traumatic experiences and move forward strongly, carry it off, raise their children, and want to survive.

The relationships between the members of this family were deep and intense - attached to each other, emotionally connected and united, they knew each other's vulnerabilities, they laughed and cried together, they were very intimate with each other, they shared secrets, they were by each other's side in the most challenging moments, which they passed together. For them, the family had a powerfully transformative role, and the egregor of the family tree could process and alchemize feelings, turning them into real inner resources and treasures.

The natives with this aspect have very strong psychic abilities, are sensitive, and perceptive, and feel everything that is hidden, with a great power of penetration. They quickly sense behind someone's words or actions, make connections, and put things together, like a lie detector or a radar.

They are very good mediums, psychologists, and psychoanalysts, they receive the emotions of those around them and can see deep inside them, finding the root of the problems, but also the solutions for healing. They can introspect very deeply, can dive into symbols and signs, and are also good detectives.

When they attach to somebody, they do it totally, all the way, to death. Their relationships are intimate, intense, and passionate, and emotions boil in their veins. The sense of belonging is strong, and so are their attachments, which they can chain any partner with.

Emotionally and relationally, they want and offer total sincerity, unveil their emotional side, show their vulnerability and penetrate emotionally the partner.

◊ **Famous people with harmonious aspects between Pluto and the Moon:**
◊ Nicolas Cage

Hard aspect

Fear, terror, panic, horror, frustration, guilt, all of these undermine this tree, which tends to hang heavier and heavier, to grow in shadow or darkness, haunted by many demons and horrors. Family relationships are the main scene where this pattern unfolds. Here lies hidden deeply buried secrets, toxic family relationships, abusive sexuality, rape, deep trauma, painful relationship with the mother, abusive, obsessive or manipulative mother; destructive family relationships; family breakdown; orphans; shattered motherhood, abortion, suicide, death of a family member, bankruptcy; emotional blackmail, threat, intimidation, emotionally unbalanced mothers who threaten suicide, with many secrets or trauma; blame, shame and guilt - the blame for the mother's actions placed on your shoulders; terrible remorse; constant reliving of a painful moment; mother causing fear, panic, intense emotions; mothers emotionally dependent on children; mothers struggling with life; privacy violated; excessive jealousy and possessiveness on the part of the mother; mourning, inability to let go of pain.

It is possible that the maternal figures of this system, or important members were abusive, or emotionally or sexually manipulated: incestuous, compromising relationships, perversions between themselves, between parents and children. It is a system where abortions have been performed, children have been killed, many relationships have been carried out behind closed doors, and many shameful, taboo secrets have been hidden.

Over the years, the aspect brings to the surface the deepest fears, and problems related to abandonment, guilt, jealousy, manipulation, depression or obsession, and their effect can subsequently generate a series of very intense psychological and emotional experiences, where repressed feelings blow out.

Due to traumatic family relationships, the breaking of family ties, and the death of the mother or other important members, the natives who failed to integrate the aspect attract obsessive and destructive domination or dependency relationships or become so themselves.

Although they have a problem opening up and letting someone enter their intimate environment, when they do, they unveil their most vulnerable parts and ask for their deepest wounds to be healed. They need protection, comfort, a mother, but also a stable environment. Unfortunately, not many are able to understand or help them, as their wounds are very deep.

They tend to be consumed inside with their greatest fears, to wander into the darkness of their soul. The feeling of broken-up attachments horrifies them, so they hold on to love, become possessive, and unstable and may resort to painful manipulative techniques. On their way, due to the unconscious content, they meet malevolent and perverted people, whom they must face, and free themselves from them, first by cleaning themselves inside. What they feel is difficult to control, many emotions paralyze their body and cloud their thinking, making them react unexpectedly, intensely and destructively. If their desires and needs are not fulfilled, they can end up with emotional blockages, depression, anxiety and even suicidal tendencies. Dark emotions and destructive-compulsive behaviour can drive them to annihilation.

In order to balance themselves, they need deep spiritual and emotional healing, where intimacy no longer seems like a problem, where they heal the wounds of abuse towards them and feel that they belong somewhere, that they are contained, loved and accepted!

They need deep love, understanding and compassion, healing and release, forgiveness and acceptance, otherwise, there will always be painful struggles within them. Hard as it is, they have to admit that they are vulnerable, in pain and hurt, and they can be crushed at any time. They have to release the pain, the frustration, the hatred, the thoughts for revenge, the obsession, the guilt, the resentment, that burn them alive.

The natives need to understand the human being deeply, to integrate both their positive side and the dark, demonic side. They must dive into the psyche and unconscious of the other and of their own, merge with it and reveal the parts hidden in the shadows.

At the same time, they need regeneration of soul, mind and body, understanding that birth and death, good and evil are part of existence.

Somatization: cystitis, reproductive system diseases, stomach acidity, internal toxicity, ulcers, gastritis, water retention in the body, genital discharge, poisoning - intoxication, fibromatous uterus, candida, mastitis, anaemia, breast surgery, stomach or uterine wound, paranoia, emotional imbalance, psychosis, obsession, anorexia, dehydration, mouth ulcers, canker sores, oesophagus burn, resection of stomach, uterus, ovaries or breasts, cancer at breast, stomach or reproductive system, inability to maintain pregnancy, abortion, toxic pregnancy, hernia, abuse of drugs or toxic substances - tobacco, alcohol, drugs.

Stages of awareness and healing phrases

◊   I honour my mother and my membership in this system

◊ I understand the trauma, violence and abuse endured by my ancestors
◊ I understand their unexpressed pain, fear and helplessness
◊ I understand that no matter what life my parents had, thanks to them I was born
◊ I am ready to release all pain and discover my roots
◊ I am ready to heal the wounds of the past
◊ I give forgiveness, compassion, love and understanding to my soul
◊ I release myself from guilt, remorse and suffering
◊ I rise from my own ashes in my best version
◊ I find inner peace by recognizing my nature
◊ I release myself from unhealthy relationships in my life, and I release those I have chained
◊ I have the right to life and safety

Transgenerational transmission

Unintegrated experiences related to this aspect can occur in offsprings who have Moon in Scorpio, Moon in the 8th house, Pluto in the 4th house, or the Moon in a hard aspect to Pluto. At the same time, repetitive or revelatory experiences can take place during Pluto's transit to the Moon or during Pluto's transit through the 4th or 7th house.

◊ **Famous people with a hard aspect between Pluto and Moon:**
◊ Elvis Presley, Margaret Thatcher

Pluto - Mars

Harmonious aspect

The masculine energy of this family tree is very strong, reminiscent of fighters, and influential people with great inner strength, power, determination, ambition, sexuality and controllability. Very likely, the male figures held important positions in the community or were very wealthy people.

Trans-generationally, the natives who inherit this aspect have a great self-identity, focus, determination, power and physical strength, as well as great handiness. They can control great forces, and very powerful machines, and they can also go very deep, or very far.

They feature great self-control, vitality, virility, determination, and endurance, but also strong desires and passions. When they want something, they are compulsive and impulsive, and go to the bitter end to get it! Since they have money, sexual power, physical power or determination, they have the ability to manipulate and control those around them, who become fascinated by them.

In their career, they are wonderful strategists, good business people, surgeons, and detectives, are very enterprising, but also persuasive, and persistent, people who can move mountains. Dominated by strong sexuality, they take control in relationships, know what they want, and are honest and fair, but also very carnal. Physical energy burns endlessly like an engine, but they have the ability to channel it properly. Not at all fearful, able to face death, can handle high-tension and high-pressure situations.

They receive energy and strength from their entire tree, which place them in a spearhead to cut through and evolve further! Not eager to come into the spotlights, they can work behind the curtain, on their own, for secret or occult interests, which do not need the approval of those around. Self-controlled and confident, they can die and reborn, each time stronger!

Their masculine energy is turned into something much more subtle, more refined, into art.

◊ **Famous people with a harmonious aspect between Pluto and Mars:**
◊ Steve Jobs, Jackie Chan

Hard aspect

This family system is impregnated by a past where the desire to preserve identity in the face of domination, assertion, manipulation and seizure situations took precedence.

Possible situations: murder, abuse, dominance through sexuality, money or personal power; violence, fighting, war, aggressive sexuality, rape, dictatorial temperament, lack of consideration for the feelings, emotions and wishes of others, coercion, blackmail, kidnapping, destruction, deprivation of freedom, death by poisoning, racking, ill-treatment, physical penance, cutting, sword, burning, horror; aggressor or abused man; suicide, fight for power or control, penance, torture, iron marking, imprisonment, humiliation, fear of death, slow and painful death, torment, agony, persecution, hunting, haunting, defeat, possessiveness; executioner, desecrator; demonic figures; undermined masculinity, castration.

The natives with this aspect inherit great inner frustration, suffocating repressed energy, and inability to properly direct the energy, which tends to implode. Very undisciplined, with a hard-to-bear type of character, dictatorial in decisions and opinions, they abuse anyone who stands in their way or is reluctant to obey them. Their masculine energy is difficult to control, their sexuality deviant, they like to torment or be tormented, but most of all to feel they are in power, they dominate, the others obey them and they are influential.

They have the survivor instinct, no matter the consequences!

Due to their hot-headedness, they end up in the worst and most precarious situations, attracting aggressive dependency and control relationships. When rejected, they become obsessed, want more and heat up, and are prone to destructive and self-destructive actions, driven by an impulse much stronger than themselves.

They attract secret enemies, dangers from the shadows, maniacs, and perverts, who track them down, or feed on their energy, and they, in their turn, feed themselves on discord, suffering and wounds.

The loss trauma creates a desire for power, well-being, and success, but it may also lead them to unfair, Machiavellian actions. It is quite possible that the aggressive or fighting spirit comes to the surface, and old repressed fits of anger are expressed. If exposed to dangerous situations, they may deal with violence, aggression and bodily harm, and even if they are surrounded by people with a lot of influence if they indulge themselves in such situations, they may quickly be turned into victims. They need to regenerate completely, lay the axe to the root of the tree, free themselves from the poison and be reborn with a new identity. To do that, they must learn to treat others on equal terms, to cooperate, to act calmly and to provide freedom. They must learn to act on their own, but also in intimacy with the other, to create healthy bonds, to reevaluate their actions and how they engage, and to test the limits of how far they can go on their own.

If they were hurt, they must mourn their pain, wallow and mourn, then empower themselves, pick themselves up, and draw the boundaries of their personal space.

No one is allowed to abuse them, especially because they know themselves, are confident in themselves and no longer get into degrading or destructive situations.

Somatization: aneurysm, sexually transmitted diseases,

inflammation of the genital organs, abscesses, gynaecological surgery, herpes, furuncle, haemorrhoids, stinging irritations, prostate diseases, vaginitis, urinary problems, oedema, inflammation of the bladder or urethra, pituitary and adrenal gland problems, cystitis, prostate adenoma, toxins in the colon, impotence or sexual deviance, autoimmune diseases, injuries or surgery of the face, skull or teeth/jaws; dysregulation of testosterone or adrenaline release, panic attack, anxiety, phobia, allergy, rash, resection of reproductive organs, impotence, premature ejaculation or impossibility of ejaculation, sadomasochism, pain in intimate moments, impossibility to perform sexual intercourse, cerebral oedema, cervix wound

Stages of awareness and healing phrases

◊ I honour my whole family system
◊ I understand the trauma, violence and abuse my ancestors went through
◊ I understand their unexpressed pain, fear and helplessness
◊ I understand that no matter what life my parents and grandparents had, thanks to them I was born
◊ I am ready to release all pain and discover my true identity
◊ I am ready to release the fear, anger, pain, and aggression that lie in me
◊ I am ready to take advantage in full of my power
◊ All people have the equal right to be free
◊ I draw my personal boundaries correctly and let go of the struggle within me
◊ I am freeing myself from the toxic attachments and people in my life
◊ I honour my sexuality, my right to life and my right to sustain life in safety
◊ Love is not sufferance

◊ I can maintain healthy relationships in full control
◊ I have confidence in myself and my identity
◊ I am able to support myself, develop myself and be independent
◊ I use my masculine energy in a way that is healthy and constructive for me

Transgenerational transmission

Unintegrated experiences related to this aspect can occur in offsprings who have Pluto in the 1st house, Mars in the 8th house, Mars in Scorpio, or Mars in a hard aspect to Pluto. At the same time, repetitive or revelatory experiences can take place during Pluto's transit to Mars, or during Pluto's transit through the 1st or 8th house.

◊ **Famous people with a hard aspect between Pluto and Mars:**
◊ Oprah Winfrey, Bruce Lee, Mel Gibson, Patrick Swayze

Pluto - Venus

Harmonious aspect

The power of sexuality - when you lose yourself in sensations and merge into the other, the burning desire to be with your partner, to breathe them, to taste them, to feel ecstasy, love them passionately, endlessly - creates a deep and intense connection, a fire that still burns in the soul of many generations.

The transgenerational memory of this system retains transformative, intense love relationships that tethered deep values in the idea of love - devotedness, consuming passion, pure intimacy, eroticism, enchained bodies, minds and senses, promises beyond time and space, immense longing and pure abandonment.

The power of love - when it truly exists, when passion is above all else - sets in motion tremendous forces, brings forth great inner resources, and attracts many outer riches.

For the native with this aspect, relationships are very important. They are looking for partners whom they can learn everything about, the deepest hidden secrets, a relationship without barriers. When they are in love, their devotion is total, but they need to feel in turn that they are wanted, and the other is willing to go, just like them, to the end. They know they are potent, they have a lot to offer and they want to fully satisfy their loved ones, and give them pleasure, but they also ask everything in return, a total union. When they do have such certainty, when their engine is maintained, they are capable of great transformation, creation, inspiration and great performance. They can alchemize this great passion, to sublimate it into something that takes deep roots.

With this aspect, the power of seduction is great, and the native attracts not only people, but also intangible assets, riches, beautiful objects, and amazing talents or abilities. Their family's inheritance may be in money, and they may have finances, but it may also be a much more valuable one, that is inner treasures. They have the ability to create even more, to find opportunities, to take advantage of them and people of means, to be exactly where they need to be and to see things in a strategic perspective, which gives them long-term plans , with results or performance on a large scale.

If they wish something, are willing to use all their methods to get it, to go through torment and suffering, make use of the personal magnetism and occult energies, to cloak and lurk, to play and strike. When they get that something, they really relish their getting!

The feelings, but also the attachments, are very deep for them, they have connections from which they obtain power or financial inducements, which they are not willing to give up. The comfort zone they create is very large, their intimate space is mysterious and inviting, and the people who know them and deal with them are attracted like a magnet and surrounded by a dizzying aura.

◊ **Famous people with a harmonious aspect between Pluto and Venus:**
◊ Bill Clinton; Virginia Woolf, John Steinbeck

Hard aspect

In the transgenerational memory of this system there is a deep trauma, which may have occurred as a result of love relationships tragically destroyed by the death of one of the partners, separations that caused pain, abusive relationships of sexual subordination, rape, excessive manipulation, control, toxic relationships, chaining, sexual relationships for money, prostitution, flesh-trafficking, brothels, crimes of passion, relationships with a tragic outcome, loss of values, bankruptcy, dispossession of goods and money, incest, invasion of intimate space, emotional abuse, disinheritance; abused or abusing women; perversity in relationships; hidden, taboo, mysterious, passionate, carnal, but forbidden relationships; criminal women or crimes against women or purity; frivolity, obscenity, pornography, sexual obligations; foul play in relationships or unions; enemies hidden in the shadows; obsessive, destructive, morbid love; toxic family relationships, of interdependence, manipulation and subtle control. The natives who inherit this configuration feel a deep hunger for intimate relationships, love, sexuality, but at the same time they have deep fears, unhealed wounds and tensions, that make them enter into relationships that affect both them and their partners in a destructive way.

For them, love and relationships activate an explosive, torturous or very tense energy, that triggers and activates an inner revolution. They may be attracted to unsuitable people, whom they are aware are not good for them, or whom they are not a match for, but by whom they feel fascinated. Everything is lived dangerously or to the extreme, feelings are exacerbated, and the addiction to such persons is what tears, and creates obsession or lack of control.

They project in the other the unconscious need for power, subjugation, domination and end up suffering, transfigured by the lowest and most tormenting sensations and feelings - jealousy, suspicion, betrayal.

There is a demon in the darkness of their shadow that they must meet and fight, accept and heal. It is the demon of worthlessness, uselessness, total destruction, loss of love and crime of passion. Indigence can make them humble, dependent, writhing between agony and ecstasy, between momentary pleasures and bitter falls, in transactions where they sell themselves into the wrong hands.

When they feel that they are losing, that they no longer have what they had, or the other rejects them, they pull the strings even tighter, suffocate even more, and the feeling of possession amplifies.

For healing, they need a new system of values, where they prise themselves, no longer allow themselves to be physically, emotionally or mentally dependent, have healthy boundaries, and love themselves. They need to dive deep into their wounds, experience intimate relationships on a healthy and deep level, and gain confidence and self-worth.

They may be capable of great love, but first, they need a transformation, a process of death and rebirth, to uproot the relationships that do not honour them and bring no tear peace and joy. They have great inner resources, and within them lies a great wealth they cannot reach as long as they seek it in others or in compromising unions.

Somatization: inflammation, ulceration or tumour of the throat, mycotic infections of the mouth or genitals, thyroid problems, laryngitis, burning on the vocal cords, inflammation of the nasal tract, kidney disorders, nephritis, inflammation of the kidneys, venereal diseases, uterine and vaginal problems, cystitis, acid urine, uterine prolapse, nymphomania, adrenal dysfunction, frigidity, herpes, resection of reproductive organs, painful nodules, uterine deformities, retroverted uterus, polycystic ovaries, abortion, inability to maintain pregnancy, dysregulation of female hormones, lack of pleasure, lack of appetite

Stages of awareness and healing phrases

◊   I honour my whole family system
◊   I understand the trauma, violence and abuse my ancestors went through
◊   I understand their unexpressed pain, fear and helplessness
◊   I understand that no matter what life my parents had, thanks

to them I was born
◊   I honour all the love relationships of my ancestors
◊   I am ready to release all pain and discover my roots, inner treasures and inner beauty
◊   I am ready to heal the wounds of the past
◊   I am ready to take advantage in full of my power
◊   I deserve to be loved and to love
◊   I deserve to have healthy and emotionally safe relationships
◊   All people have the right to be free
◊   Love is freedom
◊   I am a valuable being who deserves to be cherished
◊   I am freeing myself from worthless relationships in my life
◊   I can maintain healthy relationships, in full control and I can use some relaxation, peace and harmony

Transgenerational transmission

Unintegrated traumas related to this aspect can occur in offsprings who have Pluto in the 2nd house, Pluto in the 7th house, Venus in Scorpio, Venus in the 8th house, or Venus in a hard aspect to Pluto. At the same time, repetitive or revelatory experiences can take place during Pluto's transit to Venus, or during Pluto's transit through the 2nd or 7th house.

◊   **Famous people with a hard aspect between Pluto and Venus:**
◊   Justin Timberlake, Britney Spears, Goldie Hawn, Bruce Lee, Ivana Trump, Celine Dion, Al Capone, Bridget Fonda

Pluto - Mercury

Harmonious aspect

The combination of the two archetypes comes from times when words and truth meant a lot - they saved lives, transformed destinies, influenced minds, thoughts and souls. This family system had among its members very influential people, very close relations between relatives, who helped and stuck together, who had access to a certain type of information or knowledge. Secret, very important, vital information was used to gain power, control or authority. At the same time, reason helped them overcome moments of trauma, when they had to be mentally strong, look for saving solutions, resist and endure, be lucid.

The natives with this aspect are good strategists, they see beyond words, into the other's mind. They have great depth, capacity for introspection, and logical, but also intuitive deduction. They can dominate and penetrate the other's thoughts, subtly influencing their reasoning, and if they wish, they have the ability to speak in a way that touches the most vulnerable points, penetrates deeply and can produce revelations.

Always looking for answers or deep truths, they are able to discover clues that others do not notice or are not aware of, make connections and see links very quickly, and if they discover a lie, the spirit of justice awakens in them. They understand, see, and feel where the pain of the other is, and what is their vulnerability, and in this respect they can speculate or heal the trauma.

Because they have a psyche made of steel, they can easily dominate a conversation, can be penetrating, persuasive and incisive, and intolerant of weaknesses. They can see very clearly the good and the bad in the other people, they know how great influence have their knowledge, and they have the power to turn loss into advantage, and wound into strength.

They are strongly connected to the psyche of their genealogical tree, from where they receive answers, information and flashes, which they need to discharge in a constructive way.

◊ **Famous people with a harmonious aspect between Pluto and Mercury:**
◊ Brad Pitt, Bridget Fonda, Larry King, Moliere

Hard aspect

Possible past situations: death of brother, abusive brother, breakage of family relations; mental abuse, baneful words, mental trauma, toxic living environment - verbal assault, bad words, swearing, humiliation, terrorizing, yelling, screaming, scandals, nervous pressure, borderline situations, mental strain, indoctrination, manipulation of speech and mind, compulsion to talk or think in a certain way, obsessive, manipulative, tyrannical members; destruction of documents, manipulation of information; confrontation with occult or very powerful forces; mental or nervous trauma, terrorizing, mind penetration, thought manipulation, nerve and psyche destruction.

The natives with this aspect feel a very high intra-psychic tension - on an unconscious level, they are tormented by obsessive, destructive thoughts, unpleasant memories, and horror scenes, which they can hardly get out of their system. They are harsh in nature, aggressive in expression, uncompromising, incisive, and ready for verbal attack at any moment. If somebody steps on their toes, they can strike brutally, are very acid and eager for revenge.

When they put something in mind, it obsesses them to death, and recall the scene endlessly, each time with more ardour and pain - they cannot let go easily, are strongly attached to what they believe, do not give up their opinions, are self-contradictory and, instead of calming down, put straw on the fire.

If in childhood they were forced to learn, to behave in a certain manner or terrorized, in adulthood they have an aversion to any form of control and strongly rebel against it.

Their psyche is very unstable, they don't want you to play games with them, to promise and not keep your promise, to say things that hurt them and which they reject, to defy or ignore them, because they can flare up in fits of rage, which they are not able to control easily.

Their mind is very sharp, they see deep into people and feel their weaknesses, but at the same time, they cannot help but rub salt in their wounds and show their superiority, and dominate intellectually, verbally or rationally the people next to them. They have the ability to turn white into black, to surprise with their logic, with the deductions they make, being very tenacious both in thinking and in expression.

Because their mind takes them to the darkest places, they can have very strong fears or terrors, which they project onto others. Many times, they are suspicious, secretive, pessimistic, and their thoughts about certain situations show morbid scenarios. They struggle with their personal shadow, which throw them off balance and lead them to frequent panic attacks or overreactions.

Many secrets are buried in them, traumas that they keep hidden and which, when projected outside, they see as threats: they can have both criminal minds and spy or private detective minds, which mislead them. Because they let themselves be dominated and do not use their mind constructively, they see in everyone a threat, and they suspect, sniff, smell and turn every circumstance into a conspiracy theory. From a personal point of view, they have a talent for saying bitter words, killer words, but also for penetrating deeply into the other to bring the truth to the surface and expose it. They are deep thinkers, but this depth leads them into less pleasant areas of the mind, hence the desire to dominate, manipulate, turn everything to their advantage and gain supremacy.

Awareness of their own way of thinking and expression is

needed - the process being a very intense and deep one, not easily overcome, which digs deep into the human psyche, into previously unknown and inaccessible areas.

The natives must break through the mental barriers created and open new doors to understanding and evolution, and this requires asking questions and seeking answers beyond immediate understanding. Presupposing the confrontation with the demons of their own mind and the defeat of all beliefs, introspection and psychoanalysis become the primary weapons in this process, and the more they advance into the depths of their own mind, the more meanings will they discover for the world around and for themselves.

Their mind can reach far, and once freed from fears, judgment and preconceptions, they will touch a new realm of knowledge, which they have not experienced before, but which is full of riches, meanings and resources.

Somatization: pain, injuries, arm, finger and lung surgery, nerve damage, asthma, intercostal surgery or trauma, bronchitis, fallopian tube blockage, chronic lung disease, pancreatic disorders, spleen problems, tumours and cysts of tubular formations; nervous diseases, obsessions, phobias, nightmares, dark thoughts, insomnia, brain or nerve damage; paralysis, paresis, limbs surgery or loss thereof, crushing of fingers; trauma to the mouth, impaired speech or thinking, allergies

Stages of awareness and healing phrases

◊   I honour my entire family system, with all its branches
◊   I accept the choices my parents made and I respect their personality
◊   I am ready for mind and body healing

◊ I demand the right to a real and truthful life
◊ I am freeing myself from all negative memories and trauma of the past
◊ I turn unpleasant memories into wisdom
◊ I release the secrets and bring the truth to light
◊ I free my mind from negative and obsessive thoughts
◊ I use my mind and words in a wise way, so that they do not cause harm neither to those around me, nor to me
◊ I am freed from unhealthy attachments and have clarity in my mind

Transgenerational transmission

Unintegrated experiences related to this aspect can occur in offsprings who have Pluto in the 3rd house, or Mercury in the 8th house, Mercury in Scorpio, or Mercury in hard aspect to Pluto. At the same time, repetitive or revelatory experiences can take place during Pluto's transit to Mercury or during Pluto's transit through the 3rd house.

◊ **Famous people with a hard aspect between Pluto and Mercury:**
◊ Brigitte Bardot, Bjork, George Lucas, Franklin D. Roosevelt, Oprah Winfrey, Elvis Presley, Shaquille O'Neal, Kurt Cobain

Inter-aspects of transpersonal planets

Transpersonal planetary cycles transmute energy from one generation to another, giving them the opportunity in turn to continue the story, help elevate it, or change it. They reflect the history of humanity and its evolutionary stages, the movements within the collective unconscious. Any conjunction between two planets closes and, at the same time, opens a new chapter of the book, and any aspect formed by the two during a synodic cycle is an opportunity to change the paradigm and intervene on it.

Jupiter - Saturn

Children born with an aspect of conjunction, square or opposition between Saturn and Jupiter need to change the structure of the family tree, to overcome the limits of the system, to get out of dogma and formulate their own principles and philosophies of life. Saturn represents the limits and Jupiter their transgression, what may be beyond. During periods of transit, when the two planets form important aspects, the vision within the family can be enriched, beliefs can be changed, walls can be broken down and rigidity can be given up.

In order to rebuild and evolve, the members of a family with this aspect need to dig deep into their past to identify the laws, beliefs, prohibitions, boundaries, and the blazonry that binds them. They can keep the past alive, but they can also draw it back into something that will give them freedom, knowledge and progress.

Jupiter - Uranus

The generation born under an aspect between Jupiter and Uranus can bring changes of principles within the family, usually in an unconventional manner or as a result of a radical life situation of members of the family clan, or concerning the whole society.

During the periods when the aspects are formed again, situations can arise that bring revelations, and awareness within the family, and things change, taking another turn: the direction society moves also changes the dynamics within the family, which adapts to the time they live in.

For example, the discovery of new psychological theories, the evolution of technology, economic liberalization, the incorporation of large companies, social or cultural movements, revolutions, expansionism, and religious changes, represent moments when society changes and the individuals must adjust to their time. The natives born with a Jupiter - Uranus aspect are driven to change the vision of the old generations, readjust it and formulate new, healthy and evolutionary beliefs for their system. To do this, they may be the revolutionaries or rebels of their tree, who need a new breath, expansion, a new picture of the world, balance between the monastic world and the modern, futuristic one in which they live.

If not integrated correctly, just because they rebel against what they feel inside, they can in turn create trauma in other people. They need to abandon old beliefs and break free into a new but healthy system.

Jupiter - Neptune

The aspect between Jupiter and Neptune creates new perceptions in the subconscious field of the family tree - natives with this aspect can bring to light truths, things that have been hidden, precious information about the past or have spontaneous realizations and releases.

They have the ability to dissolve old beliefs, but also to create new, ideational ones. Very sensitive, they are attached to the family collective unconscious, which they draw many concepts from.

If the aspect is not used evolutionarily, the natives may intensify patterns related to wrong family conceptions about faith and may hide personal and family truths as deeply as their predecessors, positioning themselves in a duality zone. Inside them, the conscious area intertwines with but also faces, the unconscious side. In order not to remain anchored in a spiritual world, of concepts, ideas and dreams, they need practicality and realism.

The aspect can show very idealistic people, who have the ability to see what their ancestors did not see. They are very inspired, but at the same time, they can have far too high expectations or illude the expectations of those who came before them, only to go their own way.

If their expectations are not met, they can easily become manipulators of the system, which they wish to deceive, avoid or corrupt.

In order to evolve, they need to seek a personal truth, instead of deceiving themselves or the others, to move beyond illusion and false ideals and recompose themselves mentally.

Sigmund Freud was born in 1856 during a Jupiter Neptune conjunction in Pisces.

Jupiter - Pluto

The generation born under a Jupiter Pluto aspect has a great capacity to reformulate beliefs through their own experience. Most likely, they experience the real and concrete death and rebirth of some outdated philosophies.

Because the fears and traumas of the past are magnified in natives with this aspect, they will have throughout their lives experiences that can help them integrate, live through, and resolve them. For them, there is a call to open the wound, clean it and let it heal.

In order to support their mission, they have the ability to communicate with the world beyond, to transmute all past energy and release it from the entire family system, putting an end to an entire generational cycle of family beliefs, dogmas, principles, theories, or laws.

Saturn - Uranus

Saturn is the old generation, and Uranus represents the new and the evolving one. The association between the two planets brings into question both the opposition of archetypes and the exchange that takes place between the old and the new order.

The natives with aspect between Saturn and Uranus collide with the limitations of his system, of the old generations, but are given the opportunity to rebel against it and change it.

Saturn is structure, Uranus is chaos, and for the generation that carries the combination it is time for many patterns to unravel and recreate themselves in different, evolutionary structures, both individually and systemically.

The natives with this aspect pay off the debts of their system while opening a new chapter for themselves. Ideas planted long ago are removed, and they have the opportunity to change something with every aspect they pass through.

Even if it takes a crisis, unexpected situations, tension and a big explosion to make something happen, they need to do things differently, to break free from conditioning and everything that no longer serves them.

Thus, with a new base created and a new frame of reference, they can make a huge leap into the future, can get rid of the past, but they can also use it to create further, and to evolve.

Saturn - Neptune

At first, the generation born with an aspect between Saturn and Neptune has high expectations from family, from those in charge, from the system and from the order in which they were born, and as they grow older, they are either completely submersed in illusion or begin to take off the veil that covered it.

The natives with this aspect can induce powerful awareness at the level of their genealogical tree, showing what was not seen by their predecessors. On the one hand, their faith, fidelity, and ability to see are put to test, but at the same time their skepticism is also tested. Being on the border between the two alternatives - abandoning or becoming aware, they have the opportunity to retrace boundaries, change visions, do justice and put old/new ideals into practice during their lifetime.

Neptune dissolves the boundaries of Saturn and Saturn materializes Neptune, a combination that can have a strong impact within a family: on the one hand, gaps can be filled, on the other, there can be disappointments. The world here meets the world beyond and the border is very thin - in this demarcation zone there can be lucid dreams, subtle messages, but also traps meant to hold in place, in a spirit of sacrifice.

There is a sense of guilt that needs to be flushed through

the system, something that needs to be revealed, or else it can bring about loss of landmarks, deconstruction, annihilation and dissolution.

Once boundaries are withdrawn and new structures established, revealing secrets and putting things in order, new dimensions of consciousness, of understanding the interdependence between the conscious and the unconscious world are accessed.

Saturn - Pluto

The generation born with an aspect between the two planets lives in times when the structures of the old patterns are levelled to the ground, and everything is burned to the ground so that it can be cultivated again. Because it takes time and depth for the transformation to occur, the process is intense and multi-staged, from top to bottom.

Because there are many unresolved fears and wounds behind natives, they want to be in control, to take power, to have all the weapons on their side, even if this means going to war.

There is a lot of tension and pressure within the system, within the generation, in the native with Saturn-Pluto aspect, and to release it, they have to go back, to the essence, to the core, to the beginnings. Natives can bring about changes in the value system of society and family, reaching a new understanding of what was once considered hidden, mysterious, secret, taboo. If decoded, this content can be released, healed or theorized into logical and explanatory structures, through which justice is done for past abuses, a much deeper understanding of what was is gained, and a chapter of suffering is closed.

Unintegrated, in turn, natives can become destructive, abusive, or maniacal: Saturn preserves even more strongly what was created in the shadows.

Uranus - Neptune

The aspect between the two archetypes leads to the disintegration of past family visions and ideals.

The natives aspected between Uranus and Neptune are given the opportunity to awaken the collective imagination, gain inspiration and transcend beyond, to a new form of understanding and spirituality.

They are called to release stress from the subconscious level, not to run away from reality and to move forward, adopting a broader perspective of life.

Although it is possible to face great relegations, shattered dreams and illusions inherited from family and society, awakening to reality gives them the freedom to fly very far and create something new.

They can have a big, collective vision about society or about the whole, they can reform with ease or with struggle, contributing to greater detachment from the unconscious.

The hard side of the aspect can be the dive in a virtual, artificial and utopian world, in a modern spell, where the spirit is replaced by the machine, the robot and the Internet.

Uranus - Pluto

The generation with an aspect between Uranus and Pluto feels intensely the collapses, changes, manipulation, traumas, abuse within society or the family, to which they becomes very sensitive.

The natives need to release what is deeply buried in the system, to find out and expose the crimes and experiences of the past, and what exactly caused suffering and pain, but also to obtain the resources that they have inherited from previous generations.

They must reform, shake off, balance what has been

in the shadows and was repressed, to open a wound, but also to bring a new perspective of much faster healing and transformation of it.

Even though they may be strongly shaken by the experiences they go through, the chance to break free from the pain, transform themselves, understand and not perpetuate it is very big.

Neptune - Pluto

The generation with aspects between the two archetypes needs grounding, recovery of the lost pieces of soul, regeneration, and deep healing of the shadows.

Because those before have deeply repressed ideals, secrets, dreams, pains, they need to come out of the fog, numbness and unconscious, in order to see and complete themselves.

The process is not easy, because the healing is not on the surface, it does not occur consciously, but takes place again in a hidden realm - in the dream, inside and in the abyss of the unconscious.

They need to come out of their shells, overcome their fears, break addictions and chains of torment in order to escape and transform, but for this a journey is needed, of death and rebirth, of probing deep, and far.

Unintegrated, the aspect can turn into something dangerous, in an escape into another reality where they use what they see, and a great ability to keep the manipulation of the system under control.

Part V - Appendices

Memory, Fears and Reactions of Zodiac Archetypes

Aries

Memory: enemies, defeat, surrender of arms, loss of freedom, imprisonment, trial, tribunal, injustice, dissolution, absorption, conquest and submission, the disappearance of one's identity to lose oneself in another; the extinction of an entire race; domination, entrapment, traitors, double-dealing, cover-up, covert tactics of war, disastrous alliances

Basic fear: not to be

Complementary fears and emotions: fear of death, of loss of self, of not being considered, of not being seen, of not succeeding, of not surviving, of being caught, weak, incompetent; fear of being betrayed, becoming intimate/vulnerable or being held back; fear of loss of freedom, competition or competitor; fear of being a victim or submitting to an authoritarian, totalitarian, absolutist system; fear of abandonment or dissolution; anger

Unconscious reactions: driven by a fight or flight instinct for survival, they are always on the alert; individualists, put themselves first, and think about themselves, and their needs; instinctually, they would rather attack first than be attacked; they don't make compromises, they don't form alliances easily, they prefer to be on their own, masters of themselves and their own destinies; they have a lot of inner energy, they don't sit still and don't give it another thought, they break down barriers, break down doors, rush, act quickly and tenaciously or cut everything in one fell swoop; react strongly to any form of control, of undermining, injustice or weakness; they are competitive, daring, with initiative, stand out and feel good only when they take the first place

Taurus

Memory: dispossession of property, violation of property and destruction of boundaries, destruction of their own labour, taking of property, disinheritance; loss of beauty, purity and family peace; desecration of personal privacy; demolition, loss of crops, total destruction, horror, rupture, death, predators, abusers, executioners, rapists, poverty, famine, horror; to have nothing, to be worthless, not to count, not to be valued, to have everything taken from you, death by starvation; poison, toxicity, toxic environment, humiliation, resentment, frustration, emptiness; house destruction, landslides, earthquake, fire, flood, death of loved ones, deep traumas

Basic fear: no longer having value

Complementary fears and emotions: fear of severance, of leaving the comfort zone, of not being able to guard what they have; the fear of running out, of not having enough, of dying of hunger, of being taken from them, of being stolen, of losing stability and comfort, their boundaries violated, of having what they built collapsed and what they have to be taken from them, their own territory to be invaded; fear of hidden, evil, demonic, unscrupulous people who might harm them; of secrets, hiding, manipulation, being tricked, or not seeing things clearly; the wound of helplessness and the inferiority complex

Unconscious reactions: collects, gathers, are possessive, would not let go, sink into the materiality, draw boundaries, won't leave the comfort zone; choose the known, safe, visible, traditionalist path; work hard, develop avarice and greed; fixed, attached, do not get out of the comfort zone, fearful, cautious, take one step at a time; accumulate, eat a lot, gather provisions, are fair, set limits, restrictions, are frugal; sometimes they refuse the money so as not to draw attention and suffer if a loss occurs

Gemini

Memory: inquisition, persecution for the way of thinking, strict laws, outdated concepts, conviction for the way of expression, borders closing, being subject to a certain way of thinking, dogma, superstition, cumbersome, misunderstood concepts, which are only for a certain social class; sects, cults, crusades, murder to convince of a truth; implementing by force a way of thinking; submission to outdated or absurd legislation; judgment, injustice, error in judgment; destruction of truth and information;

Basic fear: no longer being able to express themselves

Complementary fears and emotions: of not knowing, of talking nonsense, of being judged, of saying what they really think, of being silenced, of not being on time, of being listened to, of being shamed, of not being able to speak, of not understanding, of being restricted in thinking; fear of concealment; of not finding out, of not knowing what is decided, of not understanding what it is about; fear that the information will not arrive on time, or that the information will be lost;

Unconscious reactions: haste and restlessness at the mental level, duality of mind, distributive attention, following the truth/ lie, the need to always be up-to-date, and informed, to know a little bit of everything, to talk non-stop, stuttering, gossip, whiff of information, exposure, mental inconstancy, contestation, aversion to cumbersome systems of education, nervous inconsistency, right of reply, the need to pass on information

Cancer

Memory: of hard old age, loss of parents or children, responsibilities and lack of warmth, helplessness, unloving or abandoning, restricting parental figures; loss of family relationships and removal of children; hardness, authority, suffering; blockages, the inability to assert; widowhood; loneliness, coldness, sadness, indigence; loss of structure and traditions; emotional rejection, restriction of food, inability to express feelings and emotions, loss and pain; of prosecutors and persecutors

Basic fear: not to belong

Complementary fears and emotions: of losing loved ones, of not being loved, of being rejected, of losing emotional stability, of not being able to rely on those around you, of no longer having any reason to be, of being rejected, of no longer feeling love from the other, of no longer being able to feed themselves and to survive

Unconscious reactions: emotional dependence, blackmail and emotional manipulation, strong attachments, desire to control the family, uncontrolled outbursts, fear of becoming a parent, or strong desire to procreate, extreme parenting, desire to nurture, to take care of, to protect others; sadness/depression in the face of rejection; assuming the role of caring for parents, changing parental roles; the desire to be cuddled, held, to receive affection, the search for the mother and the warm and intimate environment of childhood; melancholy, the inability to let go of the past

Leo

Memory: depersonalization, collectivization, revolt, rebellion, ideological groupings; mass struggles, dethronement, defamation, annihilation of personality; masses, voice of the people, condemnation of a person by society; inability to express, blocking the creativity, ending childhood and entering the system; standardization; emphasis on collectivity, not on the individual; toxic, limiting surroundings; losing personal brilliance due to an adoptive parent; creating a mass brand, stifling of personal development and lack of originality; starting employment and becoming nobody; lack of achievement and success; limitation; getting lost in the crowd; non-recognition of personal merits, extinction; genocide

Basic fear: of uselessness, of loss of personal importance

Complementary fears and emotions: fear of being dethroned, of losing control, of not being seen, of being left out, of not being noticed, of not evolving, of not being loved and appreciated, of being powerless, forgotten or ignored; of being mediocre; of being put on the same footing as everyone else; not to remain in history; not having a good reputation; to stop playing or enjoying life

Unconscious reactions: put themselves in the centre of things, ride high horses, self-title, stand in the spotlight, are dramatic, theatrical, stand out, want fame, leadership positions, clinging to a title, want to seduce the public or the masses, want to be admired, loved, to have their merits recognised, to be toadied, to have supporters, always make a parade of their outstanding qualities, for which they think they should be praised; superior, arrogant, of noble lineage, look down on the world, are self-centred, convinced that they deserve more than others; remain forever childish or act so

Virgo

Memory: loss of mind and reality, falsehood, falsity, duality, lie, thinking error, sacrifice, sick or crazy minds, thieves, robbers, closed, gloomy, miserable, infect spaces; sickness, hospital, suffering, sanitary diseases, poverty, famine, alcohol, depravity; mourning, pain, penance, agony; sacrifice; memory of witches, spells, curses, false beliefs or opinions; hidden enemies, who sit in the shadows and cannot be sensed; ferocious animals, which prey or kill; villains or robbers

Basic fear: losing common sense

Complementary fears and emotions: of being judged for mistakes, of not seeing the error, of getting out of the system, of not being down-to-earth, of suffering, of closed spaces, of illness, of being useless, of being tricked; of what they cannot explain, paranoia; fear of chaos, dissipation, loss, nebula, fog, unknown, carelessness; of drunkenness, loss of control of body

Unconscious reactions: hypochondriac, manic, demanding, orderly, systematic, scrupulous (investigate everything), suspicious; they clean, wash, sort, criticize, point the finger, split the thread in four; fair, uncompromising, unattached, rational; in search of healing, antidotes, medicines, herbs; don't believe before investigate; try to find an explanation for everything; stick to the system; try to preserve the purity and not to be converted

Libra

Memory: of aggressors, invaders, war, loss of a loved one, accidents, injury, attack, authoritative figures, representatives of war - soldiers, army, warriors, danger, injury; burst of tension, panic; war criminals; widowhood, abandonment; suffering from love, tension in the relationship

Basic fear - loneliness

Complementary fears and emotions: of danger, of wrong decisions, of breaking out of tension, of upsetting the other, of starting hostilities, of being caught on the wrong foot, defenceless; to have their guard down; to remain defenceless, to have no leader; to be on their own; of not knowing what to do; of independence

Unconscious reactions: they don't want to upset anyone, they want to make peace, to mediate, to calm down, to avoid scandal; they are just, fair, impartial; decide hard, weigh a lot, want everything to be fair; give up any form of independence, of rebellion, they let go, are forgiving, looking for peace; they submit themselves, they mould themselves to the personality of the other; want secure alliances and certainty; they let themselves be led, want a protector, someone to help them

Scorpio

Memory: of limits, of small gains, of fighting for food, of plantation slaves; of needs and restrained desires; of the separation of the lower class from those who have become very rich; of favouritism; of the inability to have more; of false values; condemnation of carnal pleasures, sexuality and frivolity; the interdiction to have more, to want, to transcend; boundaries, limits, inflexibility, strong attachments, chaining, love of money; superficial relations, avarice, playboys, domination by the power of money; form without substance, enrichment without essence, arrogance, beauty without consistency, sufficiency

Basic fear: not getting

Complementary fears and emotions: of not being wanted anymore, of being excluded, of being left out, of not having their share, of not getting what they want, of not drawing the line and not knowing what happens beyond, of possession, of being laid bare, found, exposed; fear of separation; fear of losing, of being possessed, of not finding the meaning, of not really discovering the values

Unconscious reactions: they manipulate, spy, stay in the shadows, stalk, lurk, and seek to get what they want; in search of depths, hiding places, and treasures; their desires are ardent, passionate; sexual, intense, mystical; attraction to the occult, to the use of unseen tools; deep regenerative capabilities; obsession, struggle with emotions/desires/needs; leave nothing unpaid; destructive and self-destructive

Sagittarius

Memory: secret police, spies, informers, lack of education, ignorance, lack of culture, norm or civilization; calumny, idle talk, false opinions, misinformation, gossip; words without consistency, aberrations, preventing the right to education and schooling, slum, lower class, lack of intellect; thieves of words, people of easy virtue, without ideals and without perspective, closed-minded people; primary judgement, haste, speaking without knowing; talking nonsense and saying words just to convince, to sell, or to manipulate; no morality, ethics, or God; misunderstanding, discord, quarrel, bad words, swearing, verbal tension, non-elevation

Basic fear: not knowing

Complementary fears and emotions: of not having knowledge, culture, mediocrity, not maintaining knowledge, losing faith, dogma, the wise word, not having perspective and being closed-minded; to be ashamed, not to know, not to be noble, be the talk of the town

Unconscious reactions: they learn, try to climb the ladder to the elite, educate themselves, gain knowledge and develop their intellect; they want to belong to a certain social class, which they consider worthy to follow and represent, to access an ideological system able to protect them; they make researches, they travel, exchange opinions, are learned, intellectually superior to those around them; develop principles, are just; they want their primary side as well as their elevated side to be satisfied; are in search of truth

Capricorn

Memory: the lack of roots, of the mother, of the warmth of home and of home; uprooting; dominance through emotional manipulation; emotional blackmail; vulnerability, emotional instability, subliminal messages, emotional imbalance

Basic fear: not ascending

Complementary fears and emotions: losing control, being vulnerable, showing emotions, being stuck, not growing and not becoming self-sustained, not becoming someone, losing their structure, to hear pleas, to have mercy, to show that they were hurt, that they suffer, or have emotions, that they are longing, or they love, the fear of disappointing the mother, but also to stay with her

Unconscious reactions: introverted, serious, tough, authoritarian, cold, closed in a shell, mature, conservative, impassive; focused on status, becoming, growth; goal-oriented; they set themselves up as parental figures; take the lead; assume everything, keep their promises, do not disappoint, carry the whole family on his shoulders, moving it forward

Aquarius

Memory: tyranny, despotic control exerted by one person, abusive father, struggle for supremacy, dominance, control, lack of love, arrogance, selfishness, false brilliance, ego, narcissism, individualism, defiance, idylls, affairs, flash in the pan, illusions, theatre, drama, masks, roles, balls, luxury, adventures, bastards

Basic fear: not to evolve

Complementary fears and emotions: of getting stuck in place, of being under guardianship, of being banned, of being marginalized, of being deprived of the right to live, of being oppressed, of the dissolution of the group to which they belong; of the loss of comrades; of suffering in love

Unconscious reactions: they are not compliant with or aligned to a cause, they do not obey the rules, or enforce others, they rebel against the system, do not belong to one person, they strike a false note, or, alternatively, do not want to stand out at all; they take risks or limit themselves, defend their rights, get involved in the causes they believe in, are charitable, take care of the disadvantaged, make plans for the future

Pisces

Memory: of a painful reality, of accusations, of soulless reasoning; lack of compassion, forgiveness or mercy; of coldness of mind, dry decisions, lack of tolerance; accusation, being pushed against the wall, proof, bringing evil to the fore, persistent criticism; penance in order to be disciplined; things are white or black

Basic fear: giving up hope

Complementary fears and emotions: of faulty reasoning, guilt, sin, no God, no escape, being sacrificed, being walled up, guilt/penance, betrayal, not being understood, loneliness, pain, malice, the judgment and criticism of others, being found

Unconscious reactions: escape, escapism, they do not want to be seen, they project another world, hide, pretend not to see, lie, hide, distort, victimize, complain, are vulnerable to pain; acting in the shadows, withdraw, call on occult forces, abandon themselves in order not to take action, ramble, not showing their real face

Retrograde planets

Those who learn nothing from the unpleasant facts of life force cosmic consciousness to reproduce them as many times as necessary to learn what the drama of what happened teaches. What you deny submits you; what you accept transforms you.
Carl Gustav Jung

Although the planetary retrograde movement is apparent, the direct planets are differentiated in astrology from the retrograde ones because the former are visible, more easily perceived and externalized, while the latter are internalized, more difficult to perceive or highlight.

Direct planets project their energy forward, outwardly, while retrograde ones store or project it inward, needing a longer period to be processed, expressed or manifested.

Direct energy can be easily used in the material, outer world, while the energy of retrograde planets can be used in the inner world. The direct energies represent the archetypes that we manifest on the outside, while the indirect energies are those that have been repressed, that need integration, recovery, and greater understanding, and as such possess greater evolutionary potential.

A retrograde planet tends to move away, to reflect, to revolutionize the dynamics towards the self and the conscious-unconscious plane, being an important step towards the start of the individuation process. Any evolutionary process needs duality, inner processing and manifestation, reception and emission, darkness and light to provide a complete experience, perfectly understood, fully stored in all psychic structures.

Astrologically, the term retrogradation refers to relearning, remaking, reanalysing, and rethinking, but also to repetition, which can trigger an alarm regarding the patterns that have been repeated in the system, regarding the lessons we have to learn and what we have to repair from our own past and that of the ancestors. By correcting their way of manifestation, a cycle is balanced and closed, which concludes a long series of events and experiences.

A retrograde planet can be a stepping stone, which does not let us go further until it is untied, or it can be the source of a great evolution and a new line of destiny.

The cycles of the planets relative to the Sun

The planets revolve around the Sun, which is the symbol of the self and the conscious plane. The complete cycle of revolution around the Sun represents the phases of experimentation, integration and maturation of the archetypal concepts, the stages of evolution of the self, and the way in which generations periodically manifest, in a spiral - archetypal concepts.

The cycle of a planet around the Sun begins when a conjunction is formed between the two, called inferior conjunction, which begins with the planet in retrograde motion, and ends at the next conjunction, called superior conjunction, when the planet is direct.

The cycle of the planets around the Sun is similar to that of the Moon around the Earth, so that in their case too the moment of the new moon can be identified, followed by the waxing phase, which lasts until the aspect of the full moon appears. The moment of the full moon marks the beginning of the waning phase, which ends with a new moment of the new moon, an end and a new beginning at the same time.

*

Phase 1 and the first face of the planetary archetype begins with the retrograde planet conjunct with the Sun. The aspect has the character of a new moon, which continues until the first quarter, that is when the planet reaches its maximum elongation from the Sun.

In this phase, the archetype of the planet is forming, like a child growing within the system. Although it belongs to the system, it is a new bud, looking to strike out on its own. It is pure, innocent, in the experimentation phase of childhood, a crucial stage where it can be easily shaped or grow wings.

Because it is fragile and does not have the ability to discern everything on its own, it can be easily influenced - it either follows the line of the system further or creates new patterns. It has a whole lot of potential ahead of it, but it still hasn't got the strength, experience or maturity to manifest it. It first needs information, research, knowledge and guidance to develop. It needs to distance itself from the old patterns, from reflection, introspection, from the gathering of information.

It is a stage where it grows roots.

Even if it is a branch at the beginning of the journey, the psyche of the planet is looking for new solutions to grow, to move forward, or to move away from the main branch. Although it still seeks to keep being a part of the old system, it will also seek to express itself differently than what was handed down in the family.

It can be ahead of the times, avant-garde, oriented towards a new form of expression, or it can be caught between what it was and what it wants to become, still afraid to distinguish between its family and its personal desires. Even if it is no longer where it is, it is still afraid of loss, suffering or abandonment.

*

Phase 2 and the second face of the planetary archetype

begins at the maximum elongation of the planet with respect to the stationary Sun and ends when the superior conjunction takes place, with the planet in direct motion.

The phase is similar to the vibration of the second quarter, which culminates with the moment of the Full Moon.

It is a much more active phase than the first, because the planetary archetype has gained more security, and now it wants to assert itself, to express itself energetically, to better itself. It has the ability to express itself and feels the need for its ideas, feelings and visions to materialize and get implemented. If something goes wrong during this stage, it has the power to overcome the moment and move on. It pursues its desires with great interest and has values that are built on the fly, based on immediate experiences. It tends to adapt to the times and integrate into them, rather than the earlier phase where it felt like breaking away from them and striking out on its own.

The closer the planet gets to the Sun, the closer it gets to the ego.

*

Phase 3, the third face of the planetary archetype begins from the superior conjunction until the time of the next retrograde motion of the planet. It is similar to the waning moon phase, the third quarter.

The phase begins at the superior conjunction, similar to the moment of the full Moon when the planet is illuminated and comes to understand, integrate the experience of the past, and dissolve it in itself. It no longer moves forward by instinct, because it already has a broader perspective, it has accumulated the information it needs to gain greater wisdom.

Its archetype is more rigid and anchored in the past patterns of itself and its system, which it has had time to beat. It is more analytical, organized, and structured and sees things from a statistical, historical perspective, from the Psyche of its tree. In this phase, it can theorize and have a greater impact on the collectivity, or a larger group of people.

Because it is deeper, if something happens in this phase, it is harder to integrate and recover, keeping trauma inside for longer. Although it is more intense, it does not open so easily anymore, it is much more traditionalist. It is patient and endures longer, but when it explodes it does so with more force, it is tougher and more radical.

*

Phase 4 and the fourth face of the planetary archetype begins from the retrograde motion of the planet to the next inferior conjunction, which marks the end of the cycle, but also a new beginning. The phase is similar to the last quarter, culminating in the New Moon aspect.

At this stage, the planet is retrograde and preparing to close the cycle. Both the planet and the Sun are moving towards each other. It is a phase of inner illumination, introspection and analysis, but at the same time challenging the rigidity. On the one hand, the planet has gathered a lot of information and knowledge, being traditionalist, but on the other hand, it is preparing to close the cycle and be born into something else. It questions itself and questions what it knows, having the ability to dive into itself and understand itself

Although it can fall into a deep hole, immerse itself in it far too much and not be satisfied with what it finds, it has the ability to understand the roots of the problem and get closer to the truth, creating something new based on its frustration. It is deeply connected to the system, its experience spans a long transgenerational past, having a great power of self-sacrifice, dissolution, dissipation or completion of the entire cycle.

Degree of Planets
in the Transgenerational Astrology

The partner is the sum of unconscious images related to ancestral loves or important system figures.
Elisabeta Horowitz

Although the degree of a planet may not be of major importance in the context of a single birth chart, it gets great importance in the astrological study of an entire family system.

When several members of a family have planets positioned in any sign in their astral chart, but at approximately the same degree (1-30), with an orbit of a maximum of 5 degrees between them, the transits of the planets affect them all at the same time - some by conjunction, others by sextile, trine, quadrature, inconjunction or opposition.

Everyone acts in their own name through the life experiences they go through, but at the same time, the system acts in their joint interest. The whole system depends on the actions of each member, and everyone is involved in it, whether they are still alive or not. A transit of a living person activates patterns of people who are no more with us and, depending on how the native reacts to them, they undo, release, honour or carry forward what they have inherited!

The morphic field that connects all family members acts in all directions - both in the present and in the past or future. By studying the synastry of family relationships, one can understand the subtle reasons why two people are attracted to each other, the moment of a person's birth into the system, how patterns are perpetuated, and how multiple trees complement or compensate each other.

Events propagate starting from a common situation, or each on its own level, but they are chained to each other.

Part VI - Case studies

The British Royal Family and Neptune

The royal family of Great Britain has been at the centre of several scandals in recent decades that have drawn the attention of the whole world, most of them being cases of infidelity.

In the picture herein, the family tree of Prince William is sketched, where only part of the direct ancestors have been traced. Next to each member, the aspect formed between the planets Venus and Neptune is noted.

Queen Victoria (Neptune retrograde in Sagittarius trine Venus in Aries)

Queen Victoria (b. May 24, 1819, 4:15 AM, London, Great Britain), inherited the throne of England at just 18 years of age, and shortly after the coronation she married Prince Albert. Unlike most marriages in the royalty world, theirs sprung from true love and they happily lived until the death of Prince Albert did their part. Her highness was wretched ever since. Although there were other men in her life, she mourned the man she loved to the end of her life.

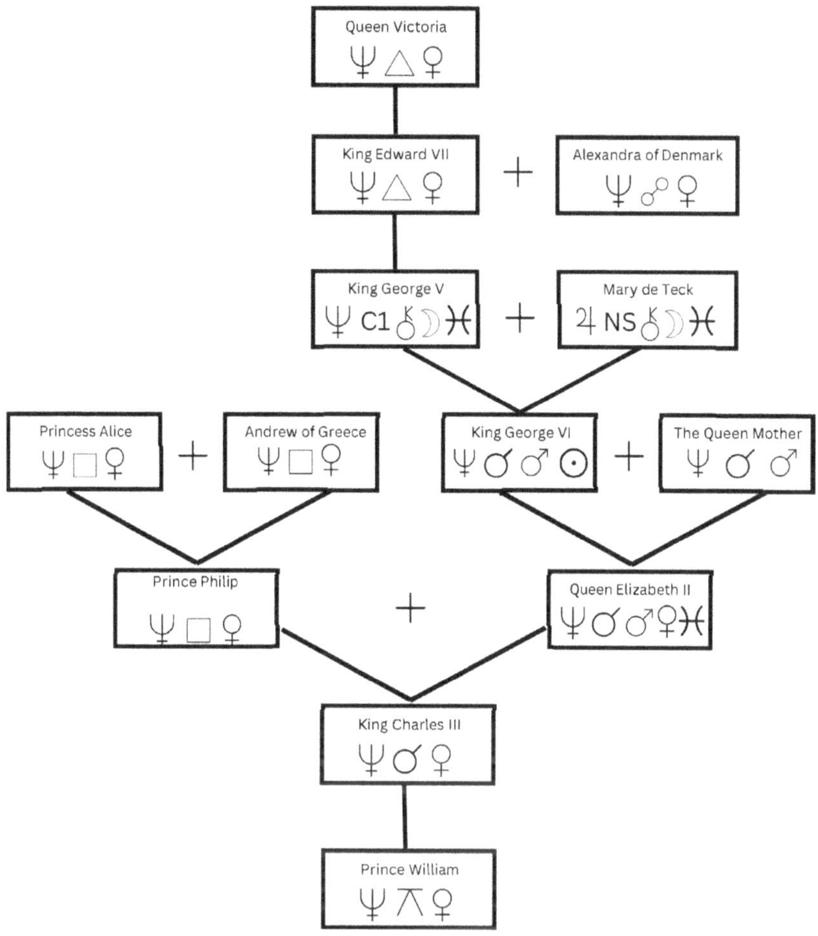

King Edward VII (Neptune in Aquarius trine Venus in Libra)

Alice Keppel, one of the most prominent social hostesses of the Edwardian era, described as witty, kind-hearted and always with a smile on her face, became King Edward's (b. November 9, 1841, 10:48 AM, London, UK) mistress while he was 56 years old and was still a prince at that time. Despite a 26-year age difference, their relationship lasted through his ascension to the throne, until his death in 1910.

Queen Elizabeth II (Venus in Pisces, Neptune in Leo, 8-degree orb conjunction) and Prince Philip (Neptune in Leo square Venus in Taurus)

The love story between the Queen of England (b. April 21, 1926, 2.40 AM, London, Great Britain) and her husband (b. June 10, 1921, 9:46 PM, Corfu, Greece) lasted 73 years, but it was not always the same, as it was shaken by the prince's infidelity even while she was eight months pregnant with Prince Charles. In 1948, rumours about the consort's affair with one of the London stars, Pat Kirkwood, were unstoppable. Philip and Pat did not hide from the eyes of the world at all, they dined in restaurants and danced in nightclubs like any other lovers.

Princess Margaret (Venus in Libra square Jupiter in Cancer and Saturn retrograde in Capricorn, Neptune in Virgo)

The younger sister of the future Queen Elizabeth II, Princess Margaret (b. August 21, 1930, 9:22 p.m., Glamis, Scotland) fell in love with a divorced man, 16 years her senior, Peter Townsend. After a 5-year relationship, torn by the dilemma of having to choose between the royal family and leaving Great Britain, Princess Margaret finally chose to honour her royal duties: 'But mindful of the Church's teachings that Christian marriage is indissoluble and conscious of my duty to the Commonwealth, I have resolved to put these considerations before others.'

Margaret later married Lord Snowden, but, ironically, their marriage ended in divorce, caused by rumours of her husband's infidelity, drug and alcohol addiction, controversies about his sexuality and even speculations that the lord fathered a child just months before their marriage.

Prince Edward VIII (Venus in Taurus, Neptune in Gemini, Moon in Pisces)

The scandal caused in 1930 by the love between Edward (b. June 23, 1894, 10 p.m., Richmond, Great Britain), Prince of Wales, and the twice-divorced American, Wallis Simpson, was so great that the prince waived his right to ascend the throne to live with the woman he loved. When his father, King George V, died, the prince told the whole country: *"I have found it impossible to carry the heavy burden of responsibility and to discharge my duties as king as I would wish to do without the help and support of the woman I love."*

Princess Anne (Neptune in Libra square Venus in Cancer)

Princess Anne (b. August 15, 1950, 11:50 a.m., London, Great Britain), the only daughter of Queen Elizabeth II, was on the front page of the world's tabloids for a long time. In 1973 Anne married Mark Phillips in a lavish ceremony, but their nearly 20-year marriage was reportedly unhappy amid rumours of both husbands' infidelity. The couple divorced in 1992, and eight months after her divorce from Phillips, Anne married Sir Timothy Lawrence, her lover.

Prince Charles (Neptune conjunct Venus in Libra)

Prince Charles (b. November 14, 1948, 9:14 p.m., Buckingham, UK) married Princess Diana in 1981, but soon after their marriage collapsed after many disclosures about her husband's infidelity. After the divorce, Diana declared: *'There were three of us in this marriage, so it was a bit crowded.'* It was later revealed that she was also having a five-year romance with James Hewitt at the time.

Prince William (Neptune in Sagittarius inconjunct Venus in Taurus)

Head over heels in love with Prince William (b. June 21, 1982, 9:03 p.m., London, Great Britain) since high school, Kate Middleton was nicknamed "Princess-in-Waiting" by her schoolmates. As fate would have it, in 2001 Kate and William became schoolmates at the University of St. Andrews, where they studied art history together. He fell under her spell, and the two began a relationship with many ups and downs. Between 2002 and 2007, they broke up many times, and in 2010, after 8 years of relationship, Will took the big step and gave Kate the engagement ring that belonged to Princess Diana.

In 2019, their marriage repeated the pattern of their predecessors - Lady Di, Prince Charles and his mistress, Camilla Parker Bowles, now Queen Consort of England - the first news was broken about the infidelity of Prince William, who started a relationship with his wife's best friend, Rose Hanbury.

The five Rothschild brothers

The Rothschild family (or House of Rothschild) is a European dynasty of Jewish-German origin, who established their banking business in Europe at the end of the 18th century, becoming one of the most financially powerful families in the entire world.

The family's ascent to international prominence began in 1744, with the birth of Mayer Amschel Rothschild in the Frankfurt am Main ghetto.

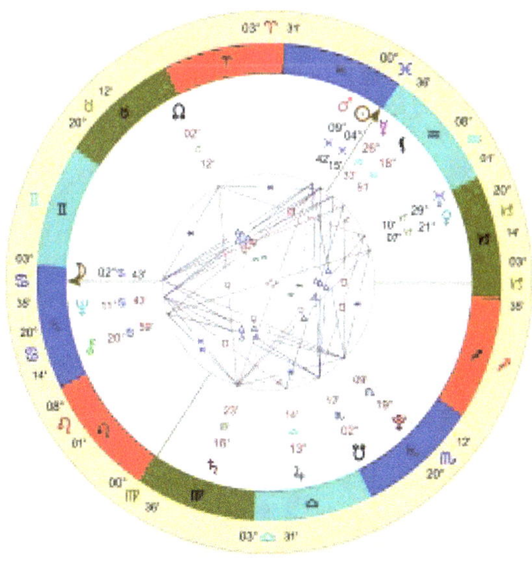

The son of Amschel Moses Rothschild, a money changer who had traded with the Prince of Hesse, Mayer developed a finance house and spread his empire by installing each of his five sons in the five main European financial centres to conduct business: London, Paris, Frankfurt, Seville and Naples.

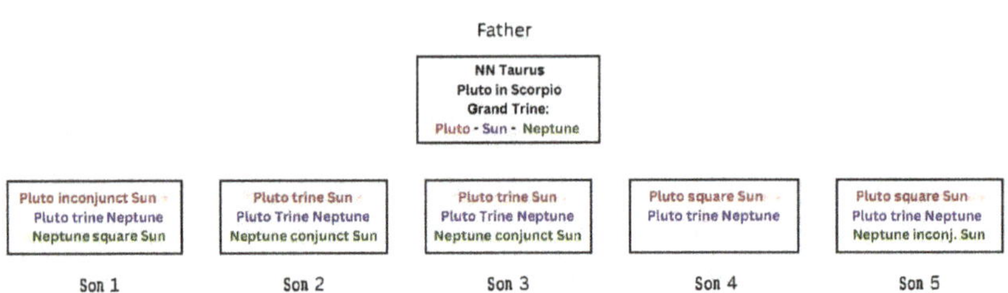

The Rothschild coat of arms contains a clenched fist with five arrows symbolising the five dynasties established by the five sons of Mayer Rothschild, in a reference to Psalm 127: "Like arrows in the hands of a warrior".

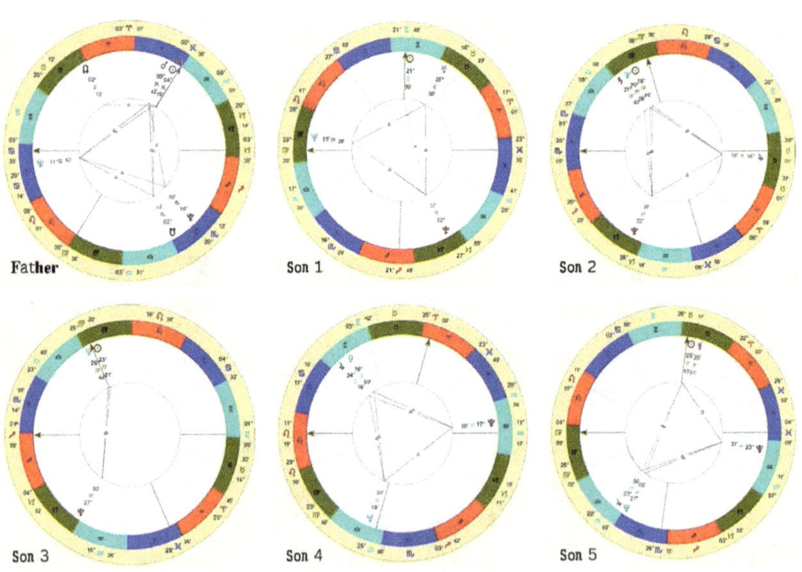

Amschel, the father, was born with a royal trine configuration in water signs, which includes: Pluto in Scorpio, Neptune and Moon in Cancer, Sun and Mars in Pisces. At the same time, this configuration was completed by the axis of the lunar nodes in Taurus - Scorpio, which transforms it into a kite, with the orientation of the North Node in Taurus.

The interesting thing, all five of his sons, born 1, 4, 15 and 19 years apart from each other, have the same pattern, part of the father's configuration.

Birth dates:

- Father - Mayer Amschel Rothschild - 23/02/1744
- Son 1 - Amschel Mayer - 12/06/1773
- Son 2 - Salomon Mayer - 9/09/1774
- Son 3 - Nathan Mayer - 16/09/1777
- Son 4 - Karl Mayer - 24/04/1788
- Son 5 - Jakob or James Mayer - 15/05/1792

The Romanovs

Story 1

Ivan the Terrible
Natal Chart
25 Aug 1530, Thu
12:00 LMT -2:30:20
Moscow, Russia
Tropical
Placidus

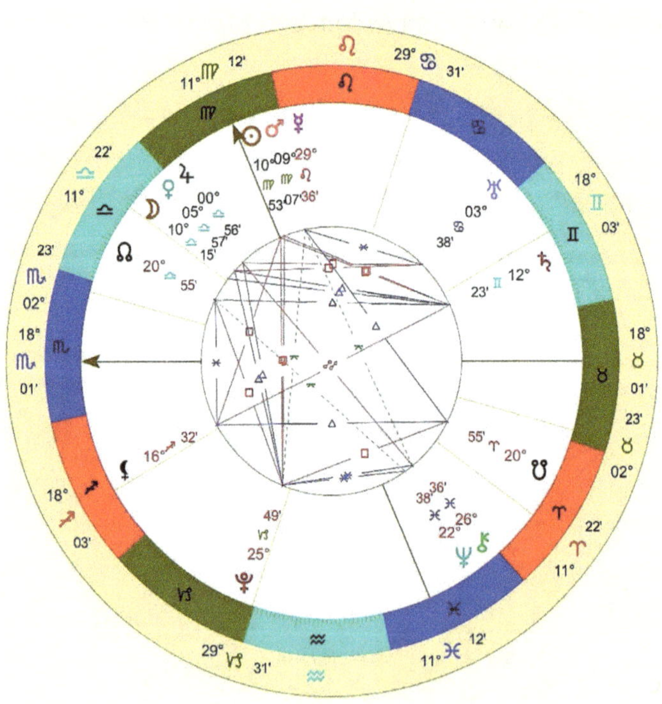

On August 25, 1530, comes into the world Ivan, the long-awaited son of Vasili III, Grand Prince of Russia. Unfortunately, the life of Ivan, later known as Ivan the Terrible, is littered with a long series of bitter events, murders, persecutions, suffering, pain, manipulation and control, which not only mark his own existence but also that of all subsequent generations, i.e. of the entire Romanov dynasty, whose destiny ends tragically.

Natal astrological aspects:

- Saturn square Mars - Sun
- Uranus square Jupiter - Venus - Sun
- Pluto retrograde conjunct Mercury retrograde at anaretic degree
- Neptune conjunct Chiron
- South Node in Aries - North Node in Libra

When Ivan was three years old, his father died, leaving him under the tutelage of his mother, Elena, and the boyars of the time. Due to the latter's desire for power, his mother is assassinated, and he remains until the age of 15 in the care of two boyar families, where he spends his childhood in an atmosphere of hatred and death, constantly afraid that he will be killed. Here he knows hunger, cruelty, malice, beating and indifference.

In a letter to Prince Kurbski[6], he reveals how he and his brother, Yuri, were brought up: "*of shame and misery, like vagrants and children of the poorest, or of the last of servants!*" "*Sometimes we had no clean clothes, everything was shabby, old and dirty. [...] Sometimes we were very hungry, we were starving. [...] Oh yes, since I know the poor, I know that! I saw hate.*"

Growing up like this, his passions are divided between torturing animals and mistreating the surrounding villages, showing signs of a very contrasting personality: on the one hand, he is an intelligent, very busy, dynamic man who takes responsibility

6   Andrey Mikhailovich Kurbsky (1528–1583) was a Russian political figure and writer. Intimate friend of Ivan the Terrible, his correspondence with the tsar is a genuine literary document.

as a sovereign in heart, on the other hand, is an unbalanced man with a fragile psyche, subject to violent mood swings and long-lasting depression.

At the age of 17, right after the coronation, he marries the daughter of an old family of noble race, Anastasia Romanova, who gives birth to six children: Anna (who died at twenty months), Dimitri (who died at eight months), Ivan, Maria, Eudoxia and Feodor, (born mentally retarded).

In 1560, after 13 years of marriage, Anastasia died of poisoning in mysterious circumstances. Ivan suffers a very strong emotional collapse and, not knowing who is his wife's murderer, begins to kill and torture several boyar families.

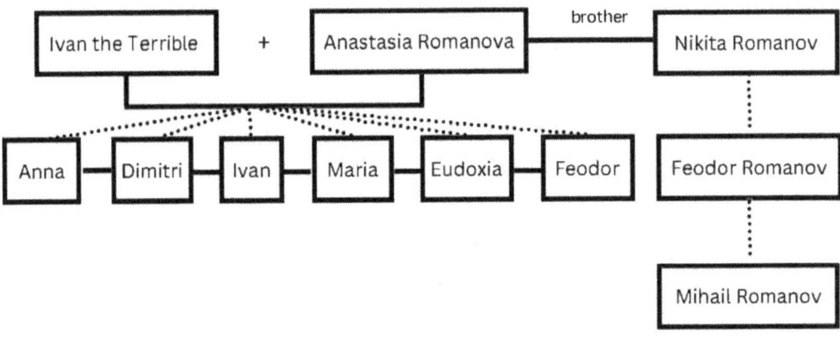

From here on, the reign of the first tsar of Russia can be divided into two periods: a prosperous one, full of great and appropriate reforms, and the second one, full of the effects of the problems caused by madness. After Anastasia's death, the restless Ivan had eight more wives: Maria, who died of poisoning nine years after the death of his first wife; Marfa, who died 16 days after the wedding; Anna Alexeievna, sent to the monastery after two years of marriage due to her infertility; Anna Vasilchikova, who died violently one year after the marriage; Vasilisa, accused of infidelity, sent to the monastery and deceased four years after the marriage; Maria Dolgorukaya, killed after the wedding because she was not a virgin, and Maria Nagaya, whom he married on the same day that his and Anastasia's son, Feodor, was marrying Irina Godunova.

The great decline of Ivan the Terrible begins 20 years after Anastasia's death, on November 15, 1581, when in a fit of rage he kills his son, Ivan, and beats the pregnant wife of the latter, Elena, very badly, which caused her to suffer a miscarriage.

After all the deaths, crimes and atrocities he went through - the death of his father, the assassination of his mother and of Anastasia, the death of his other wives (either killed by him or by others), the murder of his son and grandson becomes the final straw: Ivan can only sleep a couple of hours a night, he is full of remorse and begins to get sicker and sicker.

Since neither the doctors' potions nor the priests' prayers could stop the disease, Ivan calls astrologers, diviners and healers from all over Moscow, who calculate the time of his death as March 18, 1584. Their calculations come true, and it is on that very date that Ivan the Terrible dies during a game of chess. The story goes that he died of an impairment of the intestines and urogenital system, but after Stalin ordered his exhumation, mercury poisoning was added to these conditions.

Upon his death, the throne of Russia was occupied by his and Anastasia's other son, Feodor, and after Feodor's death, the fight for the throne took place between Anastasia's family, the Romanovs, and Boris Godunov[7], who won and became tsar in 1598. His revenge on the Romanovs was terrible: the whole family and their relatives were deported to the far corners of Northern Russia and the Ural Mountains, where most of them died of hunger, or in chains.

Anastasia's brother, Nikita, the leader of the Romanov family, was exiled, but her nephew, Michael, the only survivor, was sheltered in a monastery with his mother.

Little Michael, nephew of Ivan the Terrible and Anastasia, would continue the Romanov dynasty and its tragic destiny!

7   Boris Godunov was the regent of Russia from 1585 to 1598 during the reign of Tsar Feodor I, who was mentally disabled, and then reigned as Tsar from 1598 to 1605 (7 years).

Story 2

Michael Romanov (12 July 1596), Anastasia's nephew by his brother, was crowned Tsar at the age of 17, as was Ivan the Terrible, being the first Russian Tsar of the Romanov dynasty.

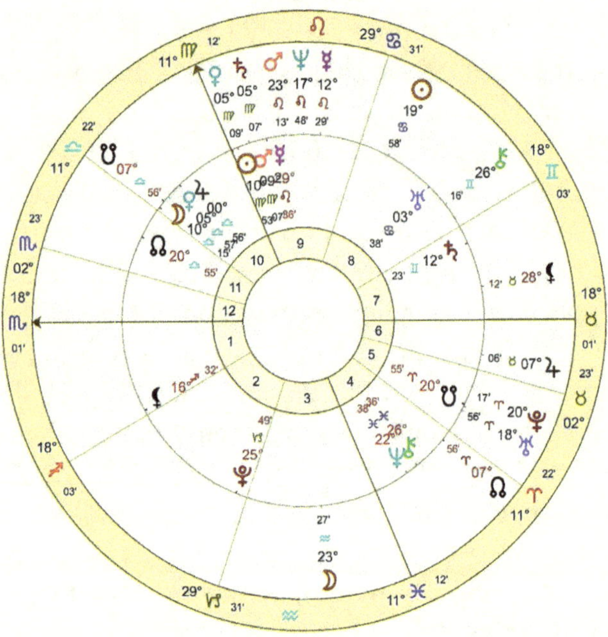

Natal astrological aspects:

- Saturn conjunct Venus
- Uranus, Pluto square Sun
- Neptune conjunct Mercury - Mars
- South Node in Libra - North Node in Aries

Michael's childhood was difficult: at the age of five, he was separated from his father and taken to a monastery, where he spent his entire youth attending endless religious services. For that reason, his mental state suffered.

Following the pattern of the first story, Michael marries for the first time Maria, but four months after the wedding he becomes a widower!

His second wife, Eudoxia, gives birth to 10 children, of which the eldest son, Alexei, succeeds him on the throne after he dies at the age of 49!

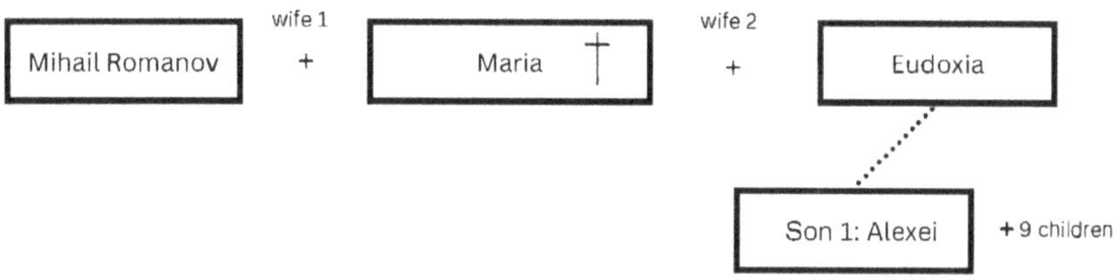

Story 3

Alexei I (b. March 9, 1629), the eldest son of Michael's 10 children with Eudoxia, became the next Tsar at the age of 16.

His education was committed to the care of his tutor, Boris Morozov, a sympathizer of Western culture, who, being accused of sorcery and witchcraft by the Muscovites, is exiled to a monastery, and Alexei, like Ivan or Michael, suffers a terrible depression after this forced separation.

From a relational point of view, he follows the same pattern: he had two wives.

The first wife, Maria, dies after twenty-one years of marriage, shortly after her thirteenth childbirth. Two sons survived her: Fyodor and Ivan, the latter being a child with serious mental problems, like Ivan the Terrible or his son, Feodor.

His second wife, Natalia, gives birth to a son, Peter.

Alexei dies in 1676, and Feodor, his eldest son, ascends to the throne.

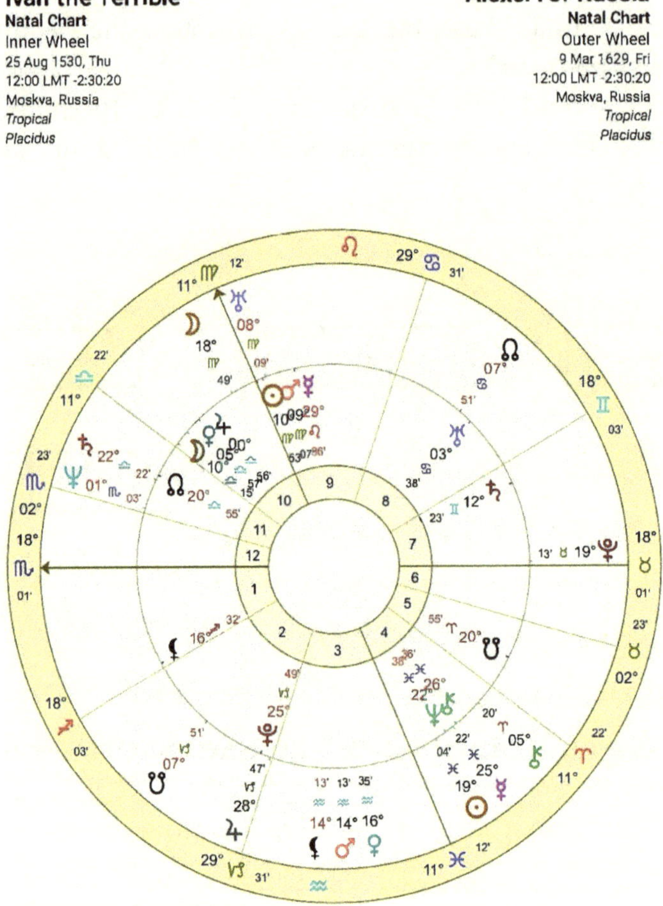

Ivan the Terrible
Natal Chart
Inner Wheel
25 Aug 1530, Thu
12:00 LMT -2:30:20
Moskva, Russia
Tropical
Placidus

Alexei I of Russia
Natal Chart
Outer Wheel
9 Mar 1629, Fri
12:00 LMT -2:30:20
Moskva, Russia
Tropical
Placidus

Natal astrological aspects:

- Pluto square Venus - Mars - Lilith
- Uranus conjunct Moon
- Full Moon
- South Node in Capricorn - North Node in Cancer

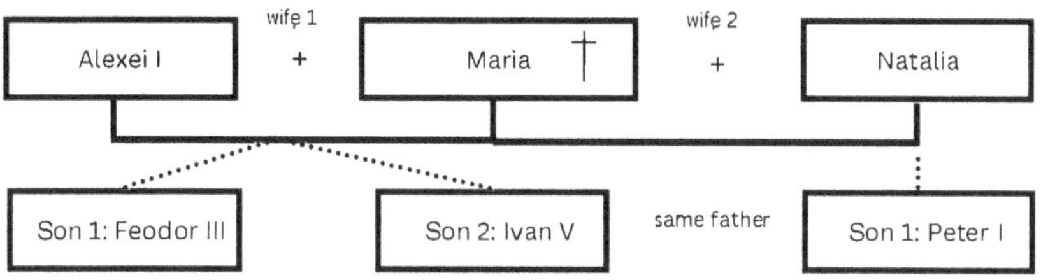

Story 4

Fyodor Alekseyevich of Russia (b. June 9, 1661) succeeded his father on the throne at the age of fifteen.

He had two wives.

The first one, Agaphia, dies a year after the marriage, along with the child she gave birth to a few days earlier.

Shortly after marrying his second wife, Marfa, he also dies, without naming any heir to the throne (as was the case earlier with Feodor, son of Ivan the Terrible).

With no heir to the throne, the families of Alexei's two wives begin to vie for power, leading to a unique concept of rule - two tsars at the same time: the first tsar, Ivan, Feodor's younger brother and son of Maria, and the second tsar, Peter, son of Natalia.

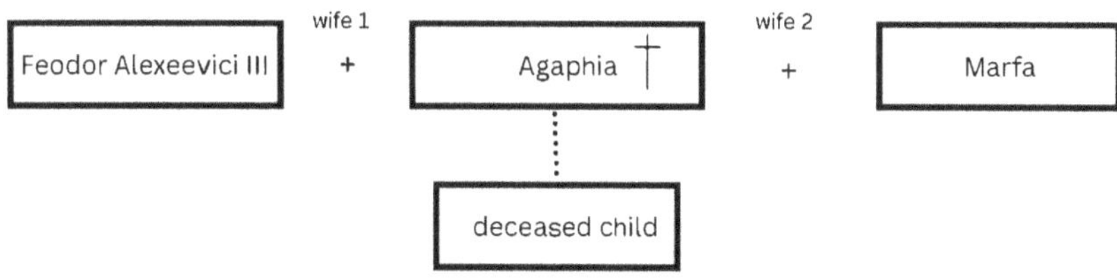

Ivan the Terrible
Natal Chart
Inner Wheel
25 Aug 1530, Thu
12:00 LMT -2:30:20
Moskva, Russia
Tropical
Placidus

Feodor III of Russia
Natal Chart
Outer Wheel
9 Jun 1661, Thu
12:00 LMT -2:30:20
Moskva, Russia
Tropical
Placidus

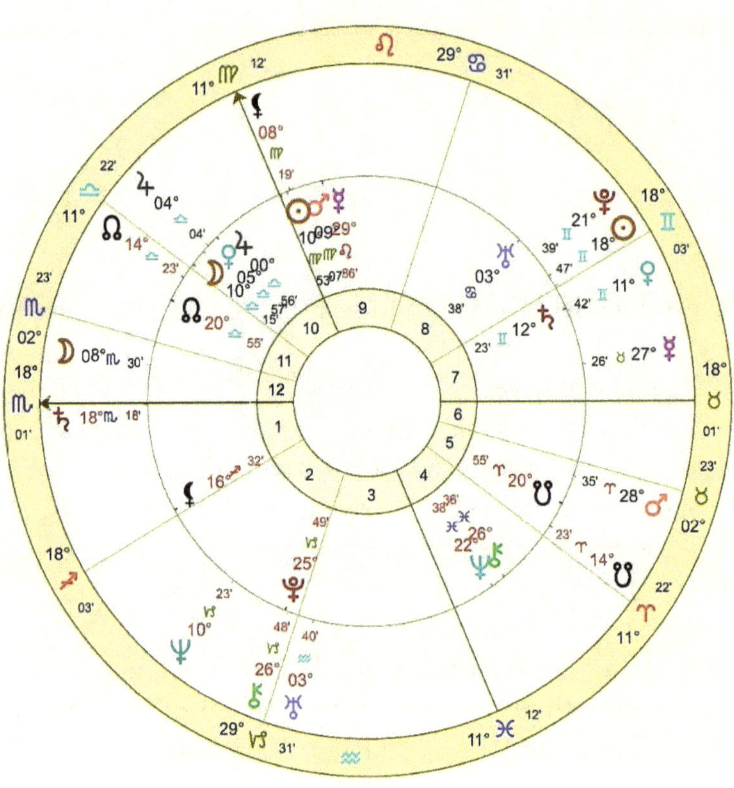

Natal astrological aspects:

- Pluto conjunct Sun
- Neptune inconjunct Venus
- Venus inconjunct Moon
- Uranus square Moon
- Saturn conjunct Moon
- South Node in Aries - North Node in Libra

Story 5

At the age of 16, Ivan V (August 27, 1666) and Peter I were jointly installed in power, with Ivan's sister Sophia as regent.

Due to his infirmity - the fact that he was feeble-minded, paralyzed and blind - Ivan's leadership is formal. He only spends his days with his wife in prayer and fasting until the age of 29, when his life comes to an end.

He leaves behind five daughters.

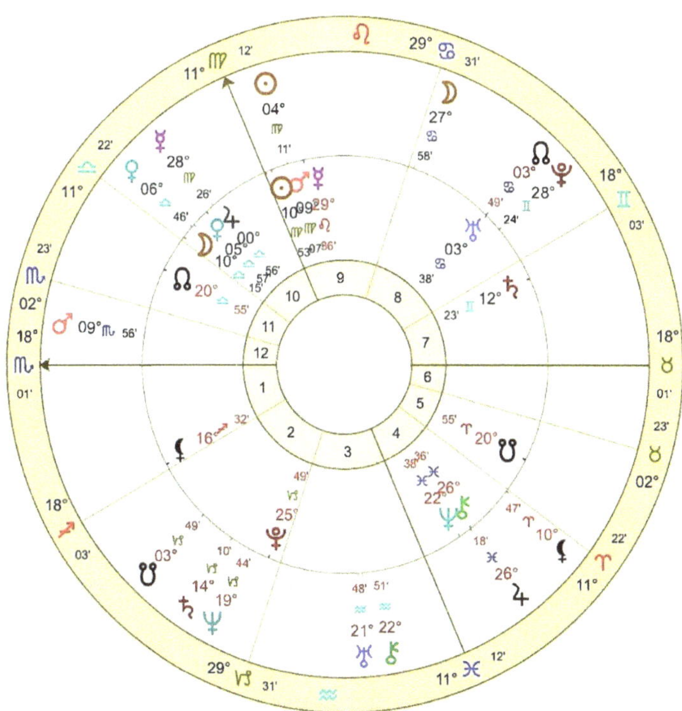

Natal astrological aspects:

- Pluto square Mercury
- Uranus retrograde - Chiron retrograde inconjunct Moon
- Saturn retrograde conjunct Neptune retrograde square Venus
- Venus opposition Lilith
- South Node in Capricorn - North Node in Cancer

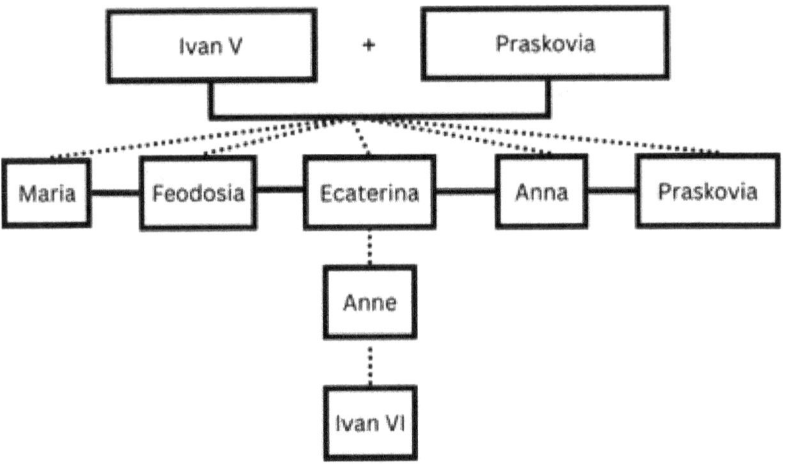

After Ivan's death, Peter remains the sole Tsar of Russia, known in history as Peter the Great.

Peter had two wives. The first wife, Eudoxia, with whom he has three children, is driven into exile due to incompatibility, and one of their sons, Alexei, whom his father could not stand, is imprisoned, subjected to torture and killed at the age of 28.

Besides the many mistresses he had, Peter's second marriage is to Martha, a Polish peasant who converts to Orthodoxy and takes the name Catherine. In total, they have 11 children, but not all of them live. Peter died in 1725, and the throne was taken over by his wife, who died two years later.

The only surviving heir remains another Peter, grandson of Peter the Great, son of Alexei, who had been killed in prison.

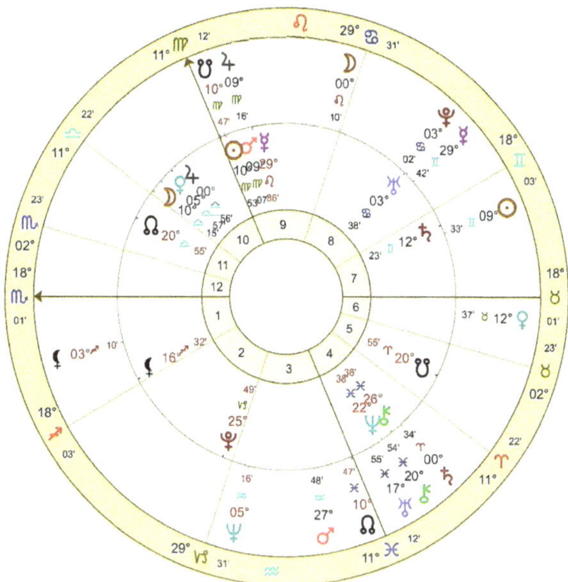

Natal astrological aspects:

- Neptune square Venus
- Neptune opposition Moon
- Saturn trine Moon
- Uranus conjunct Chiron

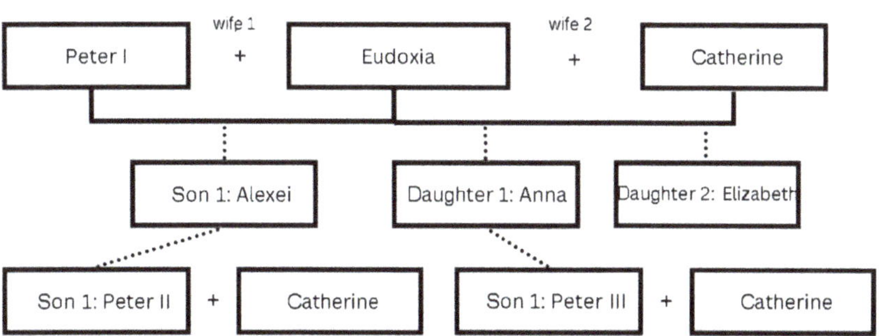

Story 6

Peter II (October 23, 1715), crowned at the age of 11, has an unfortunate destiny.

His mother dies shortly after giving birth to him, his father is killed in prison when he is three, and he dies of smallpox at the age of 15, on the very day he was to marry his fiancée, Catherine.

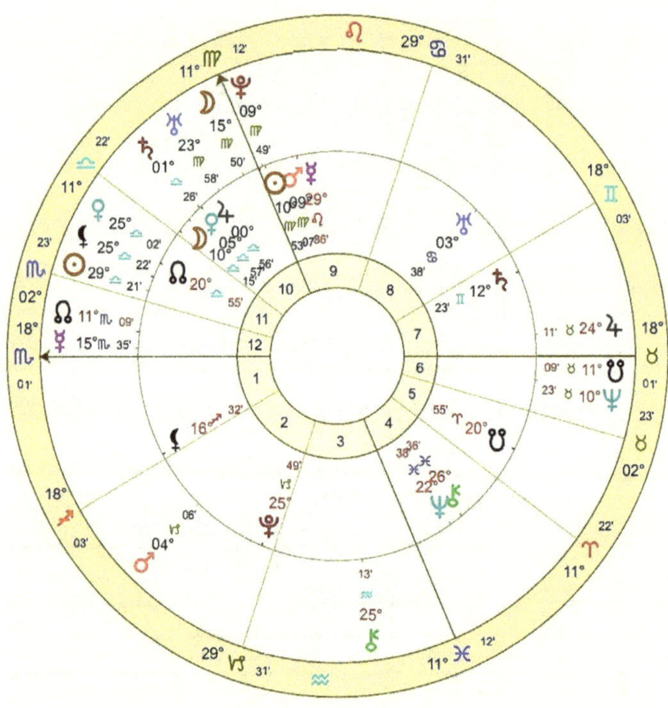

The direct male bloodline of the Romanov dynasty dies with him!

Natal astrological aspects:

- Neptune conjunct South Node
- Neptune opposition Mercury
- Pluto - Moon - Uranus Stellium
- Venus - Lilith - Sun Stellium

Story 7

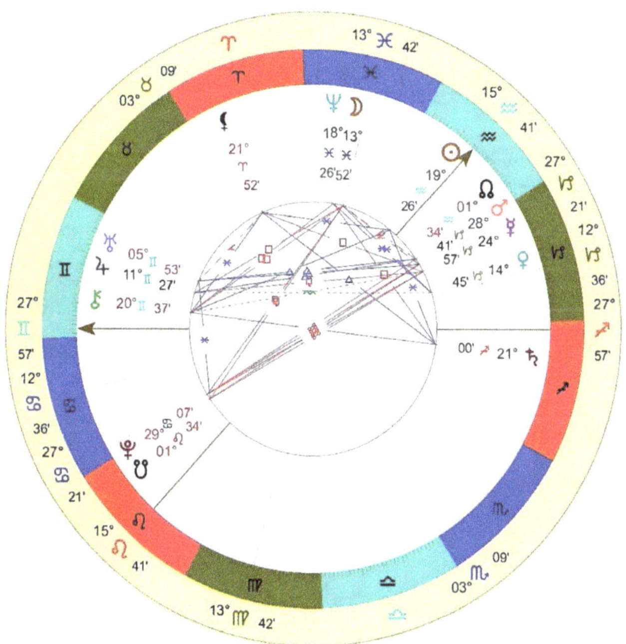

With no male heir, attention for the Russian throne turns to
the remaining women: Catherine (1691), Anna (1693), Praskovya
(1694), daughters of Ivan V, or Anna (1708) and Elizabeth (1709),

daughters of Peter the Great.

In the end, the older of the two Anna is chosen as Empress of Russia, who reigns for ten years.

By the time she was elected tsaritsa, Anna was already a widow, as her husband had died of a stroke two months after their marriage. In this context, she was offered the throne on the condition that she neither remarry nor name a successor. She signs the document of Conditions, but immediately after the coronation she tears up the document and announces her intention to rule autocratically, exiling or condemning many followers of the Council.

At the age of 47 she died, and the grandson of Ivan V (the disabled one), Ivan VI, only two months of age, succeeded to the throne.

Ivan VI (b. August 23, 1740) was an infant emperor of Russia, proclaimed when he was only two months old, and overthrown at the age of one by Elizabeth, daughter of Peter I. Ivan spent his entire life as a prisoner, and at the age of 22 he was killed by his guards.

Natal astrological aspects:

- Neptune conjunct Moon
- Pluto opposition Mars - Mercury
- Venus square Lilith
- T-Square: Saturn, Moon - Neptune, Chiron

Story 8

Elizabeth (b. December 29, 1709) became Empress and reigned for the next 22 years.

She was previously engaged to Prince Karl Augustus, but a few days after the engagement the prince died! She never remarried, but she had many lovers during her life: a handsome sergeant who ended up being deported by the order of Empress Anna, a coachman, and even a waiter.

In the end, she found consolation in the arms of a young Ukrainian peasant, who will remain known as the "Night King" because a marriage to him, a commoner, would have cost Elizabeth the right to the succession on the throne. In order to have a successor, she appointed her sister's son from Germany, Peter, only 14 years old at the time. On the afternoon of Christmas 1761, the empress dies of a stroke!

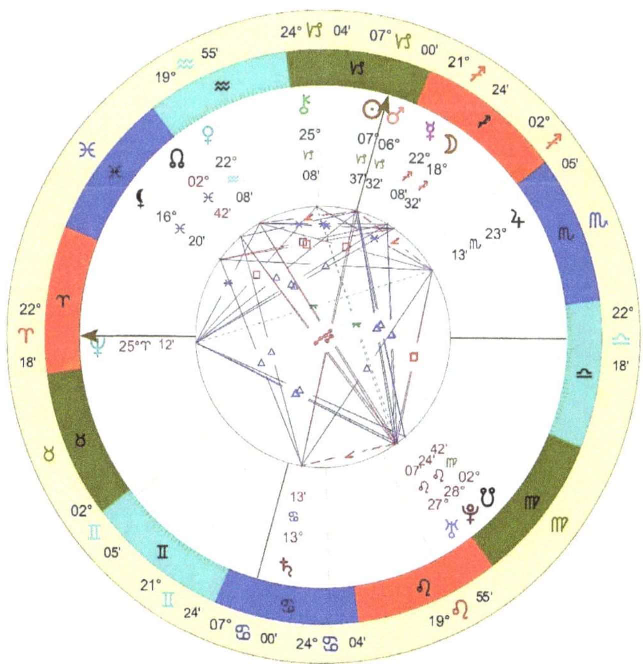

Natal astrological aspects:

- Saturn retrograde opposition Sun - Mars
- T-Square: Uranus retrograde - Pluto retrograde opposition Venus; Jupiter square Venus
- Fire grand trine: Mercury - Moon - Neptune retrograde - Uranus retrograde - Pluto retrograde

Catherine 2 of Russia
Natal Chart
2 May 1729, Mon
12:00 LMT -2:30:20
Moskva, Russia
Tropical
Placidus

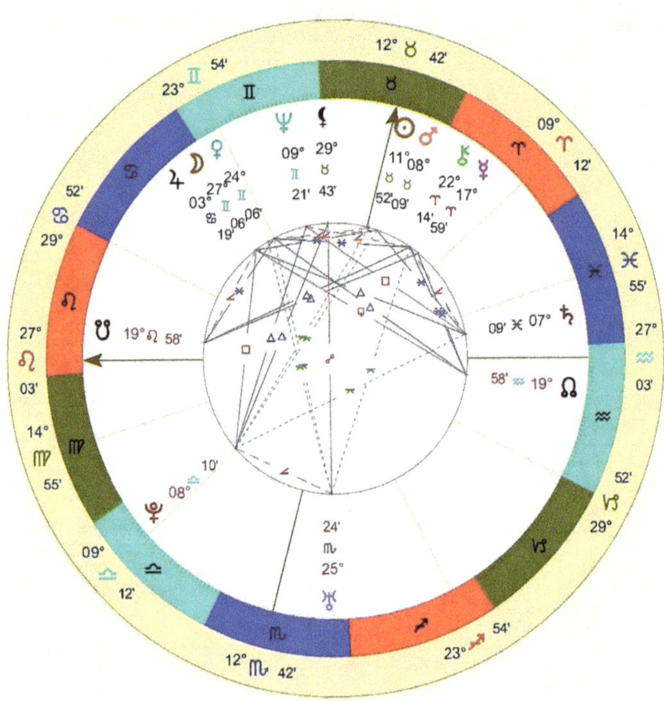

Karl Peter Ulrich (Peter III) marries the German princess Sophia Augusta Frederica of Anhalt-Zerbst, who converts to Orthodoxy and take the name Catherine. Their marriage was not a happy one, as she remains a virgin for eight years after the marriage, after which she gives birth to a boy, Pavel, who is said to be the child of a handsome chamberlain, Serghei. The second child, a girl, Anna, is the child of the Polish count Stanislaw-August Poniatowski, who dies on Christmas night (same as Elizabeth), and the third child, the boy of Grigori Orlov.

Peter III, who became Emperor of Russia, imprisoned his wife in the Schlusselburg fortress, and he settled in the palace with his mistress, Elizaveta Vorontsova.

Catherine understands what is at stake: her or him, the throne or prison, and on July 6, 1762, 6 months after the coronation, the tsar is assassinated by the friends of the empress, who succeeds him on the throne.

Catherine II (May 2, 1729) ruled Russia for 34 years, being known as Catherine the Great. She never remarries, but it is on record that she had 12 lovers in her life, some of these love relationships being long-lasting. On November 5, 1796, at the age of 67, she died of a stroke, and her son, Paul, succeeded to the throne.

Natal astrological aspects:

- Pluto retrograde inconjunct Mars - Sun
- Uranus retrograde inconjunct Venus - Moon
- Conjunction Venus - Moon in Gemini
- Saturn square Neptune
- South Node trine Mercury - Chiron

Story 10

Paul is crowned as Paul I of Russia.

He married twice: the first wife, Wilhelmina Louisa, who acquired the Russian name of Natalia Alexeievna, died in childbirth, and with the second wife, the beautiful Sophie

Dorothea of Württemberg, who acquires the Russian name of Maria, he has a son, Alexander, and 9 more children.

Throughout his life, Pavel lives with the suspicion of an assassination attempt on him. He also suspects his mother of planning to kill him and openly accuses her of trying to put crushed glass in his food.

Paul is killed 4 years after his ascension to the throne, and his eldest son follows him on the throne!

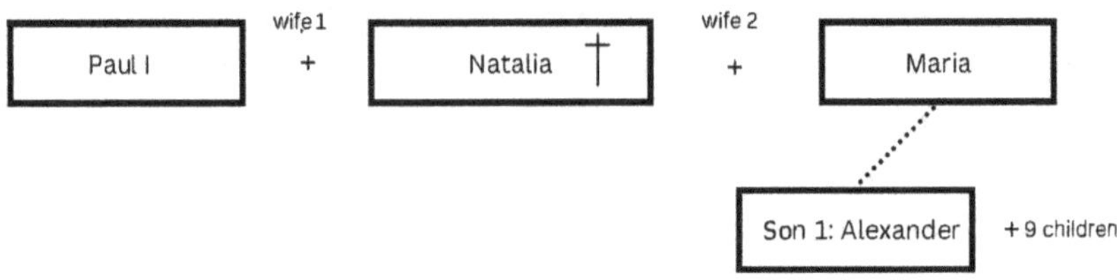

Story 11

Alexander succeeded to the throne after his father was assassinated, and ruled Russia during the Napoleonic Wars.

Soon after his birth, on December 23, 1777, Alexander was taken from his father, Paul I of Russia, by his grandmother, Catherine the Great, who hated her son and did not want him to have any influence on the education of the future emperor. Thus, both camps, Catherine's and Paul's, tried to use Alexander for their own purposes, and he had to divide himself emotionally between his grandmother and father. After the coronation, it appears that the seizure of power by killing his father caused him remorse and a sense of shame, which explains his increased religiosity throughout his life.

Alexandru I married Elisabeth Alexeievna at the age of 15. Their two daughters died at a very young age. Having no legitimate male heirs (he had many mistresses and many children with them), after his death, his brother Nicholas took his place.

Story 12

Nicholas I marries Grand Duchess Alexandra Feodorovna and together they have a son, Alexander, and 9 more children.

He reigns for 30 years, and upon his death, his son, Alexander II, succeeds him to the throne (same pattern as in the previous story).

Story 13

Alexander II and his wife Maria Alexandrovna had six boys and two girls. In March 1881, he was killed by anarchists. The first boy Nicholas had died suddenly, and his son Alexander III took his place (again, the same pattern as in the previous story).

Story 14

Alexander III married Maria Feodorovna and together they had six children, the eldest being, again, Nicholas, crowned in 1894 as Nicholas II (after his father's death from nephritis).

Story 15
The end of the Romanovs

The inheritance received by Nicholas II from his predecessors no longer aligned with the times in which he became a ruler. The Tsar believed that he was receiving guidance directly from God and that he could rule Russia based on divine inspiration alone, but he was wrong. The complexity of the modern state was contrary to this fantasy of governance, especially because it focused on the inclusion of the effort of the entire nation, not that of a single man. Like his predecessors, Nicholas II refused to accept the democratic ideal for Russia. As the last Russian tsar, he reigned from 1894 until his abdication on March 15, 1917, at the end of the revolution. On July 17, 1918, the Tsar together with his wife Alexandra Feodorovna and their children - Grand Duchess Olga, Grand Duchess Tatiana, Grand Duchess Maria, Grand Duchess Anastasia and Tsarevich Alexei, born with haemophilia, were assassinated by the Bolshevik secret police, on Lenin's order.

With this assassination, three centuries of criminal history and trauma of the Romanov dynasty ended.

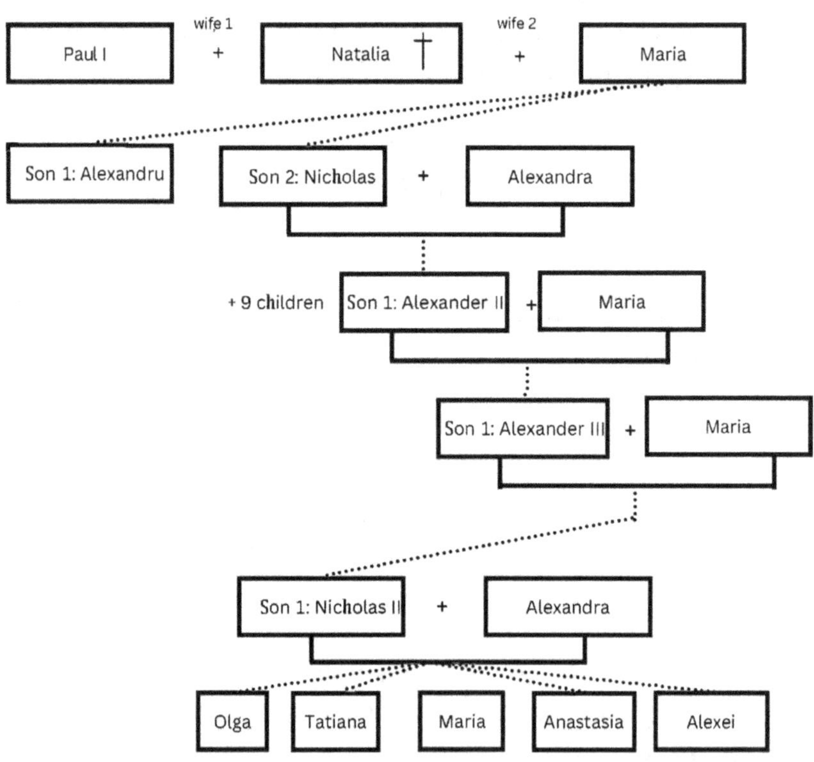

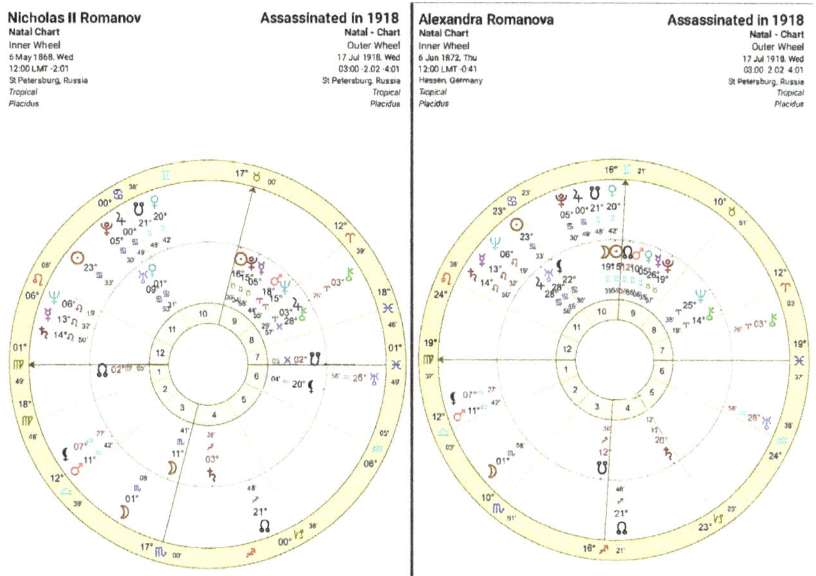

Nicholas II - Pluto conjunct Sun, Mars conjunct Neptune, Uranus conjunct Moon, Full Moon in Scorpio, yod with focus on Saturn retrograde in Sagittarius, SN - Chiron in Pisces.

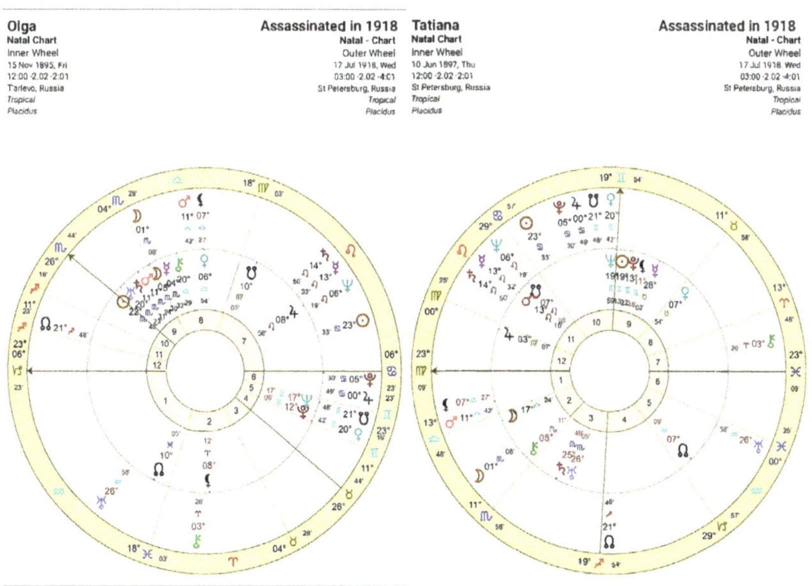

Maria
Natal Chart
Inner Wheel
26 Jun 1899, Mon
12:00 -2:02 -2:01
St Petersburg, Russia
Tropical
Placidus

Assassinated in 1918
Natal - Chart
Outer Wheel
17 Jul 1918, Wed
03:00 -2:02 -4:01
St Petersburg, Russia
Tropical
Placidus

Anastasia
Natal Chart
Inner Wheel
18 Jun 1901, Tue
06:00 -2:01
St. Petersburg, Russia
Tropical
Placidus

Assassinated in 1918
Natal - Chart
Outer Wheel
17 Jul 1918, Wed
03:00 -2:02 -4:01
St Petersburg, Russia
Tropical
Placidus

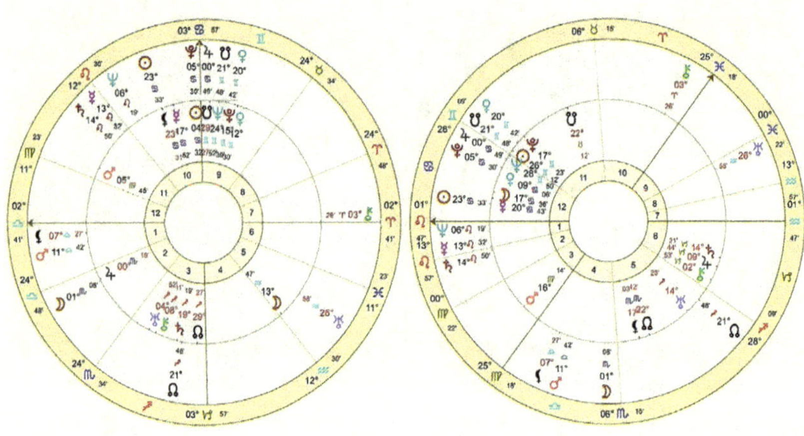

Alexei
Natal Chart
Inner Wheel
30 Jul 1904, Sat
12:00 -2:02 -2:01
St Petersburg, Russia
Tropical
Placidus

Assassinated in 1918
Natal - Chart
Outer Wheel
17 Jul 1918, Wed
03:00 -2:02 -4:01
St Petersburg, Russia
Tropical
Placidus

Anastasia Romanov, d. 1560
Natal - Chart
Inner Wheel
7 Aug 1560, Wed
12:00 LMT -2:01
St Petersburg, Russia
Tropical
Placidus

Assassinated in 1918
Natal - Chart
Outer Wheel
17 Jul 1918, Wed
03:00 -2:02 -4:01
St Petersburg, Russia
Tropical
Placidus

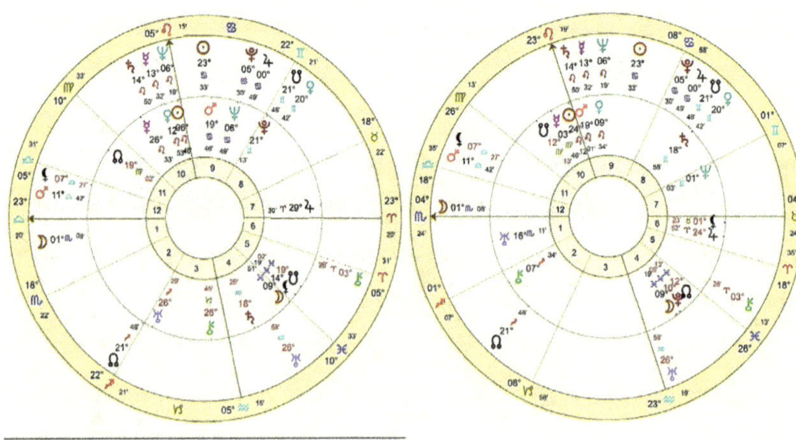

306

Nehru-Feroze Gandhi Family

Nehru-Feroze Gandhi is a family of Indian politicians who dominated the Indian National Congress for most of the early period of independent India. Three members of this family, Pandit Nehru, his daughter, Indira Gandhi, and her son, Rajiv Gandhi – served as Prime Ministers, the latter two being assassinated.

Rajiv's wife Sonia Gandhi along with her two sons Rahul and Priyanka also entered politics. Maneka, Sanjoy's wife, along with their son are also political activists, but on the opposition side.

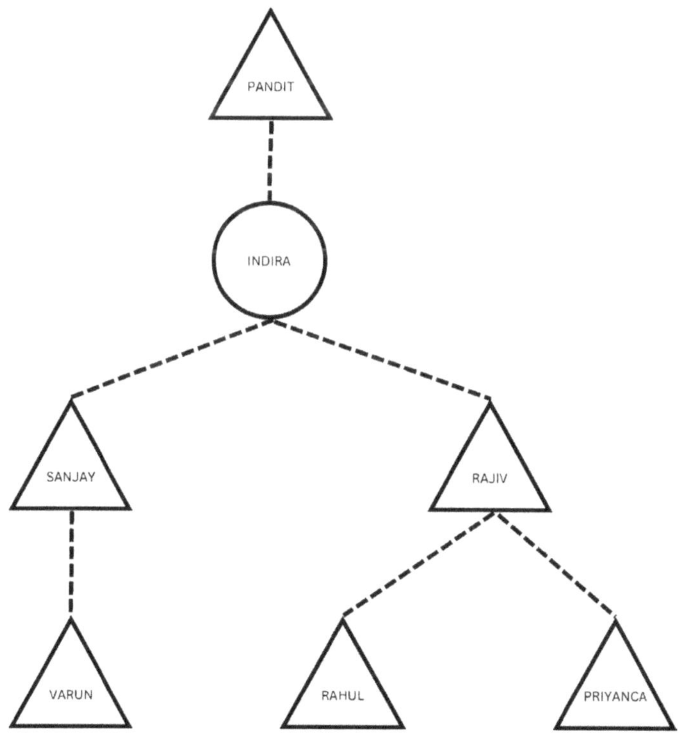

The story

Pandit Jawaharlal Nehru was one of the main founders of the Non-Aligned Movement, an organization whose aim is to ensure "the national independence, sovereignty, territorial integrity and security of non-aligned countries" in their "struggle against imperialism, colonialism, neo-colonialism, racism, and all forms of foreign aggression, occupation, domination, interference or hegemony, as well as against great power and bloc politics." The countries of the Non-Aligned Movement represent nearly two-thirds of the United Nations' members and contain 55% of the world population. Membership is particularly concentrated in countries considered to be developing countries, or Third World countries.

His daughter, Indira Gandhi, served as Prime Minister of India from 1966 to 1977 and again from 1980 until her assassination on 31 October 1984.

Growing up solely in the care of her sick mother, who actually died when she was 17, Indira developed strong protective instincts and a lonely personality. The fact that her grandfather and father were in a constant political struggle did not help her integrate into the family, where she always felt she was in conflict with her father's sisters.

During her stay in Europe, Indira met Feroze Gandhi, a young activist in the Congress Freedom Wing, and later married him. The couple had two sons, Rajiv Gandhi and Sanjay Gandhi. Their marriage started well but deteriorated along the way when Indira moved to Delhi to be with her father, the Prime Minister at the time. Eager to relieve him of the stressful environment he lived in and not wanting to leave him alone, she became his confidante, secretary and assistant.

In 1952, when India's first general election was held, both Nehru, Indira's father, and Feroze, her husband, ran for office, the latter without consulting his father-in-law. Feroze won, and at the height of the tension, Indira and her husband separated. Five years later, shortly after re-election, Feroze suffered a heart attack that brought them back together just 3 years, as he died in1960.

In her personal life, the instability of her childhood prevented Indira from developing personal interests and a lifestyle of her own. Her sense of duty to her father brought her into politics, but she was never given the space to develop as a person. Apart from political associates, she had no personal friends. After her husband's death, she became closer to his younger son, Sanjoy, who is accused by many historians of taking advantage of her emotional dependence. Indira always lived with the impression that he was accusing her of the death of his father, so she indulged him, the result being a political partnership that ended in the abrogation of democracy, corruption and abuse of power.

Rajiv Gandhi is said to have declared that he would never forgive his brother for what he had done to their mother when she was isolated, depressed and humiliated after her defeat in the 1977 elections.

On October 31, 1984, two of Indira Gandhi's bodyguards assassinated her in the garden of the Prime Minister's residence in New Delhi.

Initially, Sanjoy Gandhi had been chosen as heir, but after his death in a plane crash, his mother persuaded Rajiv Gandhi to quit his job as a pilot and enter politics (in February 1981). He became prime minister after her death, and in May 1991 he too was assassinated. His widow, Sonia Gandhi, created a new coalition of the Congress Party that led to electoral victory in 2004. Rajiv's children, Rahul and Priyanka, also entered politics. On the other hand, Sanjoy's widow Maneka Gandhi, who had a fight with Indira after her husband's death, as well as her son Varun Gandhi, are active in politics as members of the opposition.

Transgenerational legacy

Overlapping the three maps - grandfather - daughter - son,

one can see how the wishes, ideals and patterns of each generation continued.

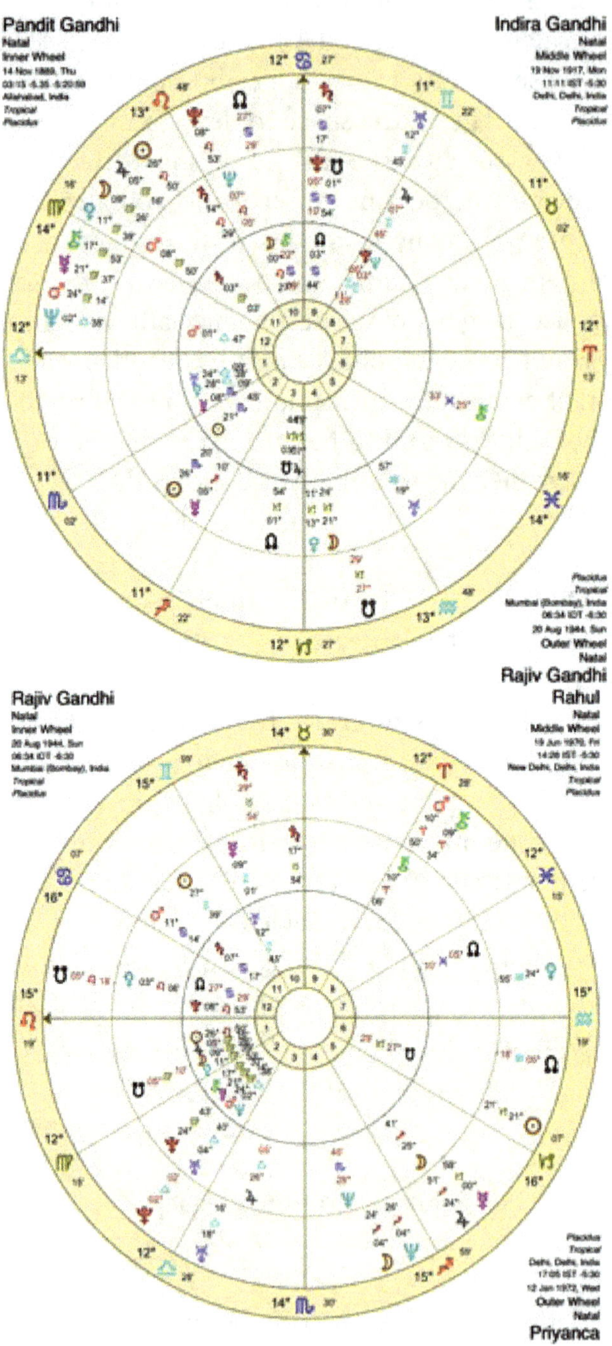

As for Pandit, his daughter Indira and his son Rajiv - all three were born with North Node - South Node axis on Cancer-Capricorn axis.

Pandit was born with NN in Cancer, as was the grandson, and Indira has SN in Cancer. Moreover, Indira completes her father's destiny line, being born with Pluto in Cancer, conjunct her father's North Node, and with Venus and the Moon in Capricorn, in the same sign as her father's South Node. Indira's son, continues the line of his predecessors, being born with Saturn in Cancer, conjunct Pluto and mother's SN and grandfather's NN.

Looking at other superpositions between the planets, we can also observe the other combinations:

It should be noted that both of Rajiv's sons have the Moon in Sagittarius, and the youngest, the Moon - Neptune conjunction in Sagittarius.

Sanjoy Gandhi
Natal Chart
Inner Wheel
14 Dec 1946, Sat
09:27 IST -5:30
Delhi, India
Tropical
Placidus

Rahul Gandhi
Natal Chart
Outer Wheel
19 Jun 1970, Fri
12:00 IST -5:30
Mumbai, India
Tropical
Placidus

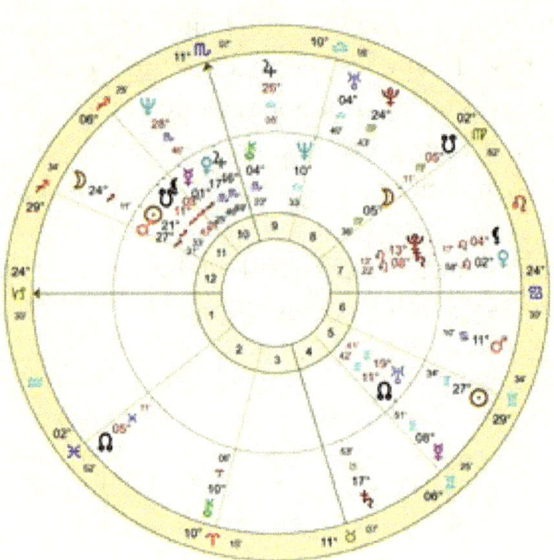

Sanjoy Gandhi
Natal
Inner Wheel
14 Dec 1946, Sat
09:27 IST -5:30
New Delhi, Delhi, India
Tropical
Placidus

Rahul
Natal
Middle Wheel
19 Jun 1970, Fri
14:28 IST -5:30
New Delhi, Delhi, India
Tropical
Placidus

Placidus
Tropical
New Delhi, Delhi, India
22:06 IST -5:30
13 Mar 1980, Thu
Outer Wheel
Natal
Varun

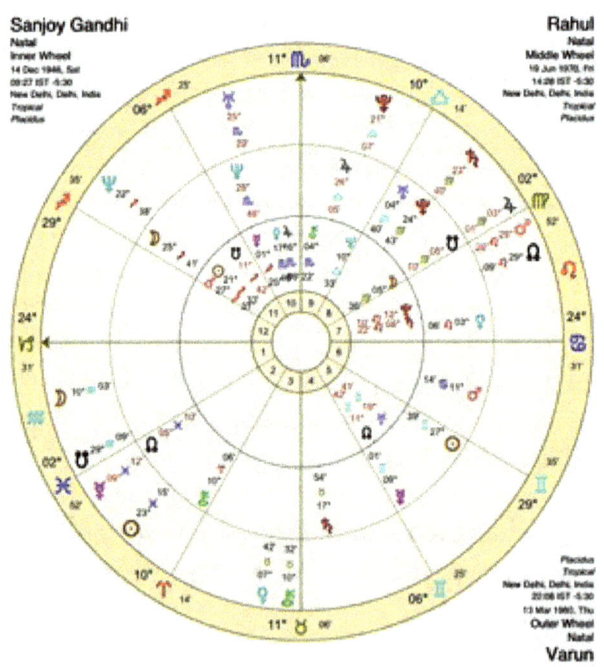

Indira's younger son, Sanjoy, dies in an aeroplane crash, and his wife and son enter politics, but as opponents.

Superimposing the maps of the two - uncle and nephew - it can be noticed that the axes of the lunar nodes are square, and the moon of each is at the south node of the other, a sign of the family debts that they carry on the mother-grandmother line.

If we add on top of the two that of Sanjoy's son Varun, who is in the opposition, we can see how the loyalty to his father is carried forward. He was born in the astral moment of Neptune in Sagittarius and Jupiter, Saturn in Virgo.

Dates of birth:

Pandit Nehru - November 14, 1889, Allahabad, India
Indira Gandhi - November 19, 1917, 11:11 a.m., Allahabad, India
Rajiv Gandhi - August 20, 1944, 6:34 a.m., Mumbai, India
Sonia Gandhi - December 9, 1946, 9:30 p.m., Lusiana, Italy
Rahul Gandhi - June 19, 1970, 2:28 p.m., Delhi, India
Priyanka Gandhi - January 12, 1972, 5:05 p.m., Delhi
Sanjoy Gandhi - December 14, 1946, 09:27 a.m., Delhi, India
Maneka Gandhi - August 26, 1956, 04:10 a.m., Delhi, India
Varun Gandhi - March 13, 1980, 10:08 p.m., Delhi, India

A bond beyond the grave
Bogdan Petriceicu Haşdeu and his daughter, Iulia

Bogdan Petriceicu Haşdeu (b. February 26, 1838, Cristineşti, Hotin, present-day Ukraine) was a Romanian writer and philologist, who pioneered many branches of Romanian philology and history. A walking encyclopaedia, jurist, linguist, folklorist, publicist, historian and politician, Haşdeu was one of the greatest personalities of the Romanian culture.

His daughter, Iulia Haşdeu was a child prodigy, a young genius: at the age of two she was learning French, at five she was writing short stories, at 11 she was writing drama, and at 16 she became the first Romanian woman enrolled at the prestigious Sorbonne University, stunning all the intellectuals of those times. She wrote poems of astounding depth, had remarkable skills for painting, was passionate about music, had a wonderful voice and graduated from the Bucharest Conservatory of Music. Unfortunately, this promising destiny would end on September 29, 1888, at just 18 years of age, due to tuberculosis.

In March 1888, a few months before her death, Iulia wrote the poem "Death", a disturbing artistic transposition of the final moments:

"I don't hate life, I'm not afraid of death, Because it's bright and warm light,

Even the dying - who in its peace calls him - Under tired eyelids new views bathe.

But the soul soars into the unknown world
And passes into other bodies when it can know how to forgive;
That's how we all drink from the sacred cup, purposely,
And never, no one can waste it"...

Iulia's untimely disappearance caused the mental collapse of his father who, from that moment on, tried day by day to communicate with her until one day, when he felt that Iulia answered him.

"It had been six months since my daughter's death. It was March: winter had gone, and spring had not come yet. One wet and gloomy evening I was sitting alone in the room, next to my work table. In front of me, as always, there was a quire of paper and several pencils. How? I don't know, I don't know, I don't know, but before I knew it, my hand took a pencil and rested its tip against the shine of the paper. I began to feel short and heavy throbbing in my left temple as if a telegraph machine had been inserted there. Suddenly, my hand went into a restless movement. About five seconds at most. When the arm stopped and the pencil fell from my fingers, I felt awake from sleep, although I was sure I hadn't fallen asleep. I took a glance at the paper and saw there very clearly: «Je suis heureuse; je t'aime; nous nous reverrons; cela doit te suffire. Julie Hasdeu» – (I'm happy; I love you; we'll see each other again; That should be enough for you). *It was written and spelled out in my daughter's handwriting"*, Hașdeu would confess later.

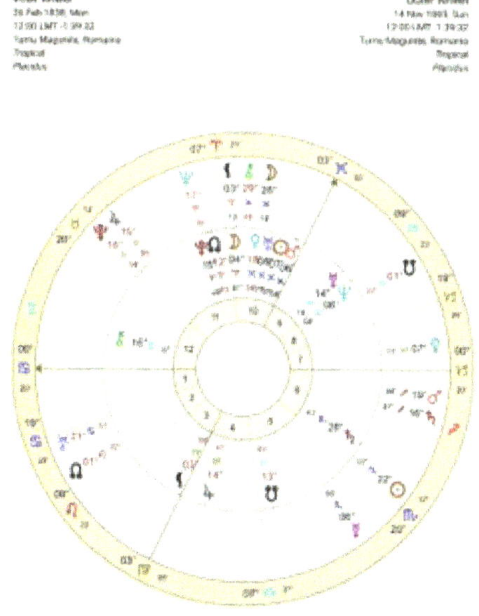

The synastry between father and daughter shows the following inter-aspects:

• Julia's Neptune retrograde is close to father's North Node and his Neptune is close to her South Node
• the father has a stellium of planets in the sign Pisces - Mars, Sun, Uranus, Venus retrograde, and the daughter a conjunction Moon - Chiron, retrograde, at anaretic degree
• conjunction Lilith - Moon (Aries) and Sun - Saturn (Scorpio)

Julia's composite chart with her father's has the axis of the lunar nodes in Gemini, squaring Neptune in Pisces. The ruler of the North Node, Mercury, is in Sagittarius at the South Node with Saturn, and the ruler of the South Node, Jupiter, is in Cancer. Jupiter and Neptune are in trine.

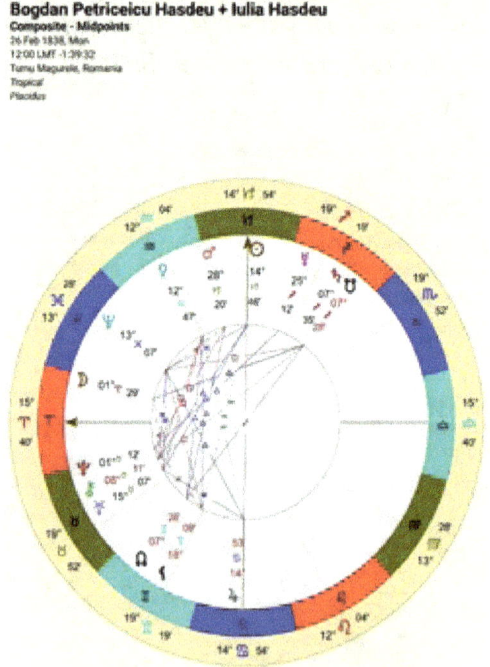

The astrological moment when Haşdeu felt the connection with his daughter can be traced in the picture below, where the

316

transit of March 1889 is superimposed on his natal chart, but also on Iulia's. I chose March 22, 1889, because that's when Neptune was resuming its transit into Gemini, joining Pluto!

At the same time, the transit was also activating the composite map of the two.

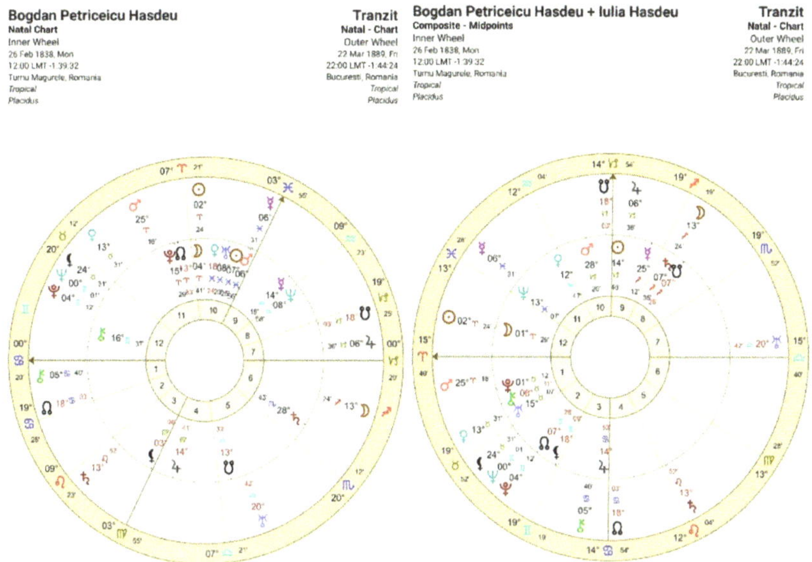

After this sign, Hașdeu made it his goal to find the spirit of his missing daughter by any means: he took refuge in spiritualism, he built a temple in memory of his daughter at the Belu cemetery and in 1893 he decided to build a castle, Iulia Hașdeu Castle in Câmpina, "The Great Temple of the Beyond". In the castle, he set up a special spiritism room, where he tried for years to get in touch with his daughter in the other world, and from his documentation, it seems that he succeeded.

*

What were the astral transits that Hașdeu experienced for 18 years (a period equal to Iulia's age when she died), from March 1889 until his death on August 25, 1907?

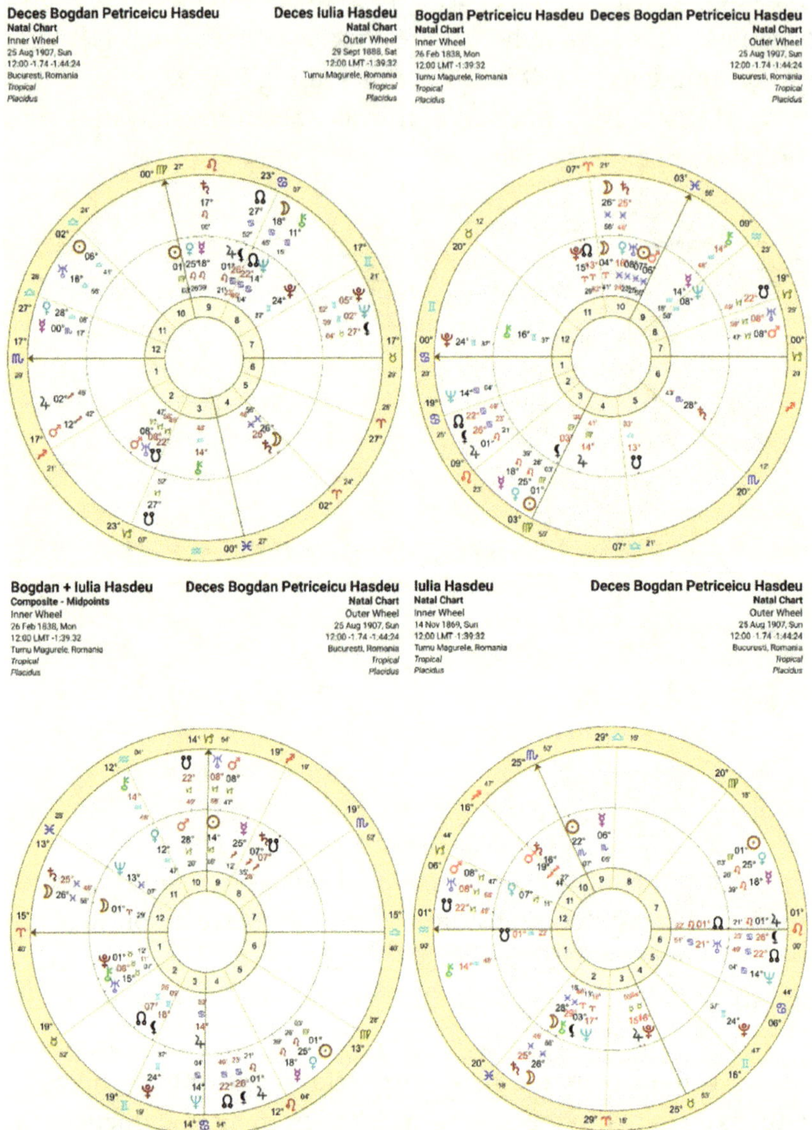

- Both deaths, Julia's and his father's, happened when the North Node was transiting Cancer. Thus, the 18-year period marked a complete cycle of the axis of the lunar nodes

- In his natal chart Hasdeu has a stellium of planets in the sign of Pisces - Mars (6 degrees), Sun (7 degrees), Uranus (8 degrees), followed by Venus retrograde at 18 degrees. Since March

318

1889, both Neptune and Pluto, in the first degrees of Gemini (communication, transmission of information) squared the natal planets in Pisces for 18 years (Neptune changed sign in 1901, Pluto completed the last square in 1906, and since then until his death, Saturn transited the sign of Pisces).

Lunar Nodes and Transgenerational Legacy

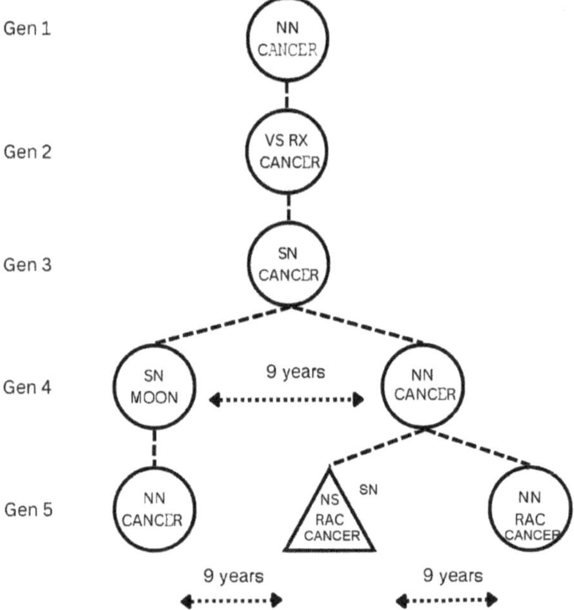

I have recently worked on a lady's family tree, where there were many women and an intricate mother-daughter relationship over several generations.

The above picture describes how the Cancer-Capricorn axis had to be integrated by the members of this system, who went through divorces, misunderstandings, and wounds, especially in the relationships between women. They took heavy responsibilities in the relationship with their mother or daughter, carried on patterns of emotional limitations or dependencies, and suffered from depression, abandonment or burden.

Very interesting, for taking their place in the system, each birth was programmed so that there was a difference of 9 years. The same thing with the cousins, between whom there is a multiple of 9 years.

Please note that there is a difference of 56 years between the 1st and 3rd generations, which is exactly the age the first analysed woman had when her granddaughter was born.

Transgenerational legacy

In the astral charts of the members of a family clan where the same axis of the Lunar Nodes (superimposed or inverted), as well as planets conjunct with them (North Node and South Node) in synastries are present, it is easy to see how the psychic content accumulated is transmitted trans-generationally like a wave.

- **Generation 1 - Great-great-grandmother - 1898**
  - South Node in Cancer
    - Saturn opposition Moon
- **Generation 2 - Great-grandmother - 1924**
  - Sun, Mercury, Venus Rx, Pluto in Cancer
- **Generation 3 - Grandmother - 1954**
  - Sun, Jupiter, Mercury Rx, Uranus, South Node in Cancer
    - Moon square Uranus and opposition Neptune (T sq)
- **Generation 4 - Daughter 1 - 1971**
  - Sun, Mercury in Cancer
    - Moon conjunct South Node
- **Generation 4 - Daughter 2 - 1981**
  - North Node in Cancer
    - Venus conjunct South Node
- **Generation 5 - Granddaughter 1 - 2001**
  - North Node in Cancer
    - Moon opposition Saturn, square Uranus, Mercury, Sun (T sq)
- **Generation 5 - Grandson 2 - 2010**
  - South Node in Cancer
- **Generation 5 - Granddaughter 3 - 2019**
  - North Node in Cancer
    - Moon conjunct Uranus

Saturn in Pisces

I have recently spoken with an acquaintance who felt extremely sick, sad and tense, since Saturn's ingress in Pisces (2023), especially due to his 13-year-old son's decision to separate from her and to live with his father, her ex-husband now. After analysing together the charts of those involved and their situation, I asked her what happened in the previous cycle of Saturn in Pisces, 1994 - 1995.

An interesting thing, at that time she was 13 years old, an age that coincided with the moment when her parents divorced, and she went through a very complicated period emotionally. By their separation, she felt cut off from her father, who no longer lived in the same house with her. Shortly after, her mother remarried, and his place was taken by another man, with whom she never got along. Going even further, I wanted to know what happened in her parents' lives a Saturnian cycle ago, also in Pisces. In the mother's case, the Saturn in Pisces period (1967) coincides with the moment when, at the age of 13, she found out that not her father is her real genitor, but the adoptive father, the second husband of her mother. Her real father had left her mother at her birth. The moment of truth awakens in her the feeling of abandonment and a strong paternal complex. As for the father, in 1966, also during the transit of Saturn in Pisces, he was orphaned by his mother at the age of 19.

Being curious and willing to go even further, I asked her what she knew about her family, that of the four grandparents from the cycle of Saturn in Pisces. The only information she has is that in September 1935 (Saturn in Pisces), her maternal grandmother, age 11 at that time, lost her 17-year-old brother in a car accident.

Her grandmother's sister was 13 years old at the time. The tragic accident did not only affect the two of them, but also their mother, the great-grandmother, who was burying her son. We do not know what happened in the personal lives of the great-grandparents in the period 1905 - 1907, but history tells about the Peasant Revolt of that period, which spread out the entire Romania. On 18 March 1907 a state of emergency, and then a general mobilization was declared, 140,000 soldiers being recruited. The Romanian army opened fire on the peasants, and entire villages were literally wiped off the face of the earth. Apparently, 11,000 peasants were killed. At the time, the historian Constantin Giurescu admitted that the army's repression was excessive.

Although the full meaning of this chain of separations between mothers, fathers and children is not fully understood, it is certain that Saturn's last entry into Pisces activated the whole set of patterns, emotions, states and feelings, triggering both for her, as well as for her tree (child, mother, grandmother, great-grandmother...) a possible moment of healing. In recent times, when her son is about to leave the country and study abroad, living with his father at the same age as his mother when she lost her father when the grandmother learned of the existence of the lost father and the great-grandmother lost her brother, it can be a moment when a circle closes or repeats itself. It is the time when he also separates from his mother and maternal sisters to go in search of his father and his lost paternal brother, who are on another continent!

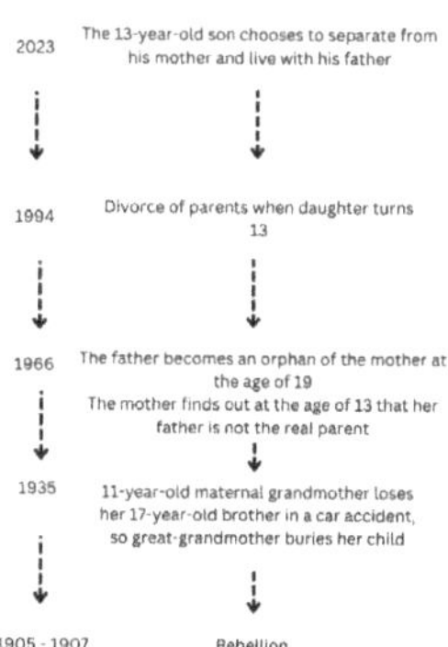

Why am I not successful?

This transgenerational analysis started from the case of a 19-year-old young man, a professional sportsman, who told me his story:

"The passion of my life is basketball, a sport I have been practising since I was 7 years old, always in teams with players older than me. At 11 I was designated as the best national player in my age bracket, from 13 to 16 I played in the national team, and then I performed at a top club in Spain. At 17, I returned to my home country, and currently, I perform with the senior team ranked 2nd nationally.

Despite my performances, natural talent, dedication and the fact that I was always the best in the team, and recognized as a very good player, my path was never easy, and the success I should have really achieved would go to the winds in the last moment.

Over time, I have suffered injuries in training (never during the game), which I can categorize as absurd, stupid or meaningless: an open fracture of my right forearm, broken skull, twice fractured nasal pyramid, countless sprains in ankle and right thumb, twice torn meniscus in right knee. For those who think that these injuries can be normal and common in the life of a performance athlete, I would like to tell them that they are not at all! At the national level, in all the teams I've been part of, it only happened to me, in the most trivial ways. Aggressive blows with painful and long recovery, as if, at the most important moments, I am prevented from moving forward!

At the same time, another wound of mine is the fact that my value is not recognized - at school, in the team or in relationships. I worked more than the others, I was the central figure in winning a game,

I had good results everywhere, but the teachers and coaches treated me with aggression, intolerance, contempt, disrespect and a lot of injustice.

The only people who have been by my side unconditionally, supported me, seen me and really understood me are my parents. I can rely on them at any time and their love and support encouraged me to go further!

All these experiences made me question my destiny and why these things happen periodically! Why do these accidents happen to me at key moments in my life? Why am I not allowed to perform according to my talent?

Although they claim that I have sports intelligence, talent, and skills, and my results were the best, why am I not seen, supported and promoted by my coaches?'

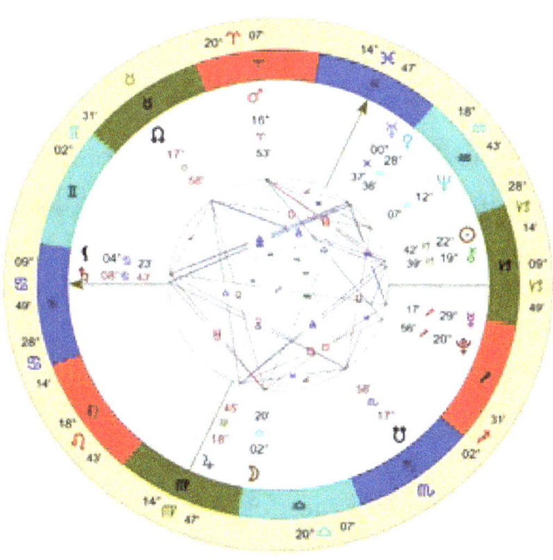

The Sun and the systemic line of the father

In order to understand what happens when the young man is about to succeed, shine and be seen, I began the study of his astrogram with the analysis of the Sun (father), and then I went on studying the system family represented by the mother (the Moon).

The Sun is in Capricorn, in conjunction with Chiron, in trine to Jupiter in Virgo and the North Node in Taurus, in square to Mars in Aries, and in sign opposition to Saturn, who is on the Ascendant, retrograde, in Cancer.

The Sun - Chiron conjunction can show a transgenerational wound, inherited from the father, related to the impossibility of proving himself, and the difficulty of achieving success and fulfilling his desires. By also adding the square to Mars in Aries, we are able to deduce the loyalty to the father's failure - at the moment when the Sun wants to assert himself, Mars intervenes volcanically and the pattern translates into injury, fall, breakage, and dive.

But why? What happened in the father's life and what is his scenario?

The father

Analysing the father's map and his life story, I find out that in his youth he was not allowed by his mother to follow his dreams, he was restrained, and his possibilities to take the path he would have meant to were limited - Saturn in Leo makes a square aspect to the Sun in Scorpio.

Although he was a very talented footballer and had the chance to attend a sports high school where he could perform, his mother did not want this and enrolled him in a theoretical high school (14 years old, a moment that also coincided with his parent's divorce). Here, his sporting talent came to the surface again, and he became a very good handball player.

When he was about to choose a college, although he wanted to choose a sports career and pursue his passion, his mother insisted that he attend an engineering college. With no support from his father either, who did not acknowledge his performances and was quite absent, he abandons once again, choosing to become an engineer.

His dream of becoming a sportsman and the talent he had are blocked, closed and repressed (South Node - Lilith in Taurus, 7th House), and during his life, abandonment and non-fulfilment become a frustration (Chiron in Aries, retrograde, anaretic degree, Saturn in Leo square Mars - Sun in Scorpio; Pluto in broad opposition to the Moon, also in 7th House, in Aries).

X's father
Natal Chart
3 Nov 1976, Wed
17:30 EET -2:00
Bucuresti, Romania
Tropical
Placidus

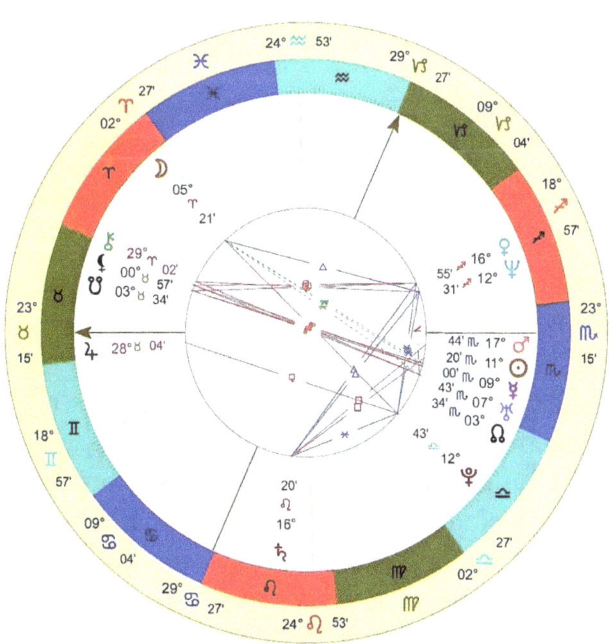

But what happened farther back, with his father?

The paternal grandfather

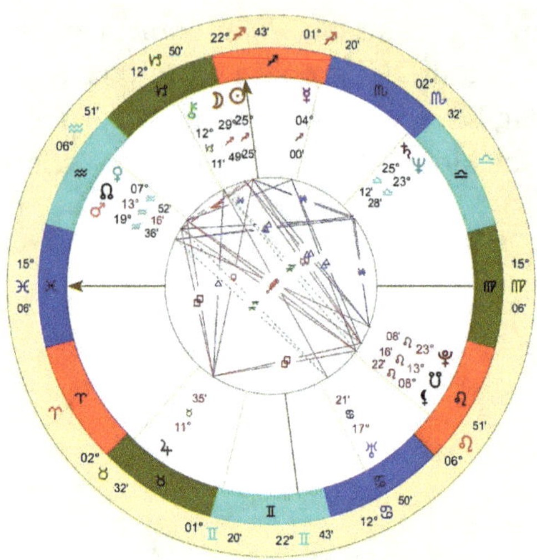

Very interesting, the grandfather was very talented at sports as a boy. Professional hockey player and he was a European champion, but when he had to choose his college, he suddenly quit his career as an athlete to become an engineer!

Later, he was professionally successful, having a great intellectual potential, but he did not leave his family system, to which he remained loyal.

The North Node is in Aquarius, as is the young nephew's North Karmic Regent, and the North Karmic Regent, Uranus, is retrograde in Cancer, from where it forms an inconjunct aspect to Mars, the North Node and, through the stellium formed, Venus. At the same time, conjunct the South Node in Leo are Pluto and Lilith, all in retrograde motion, inconjunct with Chiron in Capricorn.

Paternal great grandfather

As far as the paternal great-grandfather is concerned, I have learned that he grew up without a father, and never knew anything about his father's existence, as long as he was, as people would say, a bastard. On his own feet from the age of fourteen, he started from scratch and established a family and a home. As with his father, before this marriage, he also had a daughter, whom he never wanted to recognize.

As the identity of the great-great-grandfather is unknown, we cannot know what happened before, in his life.

*

So, the paternal grandfather, a European champion, manages on his own to get himself noticed and quits his sports career on what he considers to be his own initiative.

The father, a talented athlete, is hindered from continuing his sports career, the experience turning into a frustration, a wound.

The son, national champion, at key moments, gets injured and is left aside.

The interdiction imposed by the mother repeatedly creates a blockage in the two men - son and grandson, i.e. father and son.

What do the astral configurations look like for the two women - the mother and the paternal grandmother?

In the grandmother's chart, on the same Leo - Aquarius axis, one can identify the opposition between the Sun-Mercury in Aquarius and the conjunction Pluto retrograde - Moon in Leo, a very intense full moon aspect, to which we can also add the T-square aspect coming from Mars in Scorpio, as well as the inconjunctions Uranus retrograde Cancer - Mercury, Venus - Moon (and Pluto), Sun - Lilith, Mars - Jupiter.

In the great-grandmother's chart, a square formed on the

cardinal signs Aries (Chiron retrograde) - Cancer (Pluto) - Libra (Saturn) - Capricorn (Moon) and two crossed yods, of which the Neptune - Moon inconjunction aspect is also a part.

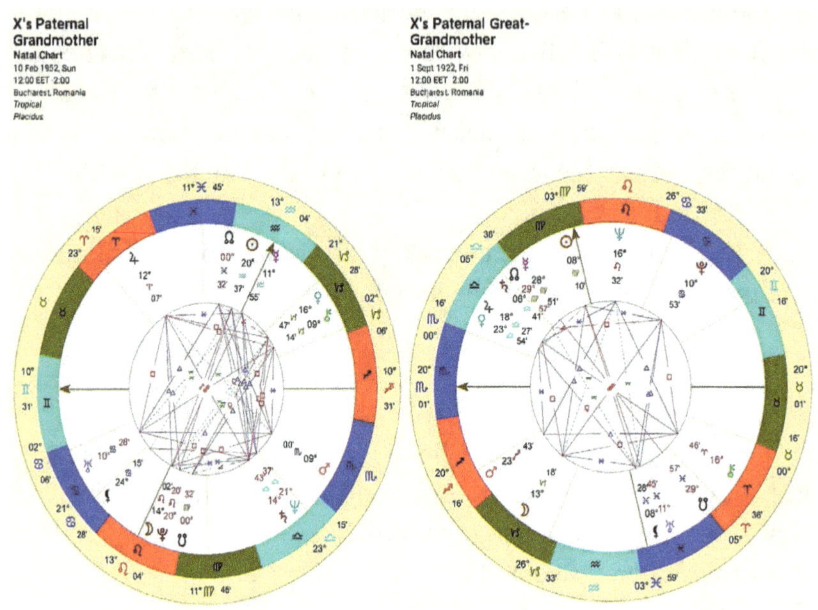

The Moon and Mother's Systemic Line
Where's My Money?

In X's chart, the Moon is in Libra, 4th house, squared by Saturn retrograde and Lilith in Cancer, located in the 12th house, but close to the Ascendant and in inconjunction with Uranus in Pisces. The layout shows a strong family pattern, and repression of a very deep, possibly traumatic psychic content.

Talking to the mother of the analysed young man, I found the same pattern of the original story - she too is faced with inexplicable situations related to money, value and possessions, which always slip through her fingers. Although she is a very good professional, appreciated by the people she works with because of the tangible results she has achieved, when there are clear opportunities for earning, business or money projects, after a short period of success, everything is lost, the people would disappear, the money wouldn't pile up and the cycle starts over.

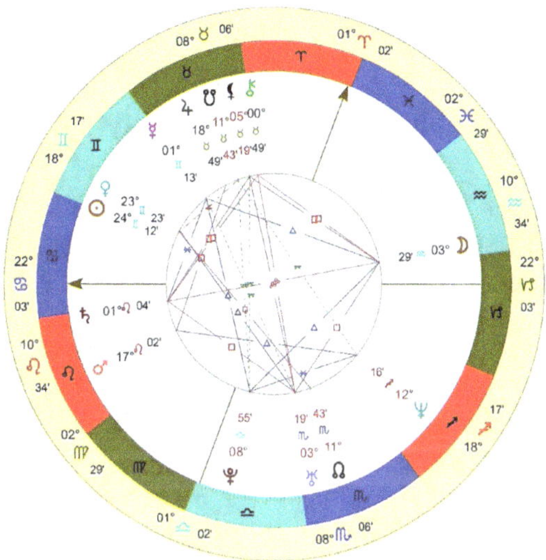

Being about money, values and earnings, the first thing that caught my attention was the positioning of the planet Venus in Gemini, the 12th House (hidden house, house of secrets), next to the Sun (father), being the ruler of the 4th and 10th houses (parents, reputation and family environment), as well as the karmic ruler of the South Node (inherited past). In Taurus (money) there is also Chiron (family wound), along with Jupiter (social condition and beliefs). Earnings and money are linked to an unconscious pattern, taken first of all on the father's line.

The opposition between Saturn and the Moon (also inherited by X, which has Moon in Libra square Saturn in Cancer in the chart) on the 1st-7th axis, with the ruler of the 7th house in the 1st house and vice versa, the ruler of the Ascendant in the 7th

331

House, shows the mirror projection of a life pattern of his parents.
What happened in her predecessors' lives?

Maternal father, grandfather and great-grandfather

The maternal grandfather's chart consists of a cosmic cross on fixed signs - Taurus (North Node) - Leo (Pluto, Mars, Saturn) - Scorpio (Moon, Mercury retrograde, Chiron, Sun, South Node) - Aquarius (Lilith), to which the conjunction of Venus - Jupiter in Sagittarius is added (strong attachment to the social condition of the family).

The maternal great-grandfather's chart also has a cosmic cross on cardinal signs: Aries (South Node, Chiron) - Cancer (Pluto retrograde) - Libra (Saturn retrograde, North Node, Jupiter retrograde) - Capricorn (Moon), plus Mars (Sagittarius) square with the Sun-Venus-Uranus stellium in Pisces and opposition Neptune retrograde Leo - Mercury retrograde - Lilith in Aquarius.

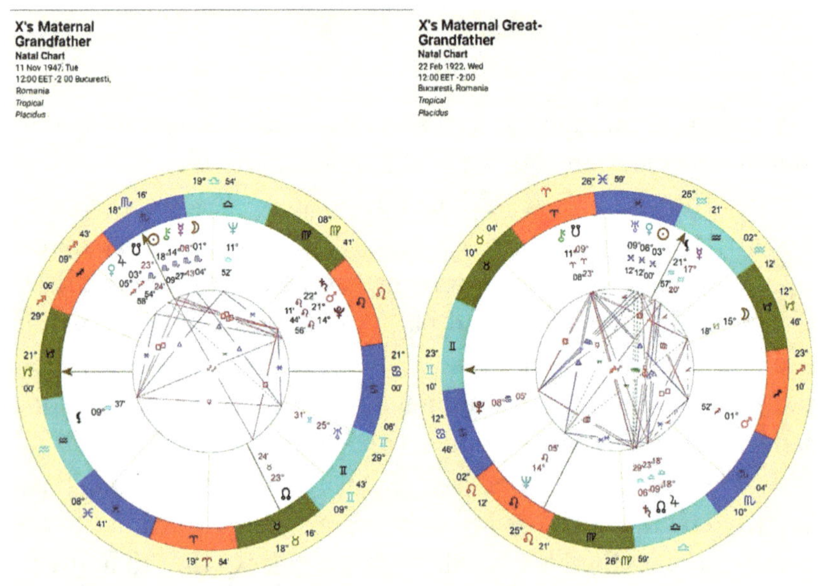

X's mother's father (maternal grandfather) comes from a simple country family, which, as I have learned from the short stories, evolved over time in the shadow of a rule: the entire family clan (composed of the parental couple, together with sons, daughters, grandparents, daughters-in-law, sons-in-law, grandchildren and, furthermore, with the families founded by them) must live in the same household. Under this rule of the clan, the members took care of the household together, shared everything, had meals together, and lived in a small family nucleus. The house they lived in would be inherited by the descendants, who would continue to live in the same place as their predecessors, carrying on the family tradition.

As they were a family that started from scratch, the father reports that the parental figures of the system (his father and grandfather) had developed a high degree of avarice and temperance - everything they earned, food or possessions, were locked up and distributed to the family members in portions, at the edge of survival.

In this environment, where life unfolded under control, austerity, limitation, fear, enforcement and surveillance, the only one who wanted to leave the clan, get out of the family system and take it on his own was himself, the father, the firstborn of the five siblings of the family.

He broke away from the system at a young age, moved to the city and started his own family, managing to accumulate, earn, settle his financial status, and build a home, where his two daughters were born. His path shows a clear ascent until, in adulthood, he begins to develop the same pattern of fear of loss as his father and grandfather: he becomes very moderate, miserly, tight-fisted, frustrated with money, and self-restricted in indulging desires or pleasures. Having a pattern of poverty in his unconscious, although he can afford to live well, he ostracizes himself, buys the cheapest and lowest quality things for himself, and does not indulge in the luxury of offering himself any pleasure. Moreover, for fear of imbalance, he even repeatedly declines all chances of enrichment, or opportunities to rise higher.

In an unwritten statement, to be faithful to his family blazonry, it is as if he unconsciously states: I do not deserve more, I refuse to be rich, I must struggle and everything must be difficult. His heritage and value remained undiscovered, locked in a pattern of indigence, duality, of struggle for money.

Following his family's rule, wouldn't share what he has got with anyone, he wouldn't crumble his wealth and what he has worked for, so he tries to move his adult daughters under the same roof with him. As he once did, the eldest daughter refuses and lives separately on her own, but the youngest, the mother of the athlete analysed, moves into his house, with, of course, her husband (the previously analysed father) and child (the boy with whom I started the analysis).

X's mother, as she stated at the beginning, although she has professional potential, chances, and opportunities, moving under the same roof and in the same unconscious pattern as the father, grandfather and great-grandfather, wastes everything that she earns in the clan's household, opportunities disappear as soon as they appear, and living becomes difficult as soon as the they overcome the family's basic condition - poverty. In his family, houses are money-consuming, and require repairs, when left in desolation they fall into disrepair, land is partitioned and sold for nothing, debts arise when everything should have been going well. In order to break free from the pattern and the debt she holds to the clan, she needs to break away from the family system, get out of the father's household (thus freeing the son as well) and build something on her own. She must become aware of the poverty pact made by her predecessors, understand it, accept it, and then free herself from it. She needs access to the restricted treasures of the system, to break the ban on having, affording, and accumulating. She has the right to wealth, and for that, she must allow herself to give herself relaxation, pleasure, fulfilment of desires, joy, good and quality things, vacations, fine food and joy.

By untying herself, she unwittingly also unties her son, who may have thus a different relationship with his own person and with his own value!

The ban on following a sports career inherited from the father's line, in conjunction with the ban on personal value inherited from the mother's line, creates in the analysed young man the situation described at the beginning.

I feel like a living dead!

This analysis starts from the endeavour of a woman to understand what is happening in her complicated life, in the relationships she attracts and in her family dynamics, where all the roles have been reversed.

Briefly, she tells her story as follows:

"I come from a family where there was a lot of turbulence, arguments, situations without explanation for me, inappropriate relationships and suffering.

There was a huge difference in age between my father and my mother, namely 34 years. Before they were together, Dad was married with a son, and his intention was to adopt Mom, who was also with someone.

In the meantime, my mother got married and my father became her godfather, but very quickly things changed, and the two fell in love. When they were lovers, he was 50 and she was 16, and she got pregnant with me. After a big scandal, in the aftermath of my birth, after they separated from their partners and formalized their union, a few years later, my younger brother was born.

Unfortunately, when I was 17 years old, my father passed away, and ever since the relationship between me, my mother and my brothers (the oldest and the youngest) changed dramatically: disinheritance, disavowal, departure, abandonment from my mother part, physical fights between us, the siblings, verbal aggression, cursing, swearing, damage to property, fights, scandals between brothers, nightmare scenes and recriminations between all family members.

In addition to all these disappointments, and overturned situations, my constant feeling is that I am not living, that I cannot find myself, that I do not understand what is happening and ... that I am a living dead!"

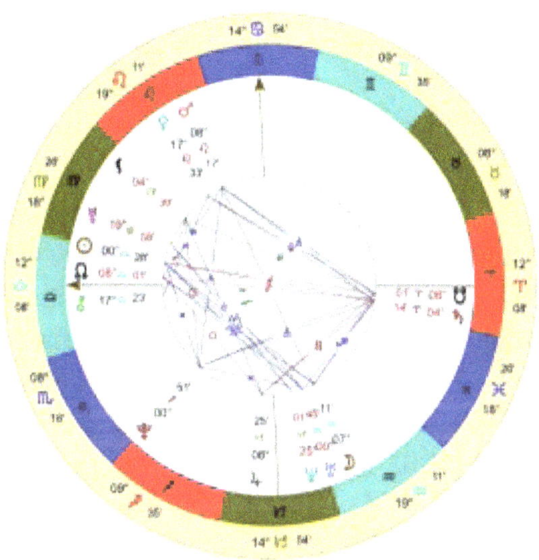

The astral chart identifies the following aspects:

• Chiron in 1st House - Libra - a wound in the family with regard to the relationships and marriages that took place in the system, which has a strong impact on her own person

• Saturn, ruler of 4th (family and roots of the system) and 5th (children and love) houses, positioned at the South Node - taking over a transgenerational pattern in relation to children and the way the family is organized

• Saturn opposition Sun - absence of or abandonment by the father

• Sun in 12th house - unconscious patterns inherited on the

337

paternal line, absent father, secrets related to the systemic line of the father

    • The position of the axis of the Lunar nodes oriented on the axis Aries - Libra - personal identity, role-playing and couple in the family

    • Mercury retrograde in 12th house - possible hidden siblings, reversed roles of siblings, patterns inherited by siblings on the father's line

    • Uranus conjunct Moon in the 4th house in Aquarius, opposition Mars - unstable relationships within the family, aggression, fighting, tense change of roles or in relation to the mother

The Sun and Mercury are in the 12th house, of secrets and hidden things, of patterns that lie in the unconscious. Since Mercury represents her siblings, I asked her if she knew anything about the existence of other siblings besides the one from the father's first marriage and the youngest one. Surprisingly, there is a secret sister! Before dying, her father had confessed to her that there is another child of his out there, whose identity cannot be revealed though, because she was born from an adulterous relationship, and the man who is raising her does not know he is not her father.

Therefore, there is a whole hidden branch of the system, an entanglement between two genealogical trees, between paternities and role-playing in the system. At the same time, the father's primary intention to adopt, and not to be with the person who later became his wife, as well as the huge difference in age between the partners, also symbolizes an unconscious father-daughter relationship, rather than a husband-wife one.

In this scenario, the husband projects the image of a daughter on the wife, the wife projects the image of a father on the husband, and the children born at an unconscious level from an incestuous relationship can no longer find themselves: who is the female figure next to them, their mother or their sister?

But what happened in the parents' lives, and why did they

choose to unite under this pattern?

The systemic line of the father

Analysing the father's chart, one can note:

• Neptune opposition Sun - father's lack of identity, changed parental role, illusion of father's role

• Saturn square Sun - absence of the father, blockage of vitality, parentification - the child takes on the role of the father

• Mars square Sun - quarrel, competition, death, accident on the father's line or on the assumed role

• Mercury retrograde in Pisces - hidden fraternal relationships

In another form, the astral configurations of the analysed girl resemble those of the father.

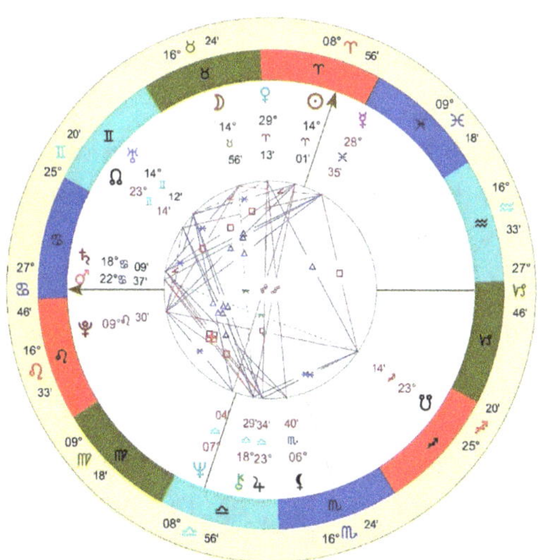

I have found out about him that he lost his father when he was young (just like her), and that his mother (paternal grandmother) had had a family before his birth, composed of a husband and a child, who had died and about whom she wouldn't ever speak. Therefore, on this level too there is a hidden branch, previous children and secrets about births or identities.

What else do we know about the father's father? His father too had died when he was young, leaving him the sole provider of the family.

Both the father, the grandfather and the great-grandfather went through the same generational pattern:

the death of the fatherly figure, the older brother of the family takes over the role of father and takes responsibility for both raising the siblings and supporting the mother. If he starts a family of his own, the roles are ambiguous: both his offspring and younger siblings are treated as children; the mother gets in line with the children, causing a conflict between herself, children, grandchildren and daughter-in-law.

On parental line:

• the first son becomes the paternal figure of the system
• the younger siblings are placed on the same line as the older brother's children
• the younger siblings and father's children compete for rights, attention and protection
• the older brother is forced to take on more responsibilities, becoming head of the clan and shouldering its weight - at the same time, he is in between the two systems, playing a double role
• the older brother's wife becomes a foster mother for the husband's younger brothers, which can create revolt or jealousy in her
• the brother's wife and his sister compete for the same roles
• under the pressure of the roles he plays - father, older brother, husband - the parental figure ends up giving in and leaving the system

The systemic line of the mother

The mother's chart has a similar configuration to that of the husband and the daughter:

- Saturn square Sun
- Neptune opposition Sun
- Mars opposition Moon

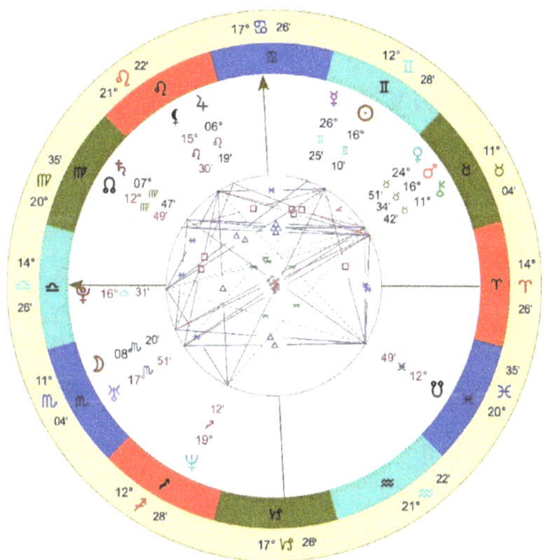

The mother was born into a family where the mother, very young, was a housewife, and the father, always on the move, was a singer. Again, just like herself later, her mother had become a mother at a very young age.

From the stories told by my client, became obvious that, due to this small age difference, the mother treated her children like a sister, and over time this took the shape of a competition for the attention of the husband/father, whose roles were confused and mixed up.

The pattern found here mirrors the paternal pattern discussed earlier: while in his lineage the parental figures died and older siblings took over, in this very system the mother figure becomes a daughter and competes with her own children for their father's attention.

On maternal lineage:

• the first-born daughter comes into conflict with her mother, whom she perceives as a sister or her rival, competing for her father's attention
• messing up the roles, after the father's departure or in his absence, the mother no longer recognizes her children, separates from them and looks for a relationship with another paternal figure, to feel protected
• in compensation, the children, abandoned by their mother, angry and hurt, take refuge under the protective wing of the elder brother or a new figure able to replace her

Union of the mirrored patterns

The union of the two (father and mother) by marriage, is actually not a union of two spouses, but a union between a father and a daughter. One wants to protect, the other to be protected, but the partnership between the two cannot be otherwise than platonic, because at an unconscious level, it means incest, and has a strong psychological impact on all those involved.

I revert once again to the original story - what kind of partners did the subject choose after the death of her father and separation from her mother, who disowned her? The answer is that her pattern moulds her parents' pattern - two years of toxic relationship with a married man with children, 24 years her senior, followed by a 4-year relationship with a man 13 years her senior, with whom she feels that she has evolved spiritually, but from whom she has finally parted.

*

In all the charts analysed for this system, the roles within the family are messed up.

The phrase "I feel like a living dead" finds its explanation in the blockage that occurred on both lines of the system, where the roots were cut by their abandonment by the mother, her refusal to grant her children the right to live, as well as by the father's departure/death.

From passion to sin

The analysis on the following pages is based on the story of a 27-year-old girl.

"I was born in a conflicting family, with many arguments and discussions between my parents, who finally could never agree among themselves and separated. My father left the country when I was 7 years old, and my mother followed him shortly after. I grew up alone, raised by my maternal grandmother, with the wound of abandonment in my soul. None of my parents ever got their lives back together, and many other inexplicable situations followed in my family: the deaths of some members on the exact birthdays of other family members, houses burning down on religious holidays, alcoholism, and accidents. On two separate occasions, Dad lost an eye and a finger. I don't have a close relationship with my mother, and my relationships with couples were uncertain: I had either mother-child relationships, or relationships based only on sexuality, which ended when my partner married someone else.

I am currently single and although I realize that my family tree is fading from all sides and there are no heirs, I do not want children.

I have only one close friend, who is always there for me, and has always been my confidant, Iustina".

Analysing the birth chart, the following aspects are identified, which I asked about and received answers one by one.
- Moon conjunct South Node in Taurus
- The Nodal Axis of the Moon on 3rd - 9th houses
- Venus in 7th house square Nodal Axis
- Mercury retrograde anaretic degree in Gemini

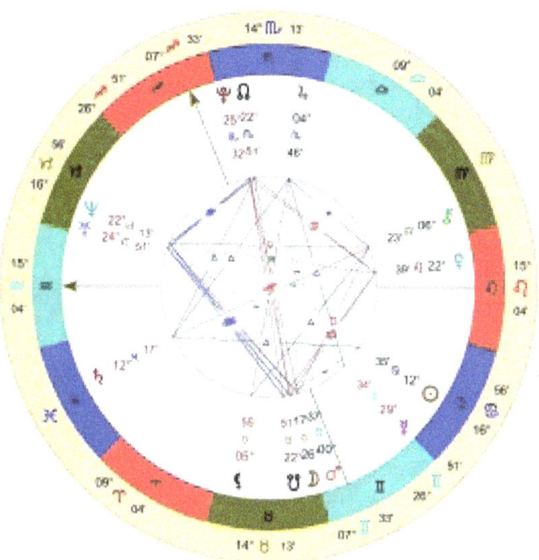

There is a big discrepancy between the mother's family and the father's family: the mother's family is Catholic, very religious and dogmatic, with solid principles related to morality, sexuality, frivolity, family and union. Polar opposite, the father's family is of the Orthodox religion, but they are not exactly devout parishioners, which often leads to upsets. The maternal grandmother grew up in a family of intellectuals, who wanted to keep the religious affiliation alive, while the paternal grandmother grew up in the forest, simple and natural, her faith being linked to nature, weeds and medicinal herbs. While in her father's family sexuality was expressed and considered something natural, in her mother's it was repressed: 'It is shameful to have children out of wedlock', 'it is bad to have an abortion', 'it is a shame to reveal your carnal desires or sexual appetite', mostly considered sins.

• T-Square - Pluto (Scorpio) - Venus (Leo) - Moon (Taurus), doubled by the position of the lunar nodes on the Taurus - Scorpio

345

axis

• Chiron (Virgo), 7th house, in opposition to Saturn retrograde (Pisces), 1st house, patterns that are found in other forms and in other people in the system.

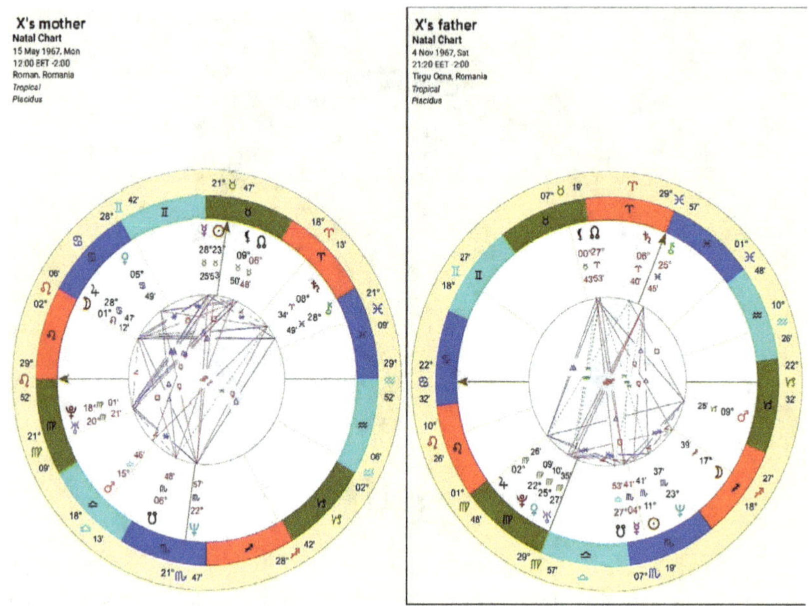

Father and Maternal Female Line:

1.   Mother X - Neptune retrograde in Scorpio opposition Sun in Taurus, South Node in Scorpio, Mars retrograde in Libra, Venus in Cancer square Saturn in Aries

2.   Father X - Stellium Pluto - Venus - Uranus in Virgo, opposing Chiron in Pisces, Saturn retrograde in Aries square Mars in Capricorn, Neptune, Sun, Mercury retrograde in Scorpio, Moon in Sagittarius

3.   Maternal Grandmother - Moon in Cancer conjunct Chiron retrograde, square Venus in Libra, Pluto in Leo square Sun in Scorpio, North Node in Sagittarius

4.   Maternal Great Grandmother - Pluto conjunct Venus in Cancer, Saturn conjunct South Node in Cancer, Mars in Aries square Venus

5.   Paternal Grandmother - T-Square - Moon in Sagittarius -

Venus in Pisces - Uranus retrograde in Gemini, Saturn retrograde in Cancer opposition Mars in Capricorn

6. Paternal grandfather - conjunction Venus - Lilith in Pisces, Moon conjunct Neptune in Virgo, North Node in Scorpio

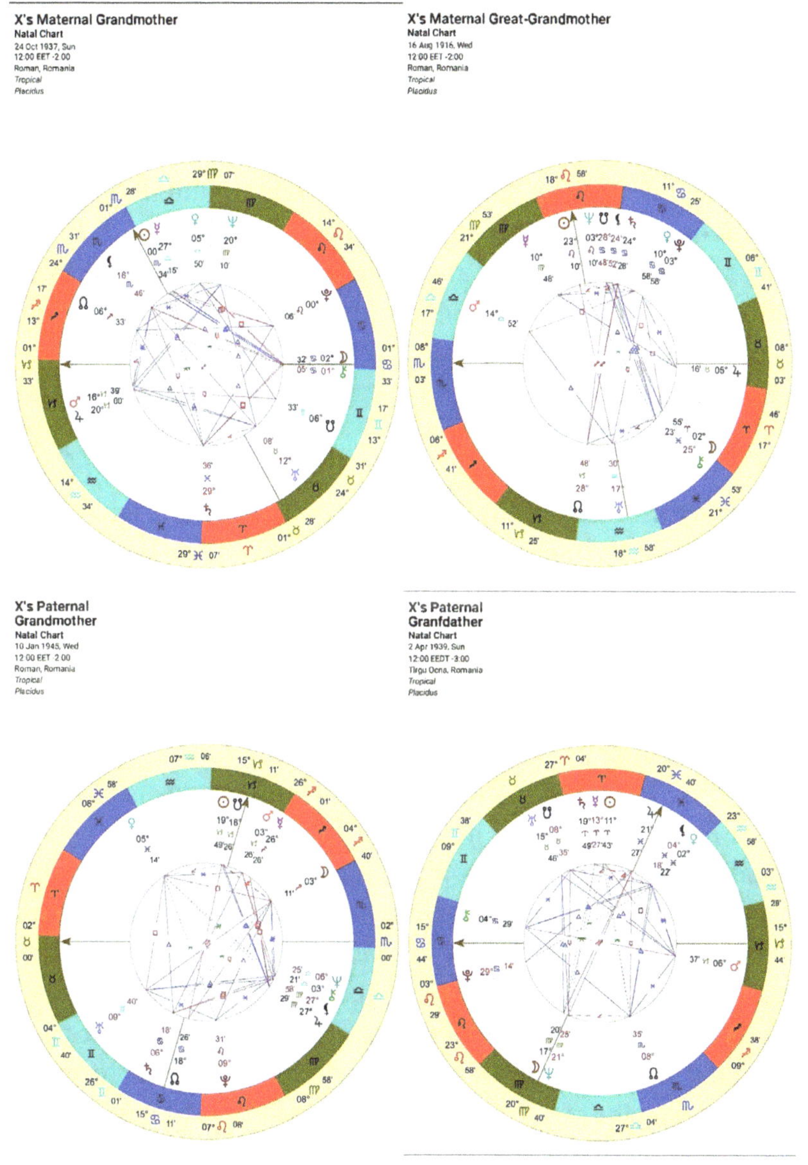

Although she did not draw experiences of physical abuse or relationships in which she was harmed, I learned about a terrible

347

drama, in which the maternal family (his grandfather and his cousin) is directly involved and which aligns with the current theme shared by the two systems - religion and sexuality. The story is told below.

Veronica Antal (b. December 7, 1935, Nisiporeşti, Boteşti, Neamţ county, Romania) was a Romanian woman of Roman Catholic religion, a member of the Secular Franciscan Order and Militia Immaculatae, the first of four children of Gheorghe and Eva (!), known in her community for her strong faith and the love she had developed for the Virgin Mary since childhood. Since it was impossible to enter a convent and become a nun (at that time, the communist regime had abolished all Catholic religious orders on the territory of Romania), Veronica, so named in honour of her paternal aunt who had died at a young age (!), took a vow of chastity in private and lived in the world, besides the parental home, as in a monastery.

In the evening of August 24, 1958 (when she was 22), while she was returning from the Holy Liturgy of a parish neighbouring the village where she lived, a young man (the cousin of the maternal grandfather of the native with whom I began the analysis) threw himself in her way as she was heading home. From later police accounts, it appears that in a failed effort to have sex with her, he fatally stabbed her 42 times. The next morning, the inhabitants discovered her body in the middle of the field: she was face down, covered in blood, on her back she had a cross made of corn cobs, and in her hand, she was holding tightly the rosary from which she never parted.

The case was widely publicized and investigated, the file was closed and reopened several times over 30 years, books were written about this event and legends were born. While it is not known exactly how and what happened, three people were arrested - Mocanu (the grandfather's cousin), considered the de facto author of the murder, the grandfather, in whose yard bloodstained clothes were found (and about which he never confessed anything) and another man, from outside the system. In 1959, the prosecutor's office of the Bacău Region at that time ordered the termination of the trial for the last two, and for Mocanu to be sent to trial, as the single author of the murder, but two years later, the Court decided to set him free, discharging him of any accusation. The crime of murder remained with unknown perpetrators and the case file was returned to the prosecutors to find the murderers.

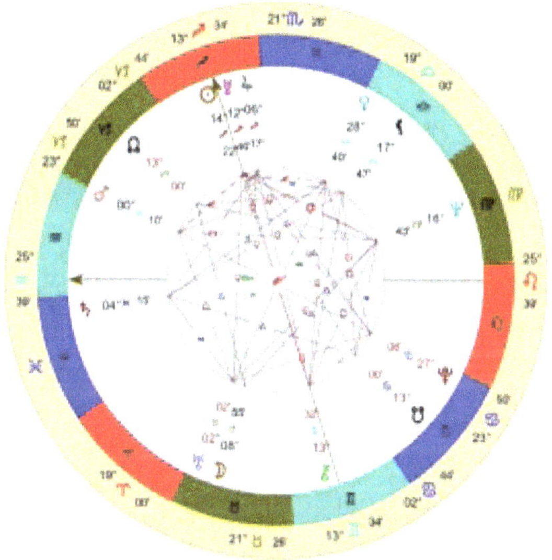

Studying Veronica Antal's chart, the following aspects stand out as relevant:

• T-square between Jupiter, Mercury, Sun (Sagittarius) - Chiron (Gemini) and Neptune (Virgo)
• Moon conjunct Uranus retrograde in Taurus
• Saturn in Pisces
• Pluto retrograde in Cancer Rac square Venus in Libra

Following the narrative in the book "Cununiţa fecioarei" - a commemorative volume published half a century after the martyrdom of Veronica Antal, authors Anton Demeter and Cezarina Avramescu, Arionda Publishing House, 2007, I have learned about her life and personality:

"I had the only task of organizing the material and rendering it faithfully, as it was made available to me.

Following the witnesses' statements, I, therefore, found Veronica Antal, all the more alive in the memory of Christians, the more the fog of years should have settled down and paled her gentle and virginal face."

"Veronica, a modest young woman, was born and lived in the midst of a Moldovan peasant family; people who were familiar with the needs and work. Top of the form at school, industrious in her household, lover of prayer, passionate about good readings, about holy songs, eager to reach heaven, she renounced married life, consecrating herself to God through a vow of purity and virginity."

"Seeing Veronica always in a good mood, cheerful, serene, with a smile and a song on her lips, one would have said that she does not know what the suffering and trouble of life is. In reality, as some of her friends tell us, and as she herself testified when she declared that Jesus also gave her some spiritual sufferings, sometimes the clouds of trials also descended on the clear sky of her soul, in the form of disgrace, contempt, shame, constraints, opposition, threats, injustices, temptations, bad premonitions and separations from loved ones." (Pr. Anton Demeter, quote p. 156).

"Apart from this, Veronica subjected herself to some penitences, sacrifices and mortifications for various causes: the return of sinners, peace, well-being in the family, in the village, the healing of a sick person, the building of the church in the village, being convinced that here on earth, we must strive to overcome every trial, as Jesus taught: In this world, you will have trouble. But take heart!: I have overcome the world! (John 16:33)".

"If you asked her why she was sad, she would answer: 'I can not say!' But we knew how things were" - Cătălina remembers.

"She sometimes was tried by heavy temptations against purity, says her friend Verona, but she fought steadfastly against them."

"However, she also had some moments of despair and was very upset because of her mother, who wanted to marry her at all costs" – sister Electa says.

"Her sister Angela, reports: In the last time of his life, she cried a lot, but we didn't know why she was crying."

Sister Rozina Antal from Nisiporeşti says: "No one suspected that the Good God had His eyes fixed on this young girl, that He would choose her to shed her blood in order to prove to Him that she had given her heart only to Him and that she feared sin more than death."

Frequently, and especially in times of temptation, says Eleonora, she repeated these words: "Oh Mary, with your name and that of sweet Jesus I hope to pass from this world and go to the heavens above."

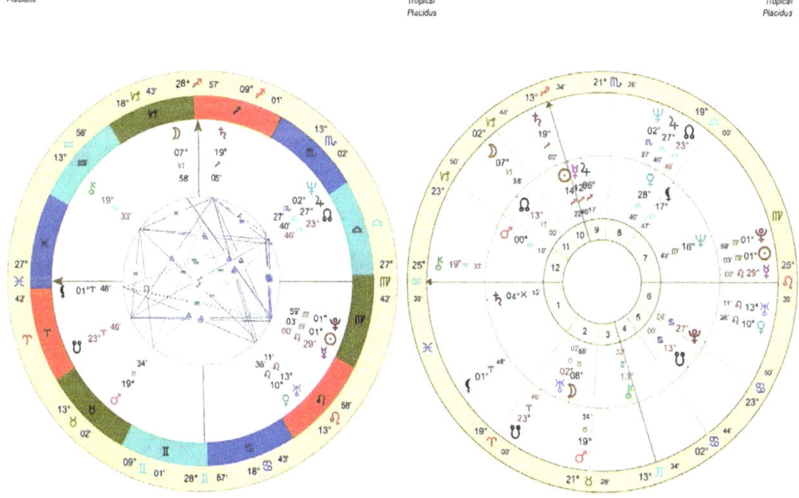

On August 24, 1958, the following aspects are identified:

- Mercury retrograde Leo anaretic degree
- Sun-Pluto conjunction in Virgo
- Venus-Uranus conjunction în Leo
- Saturn in Sagittarius

Mocanu, arrested at only 20 years of age, has in his birth chart:

• T-Square - Mars, Sun (Leo) - North Node (Scorpio) - Uranus, South Node (Taurus)
• Moon in Pisces
• conjunction Neptune - Mercury in Virgo

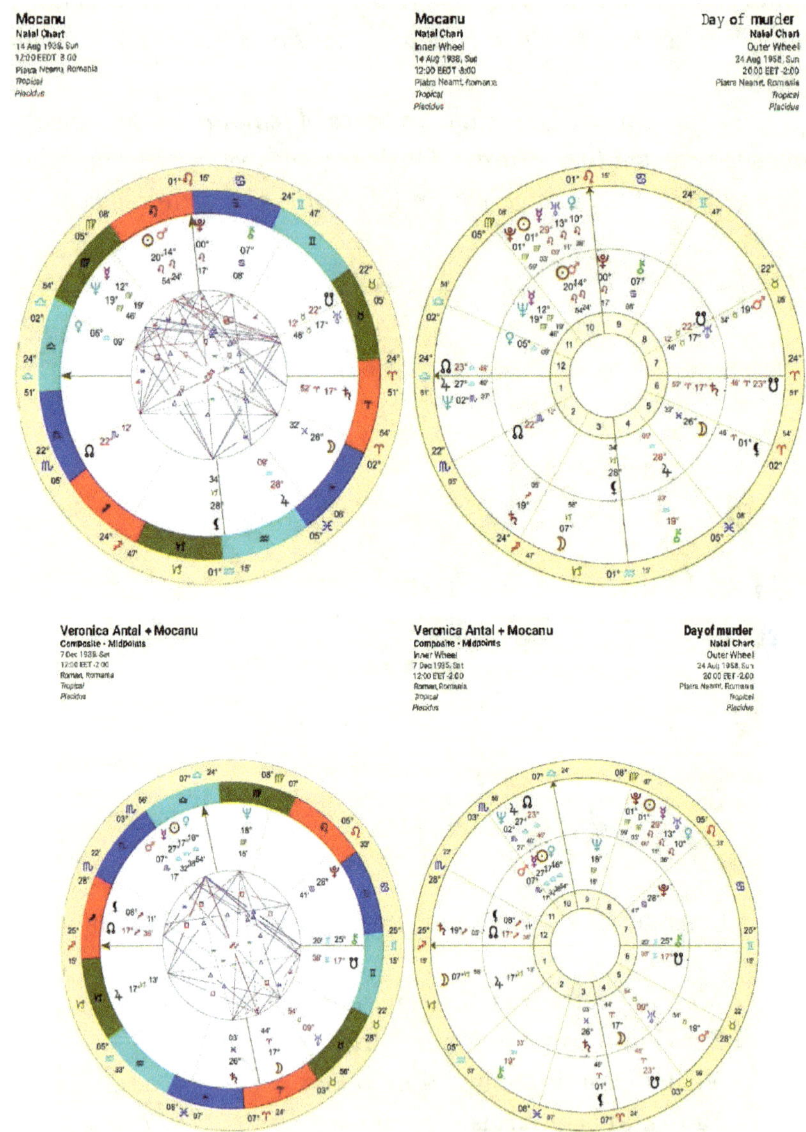

352

Surprisingly (or not), during the discussion with the subject on the topic of religion and sexuality, our attention was also drawn to the story of Saint Justina, also her friend's name which she had mentioned at the beginning. The theme is more than relevant and completes the whole picture, even if it is only a symbol.

Saint Cyprian and Justina

'In the reign of Decius, there lived in Antioch a certain maiden whose name was Justina. She came from pagan parents (…) She secretly went to the church of Christ, and often hearing the word of God, with the Holy Spirit acting in her heart, she came to believe in Christ. (…) At that time there lived in Antioch a certain youth named Aglaias, the son of wealthy parents.

Once he saw Justina as she was going to church, and he was struck by her beauty. He started to think in all manners of ways (…), he observed all the paths by which the maiden would walk, and, meeting her, would speak to her cunning words, praising her beauty. (…) Turned down every time, he became yet more inflamed with passion, and not knowing what more to do, went to the great sorcerer and magician Cyprian, and begged his help.

Cyprian invoked one of the impious spirits to inflame the heart of Justina, who marvelled and was ashamed of herself, feeling that her blood was boiling as in a kettle; now she thought about that which she had always despised as vile. But in her good sense, Justina understood that this battle had arisen in her from the devil; immediately she turned to the weapon of the sign of the cross. Having prayed long and fervently, the holy virgin put the enemy to shame. Being conquered by her prayer, he fled from her with shame. Then Cyprian called a yet more malicious demon, but the maiden armed herself with fervent prayer and mortified her flesh with abstinence and fasting, eating only bread and water. Then Cyprian, who, finding out that he had not managed to do anything, called a prince of the demons and sent him to tempt Justina, but this one too, turned back without accomplishing anything. (...) Cyprian got angry, and by his sorcery he brought diverse misfortunes on the house of Justina and on the house of all her relatives, neighbours, and friends, and struck them with illness. But when Justina prayed fervently to God, immediately all the demonic attacks ceased; all were healed from the plagues and recovered from their diseases. Having become convinced that nothing could conquer the power of the sign of the Cross and the Name of Christ, Cyprian put off the devil and from sorcerer became a great Bishop, and Justina became Abbess over other Christian maidens. The story does not have a happy ending, because not admitting his loss, the devil urged people to slander Cyprian before the Emperor, and he judged him and sentenced him to death by slaughter, alongside Iustina. After their death, both were sanctified."

In 2018, Veronica was also beatified and sanctified.

The preliminary analysis of this study ends with an awareness, which can bring liberation, healing and release, both for X and her family:

"I now understand my mother and the reason why she had a rebellious attitude over time. There was a great contradiction within her, and because of it, dissatisfaction, unhappiness and frustration. She was volcanic and passionate, she wanted to be loved passionately, but at the same time, she was religiously strict, faithful to the education she received from her grandmother, and her grandmother from her great-grandmother.

A long line of repression, shaming, silence and restraint erupted with force in a tragic, violent and harsh act that unfortunately destroyed many lives.

I understand why Mom was considered the black sheep of her family and why she wanted to get away from the system. He couldn't find her place, she needed to run and take a new path. I too recognize myself in her pattern and feel like following her actions, now much more aware - I want freedom, I don't want a relationship of complacency or without passion, nor a formal one.

I believe in God, but I also need the mysticism, esoteric or imaginary, a life lived in authenticity."

Other systems analysed

Suicidal parent

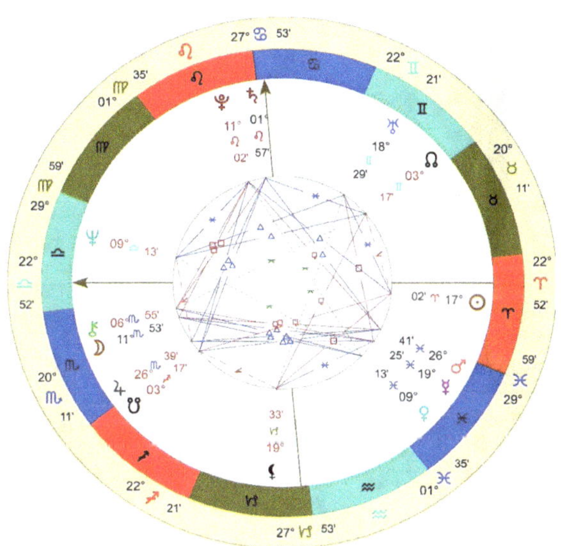

Man lost his father at the age of 17, and when he was 19 his mother committed suicide.

Hard Moon/Sun aspects: Moon - Chiron retrograde in Scorpio (1st house) square Pluto retrograde in Leo (10th house); Sun in Aries (6th house) opposition Neptune retrograde in 12th house.

Who is the mother?

A woman born to a very young mother is raised from birth by her paternal grandparents as if she were their daughter. As she grows up, she calls his grandparents mom and dad, her biological father is treated as her brother, and her biological mother is treated as her brother's girlfriend.

Aspects: Sun conjunct Mercury in Cancer, 4th house, square Chiron in Aries, 1st house; Moon conjunct the South Node, broad opposition to Mars, conjunct the North Node; Saturn opposition Neptune retrograde.

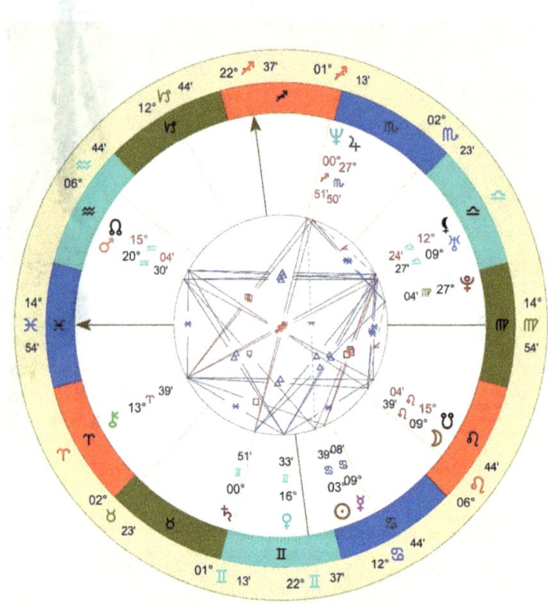

Mother lost in war

Man, lost his mother at the age of 3 when she was killed in a bombing raid during World War II. The father remarries, and, although he has a good relationship with him, is raised most of the time by the mother's sisters. He never married in his life and has no children.

Aspects: Pluto retrograde Leo square Moon in Taurus, Venus in Aquarius opposition Chiron in Leo, Moon in Taurus square Venus in Aquarius, Saturn retrograde - Lilith - Uranus retrograde square Venus - Chiron, North Node in Virgo, Mercury conjunct Sun in Capricorn.

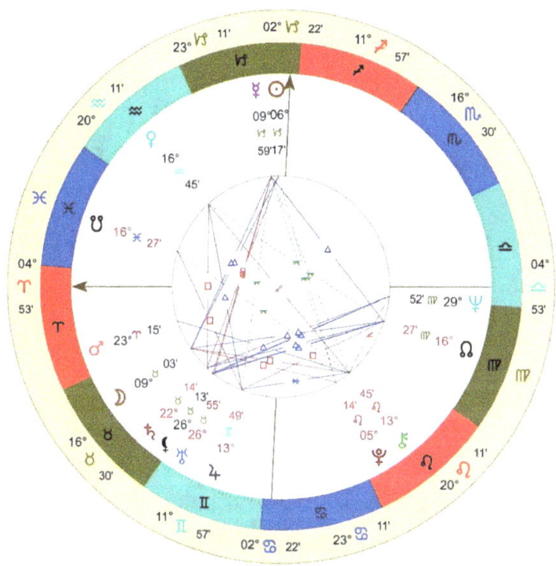

Father is the brother

Man, fatherless at a very young age. The older brother takes over the parental role and the upbringing of the whole family until the moment when the young man breaks away and sets out in life on his own, managing to assert himself and achieve status. The void left by the loss of the father was compensated by the sacrifice made by the brother, who until the end of his life, although married, had no more children.

Astrological aspects: Pluto in Leo square Sun in Taurus,

Saturn in Leo square Venus in Taurus, Chiron in Sagittarius opposition Mercury in Gemini, Mercury trine Neptune retrograde in Libra, North Node in Aries.

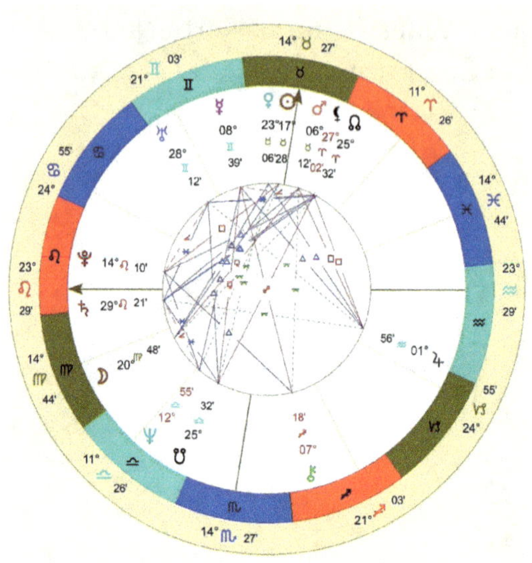

Mental illness in the family

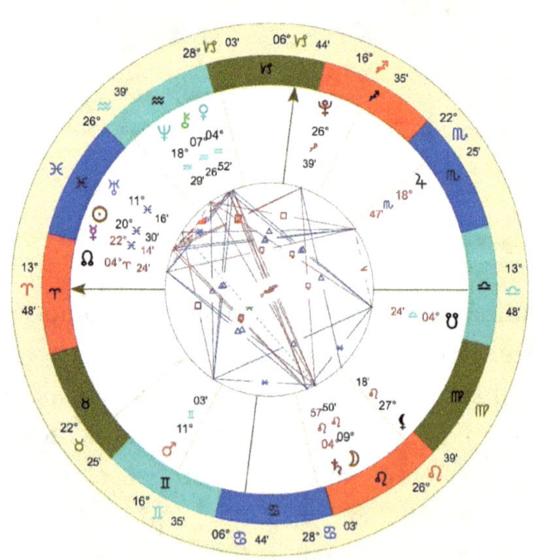

A woman has several cases of women with mental illnesses in her mother's family (maternal grandfather's sister, maternal grandmother).

Astrological aspects: Mercury retrograde in Pisces 12th house conjunct Sun, Saturn retrograde Moon in Leo opposition Venus, Chiron in Aquarius.

Bankruptcy due to fire

Man, after investing in a successful business, loses everything in a fire, which leaves him bankrupt, in debt, and never able to recover.

Astrological aspects: Mars - Saturn (anaretic degree) in Scorpio square Pluto retrograde in Leo, conjunction Jupiter retrograde in Virgo Moon, Uranus retrograde in Leo square Neptune in Scorpio.

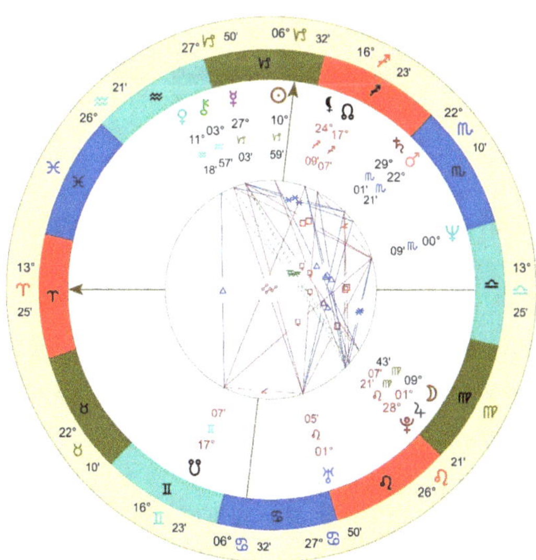

Lack of children

Female, early menopause, married, no children.

Astrological aspects: Moon in Virgo trine Lilith - Venus retrograde in Capricorn, inconjunct Saturn retrograde in Gemini South Node - Venus retrograde, square Uranus retrograde in Libra - Venus - Lilith.

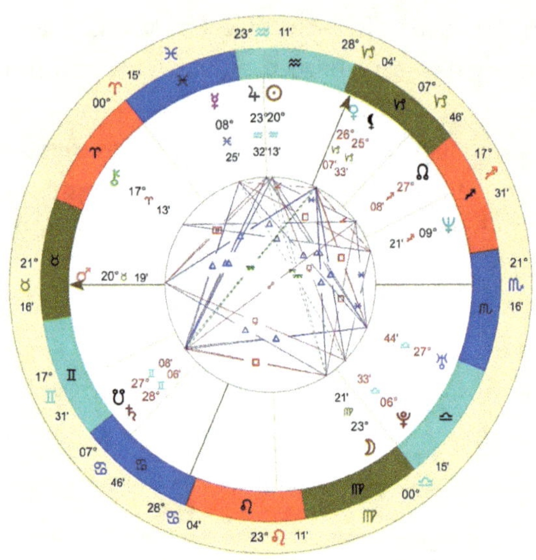

Where is my family?

Boy, his parents separated when he was 7 years old. The mother lives in Europe, the father lives in America, he has to cope with the journeys between the two residences and citizenships, not sure which one to call home.

Astrological aspects: Trine Moon in Sagittarius 4th house Sun in Aries 9th house, Moon square Jupiter in Pisces, Sun square South Node in Cancer, Saturn retrograde in Libra.

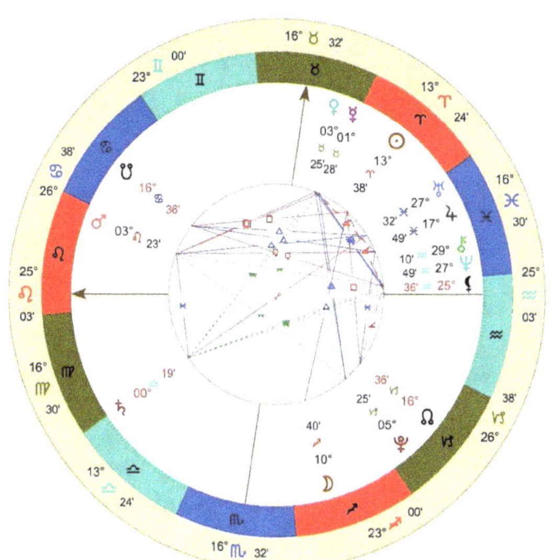

Healing and liberation

From a psychogenealogical point of view, the family is the space and landmark of the inter- and trans-generational psychic transmission. The ties that family members establish are not simple kinship or blood ties, but they follow a long history, a process of the entire family clan trying to survive and evolve, creating an unconscious algorithm according to which both the roles and births or deaths are established.

The possibility that the past has an impact on the present is explained by the existence of the unconscious, that invisible unifying field that connects what is seen to what has passed beyond, into non-being.

Therefore, apparently inexplicable and meaningless, many manifestations of the past can still be present in many forms that impact on several generations:

- the manifestation of an ancestor in a descendant, a phenomenon called 'the ghost'
- the strengths and weaknesses that a person possesses but is not aware of or refuses to see are projected onto other people, whom the person falls in love with or hates (expelling his own content from himself and projecting it onto other people)
- unconsciously experiencing events that the ancestors experienced
- attracting certain types of characters and a certain relational pattern
- family scenarios that mimic past stories

- roles, jobs, adopted status
- blockages, debts, unfulfilled relationships, and secrets that tend to surface
- reliving some pathologies or somatising the same emotion through the phenomenon of invisible loyalty and pathological mourning
- reliving the same type of trauma
- complying with an interdiction
- repetitive dates, names, events
- assuming a family blazonry
- a red thread that runs through all generations and unites them in one story

In order to heal and relieve the family tree from its traumas, shortcomings and wounds, it is necessary to go through some stages, both physical and metaphysical:

- Awareness of the roles and position of each individual within the family of origin
- Awareness of the dynamic aspects between family members
- Symbolic/emotional/psychic/decisional repositioning of the native in relation to the family clan system
- Separations and restoration of intra-family boundaries, so that each member can assume his authentic identity - family role, sex, behaviour

Since what happened in the past in physical reality cannot be changed, the psycho-genealogical process of healing must first take place in an unconscious, subtle and unifying realm for the entire family system. This can only be done through a symbolic, ritualistic dimension, which restores but also dissolves the unconscious links created with the predecessors.

The situations that could not be confessed, the statements

that were not made, the acceptances, the acknowledgements, the forgiveness, the separations, the reparations, the emotional discharges, etc. can be reconstructed, lived and continued by the ancestors, who, through the process of identification and subtle unravelling, restore the order in the unconscious plane.

At the moment, the most important techniques used by systemic psychotherapists are psychodrama - family constellations, art genogram, imago genogram, intuitive dialogue, the use of symbols as a language of communication and the ritual act, and all of which are forms by which the transgenerational past can be brought into the present, to be meaningfully reprocessed and restructured.

Thus, an arch over time is opened that releases tension and blocked energy, triggering a labour of forgiveness, understanding, healing and release, not only for the past but also for the present and future of the family. As a result of such a process, the individual is placed correctly in the trans-familial matrix to which they belong and on their unique, personal and authentic evolutionary direction.

The first consequence of the release of unconscious content is a change in the family member's behaviour, but also the fact that the blocked life situations begin to resolve by themselves.

The vein is saved through each of its members, they being equally provided with value, meaning and importance for the evolution of the psycho-genealogical being.

Barbara Băcăuanu

Founder of the School of Spiritual Sciences (Romania, 2013), astrologer (2008) qualified for individual consultation practice, trainer in the profession of specialist astrologer (2014), author of specialization programs, personal development and ongoing training (astrology, numerology, tarot, archetypes), creator of the psychotherapeutic tool for working with the shadow - Revelations, Transparent Symbols (2021), facilitator of family constellations.

.

Revelations
Transparent Symbols

For therapists, healers, and psychotherapists

The Transparent Symbols were created as a deep and complex tool for working with the self, in which the transparency allows reading in layers, exposing to the consciousness of the person who handles them a complete picture with ample details, which is meant to awaken from the memory or the subconscious, to bring to the surface and unlock the truth.

Revelations links elements of psychology, astrology, numerology, sacred geometry, and archetypes into a single concept, allowing them to communicate with each other efficiently and constructively, through a common alphabet - the symbols.

In connection with the user, it becomes a mirror of the soul, offering extremely valuable and profound revelations from within, the Universe, or from the subconscious and super-subconscious space.

Transparent symbols can be used both by therapists as a method of working with patients, by tarotists due to their transparency, and also by anyone who wants to go beyond the physical world and enter into a magical one, much more vivid than the dimension we live in - the inner world!

Enter the world of the subconscious and communicate with it through its only language, the Symbols!

Cards' transparency offers the possibility of overlappings, forming remarkable, unique and personal image combinations. Ask questions to your Self and be surprised by the amazing answers. Beautiful designed symbols form complex, detailed, and suggestive images.

Level Zero

Simple symbols form complex, detailed, and suggestive images that are not difficult to interpret.

Psychologists

The connoisseurs of Carl Gustav Jung's theories, the founder of analytical psychology, will discover concepts, symbols, and archetypes, such as Persona, Shadow, Anima/Animus, and the Self, which are directly related to the subconscious. These are the basis of the hero's journey through life and his process of individuation.

The order in which the images were placed in the explanatory book perfectly describes the circle of life, the evolution of the Self, and all the stages of a therapeutic or transformative process. Connecting with the transparent cards, you will find yourself in one of the characters and in the scenarios that resembles his life experience. Watching the sequential chain described in the story and meditating on it will give you the revelation you need to gain clarity on the past, present, and future.

Astrologers

All the elements of a celestial chart are depicted in the symbolism of several cards. You will find the archetypes of the planets (Sun, Moon, Mars, Venus, Mercury, Jupiter, Saturn, Uranus, Neptune, Pluto, Lilith, Chiron), zodiac signs (Aries to Pisces), elements (water, air, fire, earth), axes and even aspects (conjunction, trine, quadrature, opposition, quincunx) so that you will be able to interpret and understand the sequences revealed in the work sessions from an astrological perspective.

Numerologist/ Sacred geometry passionate

Although you can reduce all the symbols to a single numerological vibration, nine can be directly associated with numerology and geometric shapes (e.g., Monada, Binada, Triad, Square, Flower of Life).

Holistic Therapies

You can use the transparent symbols deck as an oracle, but even more! Its symbolism can be combined in countless ways, giving rise to very complex interpretations.

The deck of transparent symbols can be used with remarkable results by anyone as a psychotherapeutic tool, privately, without specialized knowledge, and by professionals, in therapy.

Extraordinary tool for those seeking the truth!

Step outside the classic patterns and work with the intuitive,
transparent cards and symbols reading!

www.reveland.net

www.ingramcontent.com/pod-product-compliance
Lightning Source LLC
LaVergne TN
LVHW050537200726
843506LV00001B/2